Lessons Learned from My Cat

Chicken Soup for the Soul: Lessons Learned from My Cat
Amy Newmark

Published by Chicken Soup for the Soul, LLC www.chickensoup.com
Copyright ©2023 by Chicken Soup for the Soul, LLC. All Rights Reserved.

The publisher gratefully acknowledges the many publishers and individuals who granted Chicken Soup for the Soul permission to reprint the cited material.

Front cover photo of cat courtesy of iStockphoto.com (©Linda Raymond)
Back cover and interior photo of two cats courtesy of iStockphoto.com (©CHUYN)
Photo of Amy Newmark courtesy of Susan Morrow at SwickPix

Cover and Interior by Daniel Zaccari

Publisher's Cataloging-In-Publication Data

Names: Newmark, Amy, editor.
Title: Chicken soup for the soul : lessons learned from my cat / Amy Newmark.
Description: Cos Cob, CT: Chicken Soup for the Soul, LLC, 2023.
Identifiers: LCCN: 2022948443 | ISBN: 978-1-61159-099-9 (paperback) | 978-1-61159-336-5 (ebook)
Subjects: LCSH Cats--Anecdotes. | Human-animal relationships--Anecdotes. | Cat owners--Anecdotes. | Cats--Humor. | Conduct of life. | Essays. | BISAC PETS / Essays & Narratives | PETS / Cats / General | HUMOR / Topic / Animals
Classification: LCC SF442 .C45 2023 | DDC 636.8--dc23

Library of Congress Control Number: 2022948443

PRINTED IN THE UNITED STATES OF AMERICA
on acid∞free paper

30 29 28 27 26 25 24 23   02 03 04 05 06 07 08 09

Lessons Learned from My Cat

Amy Newmark

Chicken Soup for the Soul, LLC
Cos Cob, CT

Changing the world one story at a time®
www.chickensoup.com

Table of Contents

❶

~Learning to Love the Cat~

❷

~Small But Mighty~

❸

~You Just Have to Laugh~

❹

~Lost and Found~

❺

~Meant to Be~

❻

~My Very Good, Very Bad Cat~

❼

~Miracles Happen~

❽

~Perks & Quirks~

❾

~Opening Hearts~

⑩

~Natural Therapists~

Chapter 1

Learning to Love the Cat

Two for the Price of One

Kittens are angels with whiskers.
~Author Unknown

"'m not getting a cat." Mom had been saying that all morning.

I nodded. "Right, we're just looking."

The truth was that my mother needed something to fill her empty nest. I lived in my college town for most of the year, and my father worked long hours in the city. I was home this summer to keep her company, but after graduation I'd move to wherever my job took me. So, I insisted we go to the animal shelter — just to look around.

Mom and I got there early, just as a lady with kind eyes and a wide grin was unlocking the front door. She greeted us warmly and thanked us for considering adoption.

Mom quickly stopped her. "We're just looking."

"That's right." I winked at the lady.

She gave me a knowing nod. "So, what would you two like to look at?"

Mom didn't hesitate. "A shorthaired cat, female, not a kitten, litter-box trained. Friendly. No health issues that need daily medication preferably."

I blinked. For someone who didn't want a cat, Mom sure knew what she wanted.

We walked into a small room and waited. The lady quickly returned with a black-and-white cat with bright green eyes. The black on her face looked like an ink smudge. She was adorable.

"This one just came in. The owner said she's spayed and up-to-date on all her shots. We were waiting on the paperwork to verify it, but when we called the owner back, the number she gave us was no longer in use."

Mom nodded. "What's her name?"

"Cuddles," the lady answered. "She's eighteen months, according to the owner."

She placed Cuddles into my mother's arms. I could see how she got her name. Cuddles instantly rubbed her furry face against my mom's cheek and purred. Mom and I petted Cuddles, and then we tried gently setting her down and then picking her back up again to get a sense of her temperament. She was perfectly happy, especially when held. She sank into my mom's lap, rested her head, and closed her eyes.

My mom looked at me and shrugged. "I guess I'm getting a cat."

After the shelter fee, a sizable donation, and a trip to the pet store, Mom spent nearly $1,000 on the cat she "wasn't going to get."

The day we brought her home, Cuddles took her time exploring, sniffing every nook and cranny. Mom sat patiently on the couch, waiting. When Cuddles had sufficiently surveyed the area, she hopped on Mom's lap, gave her face a nuzzle, and settled in for a rest. Mom and I gave each other a wide-eyed look. Everything was going really, really well.

We spent those first two weeks fussing over the cat. We picked her up every time she meowed and gave her all the snuggles she asked for.

But, by week three, something had changed.

I went to pick up Cuddles, and she bellowed as if in pain. I let go and stood staring. *Okay*, I thought, *she doesn't want to be held, and she let me know. No big deal.* I went back to reading my book. A few hours later, I had forgotten about the whole thing until Mom tried holding her. Cuddles meowed louder. Then she ran for her cat bed and lay down, not a bit interested in Mom's lap.

Mom and I exchanged concerned glances. "We'll keep a close eye on her," I told Mom.

The next morning, I awoke to find my mom kneeling next to the cat bed, her eyes glistening with tears. Cuddles was panting furiously and listless. "Something's wrong. We need to get her to the vet."

When I attempted to gently lift her, she howled. Although I was panicking, I managed to lift Cuddles' entire cat bed to disturb her as little as possible. Slowly and carefully, I was able to nudge her into the crate.

Luckily, the vet was close by, but Cuddles became more and more agitated during the car ride.

By now, Mom was letting the tears flow freely. "What if she doesn't make it?"

I stepped on the gas pedal. "She will. We're almost there."

The car hadn't even come to a full stop when Mom opened the door and bolted out with Cuddles in tow. The tech, seeing my mom's hysteria, led us straight into an exam room.

The vet rushed in and was lifting Cuddles out of the crate when my mom shrieked, "Oh, my god, she ate a rat!"

Something black was falling out of Cuddles.

The vet tech reached for it. "Nope. She's having kittens."

I shook my head. "But she's spayed!"

"Apparently not," the vet mumbled.

I was delighted — kittens!

Mom went pale — kittens?

Cuddles licked her new arrival and settled down. We waited in silence for the rest of the litter, but she only had one kitten.

Finally, Mom reached for the door. "I need some air."

I followed her into the lobby, and we waited, mostly in silence, as the vet finished examining them. After both were given a clean bill of health, the four of us headed home.

We spent the next few weeks watching over Cuddles and her new arrival, who we named Tuck. Cuddles was a doting mom. Each night, she'd curl up with her little man, grabbing him in her paws and pulling him close to her chest. When I was busy giving attention to sweet little Tuck, and Cuddles knew her baby was well looked after, she'd sneak onto my mom's lap for some snuggle time of her own.

I was in love with both of them, but what did Mom think? She wasn't sure about getting one cat, let alone two.

Just before summer ended, I found my mom in the den. Cuddles was in her usual spot, curled on Mom's lap, and Tuck was right there beside them, batting at his mother's tail.

It was time for me to ask the dreaded question. "What are you going to do?"

Mom looked up at me and shrugged. "I guess I'm getting two cats."

—Annette M. Clayton—

Mr. Bojangles Taught Me to Dance

Cats are something else. Once they accept you
into their life, it's forever.
~André Brink

"**Y**ou don't want that one. He's broken," said the volunteer.

"What?" I asked, thinking that I didn't hear her right. Is any animal "broken"?

"He's a stray from birth," she explained. "He doesn't like anyone: not cats, not dogs, not people. Sometimes, they're out there way too long."

I looked down at the black cat, a three-year-old who sat on my foot. When I arrived, he followed me around the shelter, trilling like a small trumpet. Yet when she spoke, he fell silent, as if he understood her words.

"I want to adopt him," I said.

"Really?" she asked, looking confused. "Why?"

"Because I've been out there way too long, and I'm 'broken' too."

Once at home, I allowed him to explore his new environment. I watched as this little panther smelled every inch of my house. Occasionally, he would turn to me and make a single chirping sound, and then he would continue his self-guided tour. Was he talking to me? If so, was he offering compliments, observations, or perhaps criticisms?

Eventually, he settled down in my lap, and I knew it was time for a serious discussion.

"Look, I'm going to be honest with you. I've only been able to love two people in my entire life, and I'm thirty-three. That's not good. I love my brother and a friend, but that's it. I could do without everyone else. I have what the professionals call developmental trauma, which causes me to have serious attachment issues." His eyes looked away, but his ears remained perked in my direction; he was listening.

"My mom stopped loving me when I was seven years old. She's not a bad person; she just wasn't capable of being a mom anymore, like how your mom wasn't able to take care of you. I guess you had to figure it out on your own, like I did."

"Chirp," he sounded, perhaps acknowledging that he was also motherless.

"It's not like one bad thing happened to me. I wasn't beaten or raped. Childhood neglect is not about what happened; it's about what *didn't* happen." He turned on his back, belly exposed, gazing up at me.

"I'm telling you this because you shouldn't expect too much from me. My therapist said that having a pet might help me attach to people, but I doubt it." I looked down, and his eyes were closed, drifting off to sleep.

"Just don't expect me to love you. I don't know how."

A week later, I named him Mr. Bojangles after the song about a homeless man who's arrested and dances in his cell to entertain his fellow prisoners. This cat was homeless and in a shelter (which likely felt like a prison), yet he continued to make music. Bojangles often chirped or trilled, a melody of peeps and trumpet-like sounds. I started to respond to this feline communication.

Chirp.

"Hello."

Trill.

"Yes, I'm home."

Chirp.

"My day was okay. Yours?"

Chirp.

"I see you've moved the kitchen sponge to the living room floor."

Chirp.

"Hunting?"

Chirp. Chirp.

"It looks dead. Good job." I petted his head.

Trill.

Months passed, and Mr. Bojangles (whom I called Bo) continued to initiate musical conversations. I continued to respond. When I was a child, no one spoke to me in my home. I was ignored or told to be quiet. I didn't want to do the same to Bo.

Chirp.

"Yes?"

Chirp. Chirp.

"Yes, you're handsome."

Chirp.

"So handsome."

Chirp. Chirp.

"The most handsome cat in the world. I don't know why humans stopped worshipping cats."

Trill.

Then, I lost him. He ran out the door into a patch of woods near the highway. My reaction surprised me. I was afraid for him. I didn't love him, but I truly cared about his welfare. I searched the woods for hours, fearing that he'd be killed by the local coyotes. At nightfall, I realized that I was not meant to be his caretaker. I reminded myself that he was a stray from birth, and he knew how to survive. Perhaps he realized that he was better off on his own. The Internet suggested that I leave a door open in case he decided to return. I was awake at 2:00 A.M. when Bo came strolling through the door as if nothing had happened.

"Where were you?" I yelled.

Trill. Trill. He rubbed against my legs briefly and then left to visit his food dish. No explanation. No apology. Just an understanding that I would resume my responsibilities as his caretaker without bias or resentment. After that night, I was careful not to let him out of the house without a harness.

A year passed, and we settled into a routine. When I awoke, Bo-Bo, as I also called him, demanded that I hold him in my arms so that he could rub his cheeks on my face. He barraged me with chirps and trills to bring me up to speed about what had occurred while I slept. When I returned home in the evenings, he requested a dance by persistently meowing until I picked him up.

In the beginning, we slowly danced to the many recordings of "Mr. Bojangles," his favorite being Sammy Davis Jr.'s. I held him in my arms, swayed and sang, "I knew a man Bojangles, and he danced for you in worn-out shoes…." Later, we transitioned to faster songs, which allowed Bo-Bo to shuttle between my legs, run around me in circles, and jump onto my shoulders. We must have looked like an uncoordinated circus act.

One night, sobbing inconsolably in bed, I was unable to dance. Twenty-seven years after she left, I realized that my mother was truly gone. She began disappearing when my father had an affair and fathered a secret child. In the long years that followed, he financially, emotionally, and sexually abused my mother. She spent most hours of every day locked in her bedroom as our home deteriorated around us. I watched as windows cracked, toilets clogged, and gangs of spiders and cockroaches multiplied.

Nothing was repaired. Nothing was made right. Eventually, my mother just disappeared. Her body remained present, and she continued to smile and engage with other people, but with me she simply wasn't there. She was "broken." She didn't have the capability to be a mother, and at sixty-five years old, with my father long dead, she still wasn't capable.

Bo-Bo lay by my head, positioning his back to my face. I moved away to give him space, but he didn't want space. He repositioned his back to press himself up against my face, and I cried into his fur. After years of trying to reach my mother, I knew she was gone for good, and the woman who was left in her wake was a shell of the woman I had once loved.

Bo-Bo's back was wet with my tears. I was sure that he would eventually leave me, but he never did. He stayed. I cried myself to sleep in a pillow of black fur. And when I awoke in the morning, he was still there. Then, I was able to say it.

"I love you, Bo."

Chirp. Translation: "I know."

Loving and being loved is a primal dance. Many are taught this dance from birth by wonderful partners who know how to embrace them, spin them, lead them, and keep the rhythm until they themselves are able to take the lead. Some of us learn this dance later in life when we find the right partners. Others, however, may never learn it. Mr. Bojangles taught me this dance. He took the lead until I was able to do so on my own. In time, I was able to dance with new friends and a lover who didn't hesitate to take his turn on the dance floor with Mr. Bojangles.

—Amanda Ann Gregory—

Not the Brady Bunch

Cats are a kindly master, just as long
as you remember your place.
~Paul Gray

We were three mild-mannered middle-aged females — a compatible trio. Buffy and Mary Kay were affectionate with me and each other. They shared lap time and bed space, ate side by side, and curled up together in yin and yang position. Peace reigned in our San Diego canyon-side home.

A hundred miles away, in a Redlands bungalow, a man — let's call him Don — lived in a companionable threesome with his boy cats. Charlie and Ditto were big guys, the strong and silent type. Friendly but circumspect, a bit skittish with strangers.

Don and I enjoyed a long-distance liaison for four years, exchanging regular weekend visits. Celebrating my birthday at his place one October, we dined at a Thai restaurant and attended a rousing performance of Rachmaninoff's "Piano Concerto No. 3," my favorite, at the Redlands Symphony.

Soon after returning home, we heard a noise on the porch. It was late, but Don often left crunchies and water for a charcoal stray, Mr. Gray, who roamed the neighborhood. We opened the door gently so as not to startle him or a creature of the night — a raccoon or possum — and were confronted by a tiny, orange kitten with long hair, stubby legs, round eyes, and a button face. It mewed earnestly and eagerly, twined around our legs and tried to slip into the house. "Go on, go home," we said, assuming it would find its way back to an anxiously waiting mama cat and human family. After a few beseeching mews, it was quiet. We peeked out; it was gone. "But how cute!" we said, with maybe a touch of longing.

The next morning, it was back on the porch, declaring squatter's rights, demanding entrance. We made inquiries, covering several blocks around the neighborhood, even on the other side of a busy, four-lane street. No one had seen the kitten or knew where it might have come from. It was there to stay.

Sweety, as he (confirmed by the vet) came to be called, was a rascal and became the alpha cat. He was never intimidated by the big boys, even though he was a midget, never reaching more than three-quarter size. He jumped on his annoyed but tolerant stepbrothers, and bit Don's fingers and ankles. Discipline was unknown, and roughhousing was indulged in this all-male household. Sweety became incorrigible in spite of my alternate-weekend attempts to civilize him. But he was adorable — poster-child, contest-winning adorable — and irresistibly sweet, which is how he got his name. He sighed with orgasmic bliss when he was petted or brushed, purring in breathless gasps.

A year later, Don and I merged lives, households, and cats. He and the three guys moved in with me and the two girls. "Love me, love my cats" was unspoken but understood on both sides — a package deal. And things were never the same.

Blended families. That's what they're called when two people with kids join forces and form a single household. Like the Brady Bunch. The kids adjust, right? Marcia, Jan and Cindy had their share of flaps with Greg, Peter and Bobby, but they became one big happy family. Ours was no televised fantasy, however, and the progeny never coalesced. My girls would have adapted to Charlie and Ditto, and vice versa, in live-and-let-live accord, but Sweety was another story. He harassed Mary Kay and Buffy day and night. He attacked them at their food bowls, attacked them upon entering a room, and attacked them just for the fun of it. With dread in their palpitating little hearts, they took to secluding themselves in one room, always on guard, creeping warily and only when necessary from point A to point B.

Over time and out of necessity, the feline five coexisted. I set up a separate litterbox and feeding station in the den where the girls felt relatively safe. Everyone paid appropriate homage to Sweety's exalted status — little Napoleon on his throne — and he, in turn, allowed the girls their private space, their DMZ. They all lived into their senior years and passed on, one at a time, to be buried in the canyon behind our house. Sweety was last, vanquishing his foes by sheer longevity to emerge the victor, commander of undivided human attention.

Among the many photos memorializing them, singly and in pairs, just one captures a rare occurrence — all five in the same room at the same time, enjoying a family evening with Mom and Dad. Just like the Brady Bunch (but without a maid).

— Alice Lowe —

Three Rotten Cats

It is impossible for a lover of cats to banish these alert,
gentle, and discriminating little friends, who give us
just enough of their regard and complaisance
to make us hunger for more.
~Agnes Repplier

My husband is a terrific guy. He spends a lot of time vacuuming up cat hair in our house. More than his fair share. I hate vacuuming, so I am happy to hand off this chore to him. I know he doesn't love the job either, but he is in charge of all things related to the cleaning of cats in this family. That was the deal we struck when our three "rotten cats" came to live with us.

We started out with only two. I say only because when you have three cats, well, it's a lot, and two cats seem like… a lot less.

I did not grow up with cats. I never liked cats. In fact, I hated them. My only experiences of other people's cats involved dead mice on the front porch and cat scratches on the owner's hands. No thanks.

But when we bought our first home, we decided we should have pets. After some discussion, we agreed that we did not live a lifestyle that would be fair to a dog. Okay, settled. No pets.

Then, one day, my husband said, "What about a cat?"

"No," I said. "No cats."

"Why?"

"I hate cats."

"You do not hate cats. And I like cats."

"Yes," I said. "I definitely do hate cats."

"Why do you hate cats?"

"Easy. I hate cats. I have reasons."

"Such as…"

"Well, they claw things. They hang out with spooky types like witches. And I heard they sit on babies' chests and suck their breath out."

"We don't have a baby," he said. "I fail to see the problem here."

"But witches…" I insisted.

Silence.

My husband did not take the opportunity presented to him at that moment to make a comment about me and witches. In his shoes, I probably would have. Like I said, he's a pretty terrific guy. But I digress.

Fast forward several months. A woman at work sent out a staff email saying she was caring for an abandoned kitten but she already had too many cats. We inquired but found that the kitty had already been promised. We were too late. (Or lucky. Whew.) However, she told us about a friend who just happened to foster for a local no-kill shelter. Would we like her phone number? She was certain her friend was currently caring for a litter that needed homes.

The next thing I knew, we had an appointment to take a long drive and go meet these cats. I was willing but reluctant. I'm sure I muttered things about "rotten cats" all the way there. When we arrived, we found that the foster lady had three cats remaining from the litter. I knew where this was going. My husband—Mr. He Who Likes Cats—wanted to take all three home with us.

"Oh, no," I said. "NO WAY!"

We agreed that we would get two—one, two—so they could keep each other company when we weren't home or whatever. NOT THREE. After some debate, we made our selection and went home the resigned but proud owners of two cats. Terrific.

Fast forward to early December. We got a Christmas card from the rotten cats' foster mom. Aside from holiday wishes and inquiries about the two boys, she explained that the remaining brother was still not adopted, had completely withdrawn from playing with other foster cats, did not engage at adoption days, and even seemed to miss the other two. Would we consider adopting the remaining one and give it a try?

I suddenly felt like I had the word "sucker" stamped on my head.

To be totally honest, I must admit that the idea of that last leftover brother haunted me for weeks before that card came. My husband, of course, had by this time decided that three cats is indeed too many cats and advised strongly against claiming the last brother.

Now what?

We took a poll, and the odds were stacking up against this little bugger. The vote came down to our two moms. His mom said that three cats are too many cats, and she would not advise having three cats. I knew what my mom would vote — she hated cats even more than I did. (It's probably where I heard the stuff about witches and babies.)

So, we asked her.

In an unprecedented show of kitty sympathy, my mother said something to the effect of, "She has one lonely brother left? And he misses them? And he's sad?"

"Yup." I was sure she would agree that three cats would be a very bad idea, and this whole issue would be settled.

"You HAVE to go get him."

Unbelievable.

So, we went and got him.

By Christmas Eve, we had upped our population to three rotten cats. All brothers. All black. (See? All set to hang with witches.) And ALL IN OUR HOUSE.

While I was strongly opposed to the idea of cats at first, I have to admit that I have become a reluctant but devoted cat mom over the years. Three cats are a lot of cats, but I don't think we'd have it any other way. Every one of those three "rotten cats" turned out to be sweet, affectionate, and highly entertaining. They never did claw the furniture or suck the breath from our daughter, they don't puke on the carpet (much), and they do their business in a box (most of the time). Very often, much to my amusement, all three might be found hovering in my general vicinity.

And the leftover one? We think he knows my mom is the one who voted to rescue him. He loves her.

She's thrilled.

— Lisa A. Listwa —

Attack of the Closet Cat People

*Any conditioned cat-hater can be won over by any cat
who chooses to make the effort.*
~Paul Corey

You know the type: anxious, awkward people, almost out of place as if from another planet. You notice them innocently enough at parties, the park, or the back shelves of your local pet store. You come around a corner, and you see one eyeing a set of mouse toys. You approach, and they turn, suddenly fascinated by a wide selection of chew bones. But you know the look. They're cat people, trapped in a dog world.

How do I know? Because I'm one of them, a closet cat person, and my story is typical. My wife and I own a dog, an adorable Teacup Terrier with a chocolate-brown goatee named Dino. I named him Dino because he's as friendly as the Flintstones' dinosaur dog, only a lot smaller and not a dinosaur. Dino's favorite trick is to burn off excess energy by running on a treadmill for an hour and then rolling his sweaty backside across my thousand-thread-count bedsheets.

I was extremely happy when he first arrived. Dino was a constant source of entertainment. But, over time, I found my eye wandering. I didn't know why. I love my dog and was committed to him. Still, the feeling pounced on me. I'd see a cute fuzzball chasing a leaf across a neighbor's lawn, and I would say to my wife, "Aaaaah! I want a kitty."

Of course, I was aware of the dangers. Cats are notoriously fickle. They do what they want when they want — unlike my Dino, who waits faithfully by the door for my return. Cats love conditionally. They'd rather sleep in the sun or sit for a half-hour watching the tub fill with water than be caught playing a game of fetch.

I knew my wife would never understand. Like me, she was raised in a strict "dog household." At any given time, my family owned at least two Rottweilers, a Pekingese, and a wide assortment of Labradoodles. But a cat? Never!

Nevertheless, I surrendered. I remember the day it happened: Super Bowl Sunday. I was enjoying the Puppy Bowl pre-show. A commercial came on, and by accident, I switched to the Kitten Bowl. I fell off the doggy wagon at the first cuddly touchdown. My pulse quickened. The sound of purring filled my ears. Before I knew it, I was out the door and heading to Petco to find a rescue.

I call my new baby, Max, after the bad boy in *Where the Wild Things Are*. He is a pure black kitten with a single white patch on his left rear paw. He had me at meow — I was helpless the moment I saw him — hooked on some cosmic catnip.

The proudest day of my life was when I presented Max to my wife. She was hesitant at first. Visibly shaken. Then, something unpredictable happened. She scratched Max behind the ear and said, "You know, I've always wanted a cat."

"Is that so?"

"Yeah," she said, with a crooked grin, "but do me one favor."

"What's that?'

"Never tell my family."

I found an app that interprets Max's meows. A long meow means, "I know I just ate, but it's GOT to be dinnertime." A short, jagged cry means, "I'm not liking this messy litterbox one bit. Get on it!" And a short, sharp meow is unmistakable for, "Squirt me with that water bottle one more time and your potted plant is a goner. I have teeth, I have claws, and I know how to use them!"

Max wasted no time in training us when to wake and when to hit the sack. At exactly 10:00 every night, he jumps in front of the TV and meows (the short, sharp kind) as if to say, "Have you noticed the time? What say we have ourselves a good lick-bath and head up to Grandma's warm, handmade quilt?"

Max and Dino were mortal enemies from the get-go. Whenever Dino tried to sniff out his new rival, two deadly swipes told him, in no uncertain terms, who was boss. At first, I fed them in separate rooms. Then, one morning, I found them nudging each other out of the same dish — reconciled over a can of Liver in Gravy. It warmed my heart to see they had reached a truce (probably celebrated by the ceremonial destruction of the backside of my sofa). The sight inspired me. It was time to come clean. The world had to know.

Since then, my wife and I admit to anyone (including our families) that there is room enough in our home and our hearts for both dogs and cats. And that barks and meows sound beautiful together. But, hold on, there's more. Last week, a fascinating, little critter caught my eye. It was cracking seeds while chirping soulfully on a rickety swing. Someday, you may run into me in the pet aisle, a mirror with a little bell attached in one hand, a cuttlebone in the other. And, I say, be prepared. Because we're coming: It's the attack of the closet parrot people.

Warning: If you are considering coming over to the dark side and joining the rest of us cat-loving dog owners, be advised. Owning a cat can lead to uncontrollable wackiness.

Possible side effects may include:

- Insisting your cat has a right to disrupt the dog park.
- Introducing your parents to your pet as Grandma and Granddad.
- Hoping your cat will watch Animal Planet, or at least a commercial with an emu in it.
- Laughing at the lump moving under your slipcovers.
- Hiding your cat in an Amazon box and surprising family members over and over again with a "special delivery."
- Wondering why no one trains police cats.
- Wondering why no one has come up with mouse-flavored cat food.
- Sampling cat treats because they simply look yummy on the package.

- Noticing your cat is by your side if you're crying.
- Arranging your whole routine, your whole house, and your whole life to satisfy the whims of an annoying little creature who you would never, ever want to live without.

— Steve Patschke —

Floating on a Pachelbel Cloud

There are two ways to forget about life's
worries: music and cats.
~Albert Schweitzer

I live alone and I'm seventy-six. I found the pandemic especially lonely. Initially, my daughter shopped for me, but — concerned about the higher death rate among elders — she wouldn't touch me. Even with hearing aids on, I couldn't understand what people said when wearing masks. Webinars and Zoom proved an unexpected blessing. Every spoken word came through loud and clear. Nonetheless, the COVID-enforced confinement morphed into a sense of disoriented isolation. I missed having guests over. I missed the outside world I'd participated in. Mostly, I yearned to touch a live, warm being. I remembered the rhesus monkey studies. Without touch, some of them died. I felt like a rhesus.

Eventually, I decided to adopt a cat. "I'm looking specifically for a lap cat," I explained over the phone to someone at the pet shelter. Everything transpired at a COVID distance.

"We have just the cat for you. She's about ten years old, brought to us from the street," the shelter woman explained over the phone. "You'll be happy with her. She's such a love bug."

They sent me photos of a cat named Bumblebee in honor of her coloring: tabby, black and gray stripes mixed with a white belly and rusty, orange-brown markings here and there. I decided to adopt her. But the name had to go. I named her Ketzeleh (Kitty in Yiddish, and a term of affection for little girls). I ended up calling her the abbreviated Ketzie.

The shelter lady hadn't mentioned Ketzie's vulture-swooping-on-prey nips on hands or arms — not skin-piercing but causing a flash of stinging pain. Maybe that's why they called her Bumblebee, I decided. The speed of attack startled me, leaving me leery of touching Ketzie.

"Those shelter people lied to me. By omission," I whined to a friend over the phone. "I asked the shelter about it later, and, yes, she'd snapped at them, too. And they aren't love nips," I explained. "They're attacks. So I'm going to give her back."

But I fretted over Ketzie's past. What fears had that cat lived through on the street? How often had she had to react with lightning speed to protect herself? Her stomach skin sagged; she'd given birth to kittens on the street. How had she cared for them? And, how could I give that cat back after she had started getting used to a safe and permanent home? I couldn't.

Ketzie wanted to get outside, back to her habitual environment. She spent most of her waking hours sitting at open — but screened — windows. When I first got her, I heard a horrific caterwauling from the kitchen. I dashed in and found her stuck fast to the window screen. Her front and back legs splayed out at obtuse angles. Her claws, caught in the meshing, held her in place. Obviously, she'd hoped to land outside, not pinned down and still indoors.

About six months in, she began to relax. She'd jump onto my lap and stand stiff-legged, her tail switching like a metronome. But she'd let me pet her. I discovered that if I rubbed her chest, she'd lie down in my lap. She'd even purr — for a minute, at best.

Then, she'd hop away. Later, she began to lie down on my lap, but she was still wary. Her tail twitched. And, more often than not, she'd nip. Ten months in, she started jumping onto my bed to wake me up with a gentle pat to my cheek. Then, she'd lie beside me, gently breathing on my face.

As Ketzie and I reached one year together, I started a new meditation routine to music. I chose Pachelbel's "Canon in D." The music swells open, then more and more, ever expanding. To me, it sounds like how meditation feels. I found a one-hour, repetitious version on YouTube.

One day, I'd settled into my comfy armchair to meditate. Ketzie sat on the couch all the way across the living room, watching birds and squirrels outside. The music started. Ketzie spun around. Her ears rotated, sonar receivers honing in on the sound. I closed my eyes and started my meditation. I felt myself inhaling. Slowly. Exhaling. Slowly.

Suddenly, I felt a bump on my legs. Ketzie had just jumped onto my lap. I opened my eyes and started petting her. She melted down. Then, she stretched across my lap. Her front legs wrapped over my right thigh. Her tail draped over my left thigh, completely still and at ease. I stroked her from forehead to tail. She purred and raised her head to meet my hand with each stroke. I closed my eyes again. Breathed deeply, in and out. So we sat for a good half-hour.

The next day, when I turned on the "Canon," Ketzie trotted from the kitchen into the living room and right onto my lap. As I meditated, I imagined Maui's turquoise waters and white-sand beaches. Felt myself basking in the warmth. As Ketzie listened to the music, did she envision herself stalking through the backyard garden? Stretching out on a piece of sun-warmed earth for a nap? Whether Ketzie envisioned anything or not, we'd become intimates — two souls floating together on a Pachelbel cloud.

— Judith Gussmann —

Help Came on Four Feet

What greater gift than the love of a cat?
~Charles Dickens

The day began with me spotting an unwelcome vine crawling on my screen. I stopped abruptly on my way to the garage to get my gardening gloves. Cleo had left his muddied paw prints on top of Dick's car again. I groaned and wiped them away before Dick could complain. His words already echoed in my head. "How much longer am I going to have to put up with that cat?"

The black longhaired feline with jade-green eyes had come to us from out of the woods a couple of years earlier. Although he had been our cat for a good while, Dick was still uncertain he would stay. My husband generally likes cats, but he doesn't like their pawprints on the vehicles.

That's intolerable. I've got to get some kind of covering for the car, I thought.

Spring had come to Saddlebrooke, where our rural community enjoys the woodsy rolling hills between Ozark and Branson, Missouri. It was a beautiful sunny day and our newly green front yard looked lovely. However, at the side of the house, the retaining wall, which is actually large boulders stacked in a graduated pile, crawled with those stubborn vines twining over them. Knowing how this can attract unwanted pests and even snakes, I went to work.

Most of the vines released their grip easily, but a more stubborn patch sent me climbing up the rocks in order to get a stronger grip. When I pulled hard at these weeds, I plummeted to the pavement some three feet below. I landed hard on my seventy-one-year-old back.

Hot pain sliced through me. I couldn't move. I couldn't even breathe for a moment.

"Dick!" I screamed through tears of agony. The slightest motion caused further waves of pain.

My husband had busied himself in the garage with the radio volume turned up. My cries did not reach him.

"Dick, help!" I strained to raise my voice as loud as I could. I did not know if I was paralyzed. I only knew the pain was horrendous. I was the perfect example of the help-I've-fallen-and-I-can't-get-up commercial. My neighbors could not see me, and it was doubtful they would hear me unless they happened to be outdoors.

Between groans and moans, I kept calling, "Somebody, please!"

That's when Cleo arrived, mewing and circling me, clearly disturbed. He made soft sounds at first, and then louder yowls. When I moaned, he moaned, mimicking the sound of my voice. My kitty actually seemed to be imitating my cries for help.

"Go get somebody!" I begged. So what if I was talking to a cat? "Go get help," I urged. He darted off, to my surprise.

Inside the garage, Dick continued his work, oblivious to my circumstances. It was nothing unusual for Cleo to appear and wrap himself around Dick's leg with a purr of contentment, but this time Dick noticed the cat's behavior was definitely not usual. He mewed loudly and kept moving back and forth between Dick and the open garage door.

"What's wrong with you? You've been fed. You have fresh water," Dick said to the cat.

Cleo ran out and back in, mewing even more loudly.

Finally, Dick decided to follow him out of curiosity. "You've caught a mouse or a bird to show me, huh?"

The cat led him straight to me, still prone on the pavement.

"Carol!" Dick began asking questions. "Can you move? Where

does it hurt?"

He managed to help me up and assisted me, in terrible pain, into the house.

Later, emergency-room doctors examined, X-rayed, poked and probed. They found I had fractured a couple of lower vertebrae, prescribed medication and sent me home with a walker.

I began a slow recovery.

How long would I have lain there on the pavement? I can only guess. But Dick decided that Cleo can stay.

In fact, my four-footed rescuing angel is now quite welcome in our home. Dick has given final approval.

—H L Ford—

8

King James

Who hath a better friend than a cat?
~William Hardwin

My son Joe, a university student, prefers to study in the garage. He concentrates best when surrounded by nature — calls of birds, chattering of squirrels, and now and then barking dogs or mewing cats. Occasionally, a groundhog, raccoon or opossum wanders by. Deer sometimes stare from a safe distance. His area is outfitted with study necessities, and Joe is a well-established occupant of that corner of the garage.

One lovely spring morning, as Joe sipped his first cup of coffee and settled in to study, a small orange-and-white face peered around the corner of the garage door.

Meow.

"Hello. Who are you?"

Meow.

The small, furry kitten strode into the garage and began an extensive inspection. After pausing to accept strokes from Joe, he examined everything — Joe's study area, stored items, the top of the workbench, behind the trash bins, and the back of the old refrigerator. An unpainted plywood storage cabinet offered a convenient place on which to sharpen his claws.

His front legs were shorter than his back legs, and his left ear was half the size of his right one. A snowy white chest extended into white forepaws. Orange and white spots splotched the rest of his body.

Returning to Joe after extensive sniffing, he jumped up onto the center of the opened geology textbook on Joe's lap.

After a moment of nose-to-nose greeting, the kitten jumped down and disappeared the way he had come.

The next morning, the kitten returned. Once more, he jumped onto the geology book and greeted Joe.

That afternoon, Joe shopped for food and water dishes, a bag of kitty food, a large bag of litter, and a litterbox. The die was cast.

Kitty came every morning after that. Joe and I wondered what we should name him. Among our considerations were Stranger, Wanderer, and Pumpkin.

On the third day, while the kitten made his daily visit, a neighbor stopped by. "Good morning, Joe," Ashe said. She got out of her car and asked, "Have you seen a small orange-and-white kitten with a left half-ear?"

Meow.

"Oh, there you are, Jim. I've been looking everywhere for you. Come on, you need to come home."

"He showed up a couple of days ago and keeps coming back every morning," Joe explained. "I didn't know you had a new cat."

"Last week, I visited a farm, and when I got home, this little guy jumped out of my car. The farmer said it was just one of many barn cats, and I could keep him if I wished. I didn't know how to get rid of such an engaging little fellow, especially since he chose to come home with me."

"Why did you name him Jim?"

"That's a funny story. You see, my ex-husband's name was Jim, and he never listened to me either. It seemed only fitting. I took him to the veterinarian who confirmed that he is male and then vaccinated him. C'mon, Jim." She picked up the kitten and put him in her car.

The next morning, Jim peered around the corner of the garage—again. Later that day, the neighbor returned. "Jim, it seems, has chosen you, Joe. Here's the bag of food and kitty litter I bought for him. You might as well have them now. I'll stop and visit sometimes. Be good, Jim." She drove away.

At first, I insisted that he remain an outdoor cat. "Do not bring him into the house. I don't trust any barn cat, and I will not tolerate any evidence that a feline lives in my home."

For the remainder of that summer and into the fall, Jim commandeered a large wicker basket in the garage into which Joe fitted a warm blanket. The basket sits atop a spare stove near the door. He enjoys the elevated vantage point. He settled into the basket every night, ate his meals in the garage, and formed a strong bond with Joe.

As Jim grew, he began to wander, but never far from the house. He inspected the entire property and, over time, encountered birds at the feeder on the deck, other neighborhood cats, geese with goslings, and frogs in the pond. He sparred now and then with turtles creeping through the yard on their way to the lake.

He familiarized himself with his surroundings and developed a daytime habit of sleeping under the largest Hosta leaves to escape the mid-day heat. Unexpectedly, Jim's head would pop up above a Hosta plant. "Looking for me?" he seemed to say. At other times, he would appear from a flower bed and sprint across the yard directly toward a large oak tree. Leaping as high as possible, he would cling to the side of the tree, looking left then right with wide-eyed wonder. At some signal, seen or heard only by Jim, he would drop to the ground and amble away.

As the months passed, Joe worried about the weather getting colder. And Jim persisted in his attempts to come inside. I continued to insist that Jim remain an outdoor cat. "After all, he's a barn cat. They're tough." But as the night temperatures dropped, I relented. "Okay, Jim, you get one chance. If there is one accident or infraction of the house rules, you will immediately be an outdoor cat again. There will not be a second chance."

By then, he had endeared himself even to me, and his bond with Joe was unbreakable. Some family members call Jim a "dog-cat." He follows Joe wherever he goes and manages to communicate his every wish. He often lays a paw upon a human leg to demand immediate attention, and then flops to be petted. He presents first one side and then rolls to the other. He is quite insistent.

Jim is a permanent occupant of our home now. He has food and water dishes inside, a litterbox to which he is faithful, and two dedicated tower beds. Occasionally, he chooses to sleep in the center of Joe's bed. The reasons for his choices are known only to him. He cuddles with me atop a snuggly coverlet when I nap in my recliner some afternoons.

Our coexistence is pleasant — Jim and Joe and me — and I often wonder if King James, as Joe affectionately calls him, already had a plan on that early spring day.

—Judith Eassa—

9

An Accidental Cat

There are few things in life more heartwarming
than to be welcomed by a cat.
~Tay Hohoff

My fourth-grade students write opinion essays every fall, and inevitably there will be one giant class debate about cats versus dogs. I used to easily take the side of dogs, citing friendly tail wagging and unconditional love, not to mention how cute they are when you dress them like a taco for Halloween.

"Besides," I'd laugh, "cats are jerks."

My husband was a cat lover, but whenever he'd mention cats, I'd quickly change the subject. My kids had asked for a kitten, and I said I was allergic. Cats fascinated me, in a way, but much in the same way I'm fascinated by serial killers.

I didn't need nor want one more thing to have to clean up after. It was too much. We continuously said no to puppies, hamsters, and fish, even when one of my children made a PowerPoint slideshow complete with bullet points about why we needed a pet. I was quite happy being pet-free, thank you very much.

On the other hand, I urged everyone else in my life to get pets. My mom needed a dog. My single friend? Yes, get a puppy as a companion.

My mother-in-law had been widowed for ten years, and I think I'd been urging her to get a pet since the week my father-in-law died. She loved cats. I'm pretty sure that the only gifts I had ever gotten her involved a cat trinket, cat calendar, cat socks, or cat sweatshirt. She'd had two cats, Sage and Einstein, when I first met my husband, but they'd both passed away over the years.

She was not easily pleased, and she'd grumble about the winter months being lonely. "Okay, just get yourself a dog!" I'd urge. "Or, I guess, even a cat…" She didn't want the responsibility. She didn't want the mess. We had helped her do work around the house, and she didn't want an animal to ruin the new things she had. She always had a reason to refuse.

And so, eventually, I stopped trying. She'd made it clear that it wasn't going to happen, and I moved on to other things. And then one day, completely out of the blue, she called me. "Christy, can you come over right away? I need your help!"

I went rushing over, thinking something terrible had happened. Instead, she handed me an already opened can of tuna. "I can't find the cat," she said.

I stared at her. "Um… what cat?"

"The cat! The kitten!"

As it turns out, just the day before, she'd gone to the Humane Society to adopt a kitten. She'd seen a commercial for a "Name Your Donation" promotion and decided, on a whim, to go for it. But this (unnamed) kitten was already a nuisance. My mother-in-law wasn't very steady on her feet, and the kitten had gone downstairs and lodged itself somewhere.

After two hours, an entire can of tuna, a broom for nudging, and help from my children, we had the kitten back upstairs.

We stared at that thing for hours. She hopped and climbed and purred and rubbed her furry head on our legs. Her startled expression when there was a thud or noise made us laugh until there were tears in our eyes.

We (yes, even I) were in love.

The next day, we went back over just to play with the kitten. My daughter really wanted one of her own. She asked her grandma to borrow the kitten overnight, but nobody thought that was a great idea. So, instead, we just went and played. And laughed. And watched.

Sadly, the next Saturday, just one week since the little kitten had been adopted, my phone rang again. This time, it was a family member asking if I'd been in contact with my mother-in-law. I'd seen her just two days prior, I said. My husband was in France, and the kids and I had gone to see my mom, but we were back now.

I quickly found someone to watch my kids, and I drove over. The car was in the garage. The TV was on. I unlocked the door and found my sweet mother-in-law dead in her bed. And curled up next to her was that kitten.

Of course, I panicked. I called the police, funeral home and family. But while I sat alone, frightened and upset on the couch, waiting, that little kitten sat right next to me. As I left the house later that night, I called a friend and asked her what I should do about the cat.

"Christy, you know what to do," she said. And, of course, I did. And so she and all her things came home with me. Her name is now Little Anne, after Julianne, my mother-in-law.

I tell people who ask about my cat, "Oh, I hate cats. I just accidentally got one." And I laugh.

But, the truth is, I don't hate cats at all. And although I don't always know what I believe, I'm also pretty sure it was no accident.

— Christy Wopat —

10

This Is Gus

Cats need to meow because we humans
are generally so unobservant.
~John Bradshaw

Gus came with the house. Not exactly like a light fixture or a refrigerator, but a feral tabby who thought all five acres were his. Actually, before we closed on the property, the former homeowner asked if we wanted Gus. Otherwise, he would re-home him. Hubby-Jeffrey was at work when this offer was made.

"My husband hates cats," I said.

Then, Former-Homeowner mentioned something that clinched the deal. "You're in the country now. Lots of mice. Gus is a good mouser."

Mouse. That one word brought back a tidal wave of memories. We were living in a condo in Brookline, Massachusetts and had a mouse problem. They were brazen, too. One skipped joyfully across our bed. Another built a nest in my teenage son's backpack.

I promptly said, "We'll take the cat."

"What about your husband?"

"What about him?"

Hubby-Jeffrey was not convinced. He came from a cat-hating family. They weren't even allergic, just appalled. I, on the other hand, grew up with felines. My mom loved the kitten I brought home from the mall when I was ten and the dirty white fluff ball that followed me home from school when I was twelve. Jeffrey's mom had a revulsion of cats, its inception unknown, but passed down to her son like a genetic disease. Unfortunately, she didn't have a loving relationship with her son either. She was gone by the time I met Jeffrey; their unresolved feelings and her cat-revulsion reason were gone forever.

Sometime during the first year of our marriage, I suggested we get a pet. "As long as it's not a cat," Jeffrey said emphatically. We decided on a Springer Spaniel. Thirty years of marriage, four Springers, a bunny and two grown kids later, I convinced Jeffrey.

"Okay," he said suspiciously but added in a warning tone, "but he stays outside."

"That's fine," I said. "Former-Homeowner told me that the feral kittens who grow up outside know how to take care of themselves." I was smug while imparting my feline wisdom.

In the coming weeks, Gus made a few appearances, looking at us askance, probably wondering where that nice family with the teenage girls and friendly dogs was. (Ours was a true Spaniel. Apollo chased bunnies, squirrels and Gus.)

One day, Jeffrey and I walked the property and spotted Gus hiding in the shade, eyeing us.

"Gus," Jeffrey called, inching closer, at which Gus promptly hissed and took off.

"See?" Jeffrey said. "Cats are demons."

Soon enough, our sly cat started showing up at the back door when he realized we were the ones who put out the food and water and lived in the dwelling on his land.

About a month into our new living situation, while Hubby and I were lounging on the deck, Gus leapt onto Jeffrey's belly, curled up and closed his eyes. Jeffrey didn't budge. He looked at me, panicked. I mouthed, "Pet him." Jeffrey looked down at his torso and froze. He thought cats were jeering devils. After all, Gus had hissed at him a few weeks ago. But this sleek, orange feline was cuddling and drooling. (We later learned that some cats drool instead of purr.)

Jeffrey tentatively slid his hand along Gus's back, which made Gus rub his head into Jeffrey's belly like it was the best pillow ever. Little did we know that this orange feral cat enjoyed human interaction — and, most of all, with Jeffrey. In fact, as time went on, Gus chose Jeffrey over me. Gus would meow at the back door even though he already had food and water in his bowl, and if I merely turned the handle to go outside, he would take off. When Jeffrey slid through the door, Gus would jauntily follow him onto the lounge, hop onto his belly and promptly drool. He only wanted to cuddle with his new buddy.

Jeffrey fell hard for Gus.

A month or so later, as Jeffrey walked the property, I noticed Gus appear from a hedge and follow him. This wily tabby sipped at the stream while Jeffrey looked for salmon.

On the nights when we used the fire pit, Gus would spy on us and then meow to let us know he was near. If the coast was clear and Apollo was indoors, Gus would leap onto Jeffrey's lap, curl up and sleep.

Gus and Jeff. It suddenly made sense. Jeffrey loved the outdoors more than inside. He preferred grass to carpet. He decompressed amongst the trees and enjoyed late-night walks down the long driveway. He was just like Gus, who was always there, an orange shadow, prancing beside him.

"So, I guess you like cats now," I said. The light from the fire pit made him and Gus glow.

Jeffrey sighed and shook his head, regretting all those years of cat-abhorrence. "Gus is a pretty cool cat."

"Why did your mom hate them so vehemently?"

Jeffrey shrugged. "She never met Gus."

"Maybe your mom sent him from heaven. An olive branch," I said.

Jeffrey grinned. He liked this notion. "Maybe," he said. "Maybe."

— CK Steefel —

Cat People

Cats are endless opportunities for revelation.
~Leslie Kapp

"I'm so glad we're not cat people," I told my wife, Rachael, with a slight laugh as we walked by an overpriced wooden cat tower covered in shag carpet at the supermarket.

"Me, too," she replied. "The litter smell and fur all over the couch? No thanks."

Just a few weeks later, our opinion changed. On an early summer evening, we walked to the park down the street from our house for a quick game of tennis.

"Look, a kitten," Rachael said as we approached the tennis courts.

I noticed a small gray cat under the bench next to the last of the three courts. As soon as we walked through the chain-link fence gate and onto the court, the cat ran toward us. Desperate for attention, she began to purr as she rubbed against my leg, so I knelt down to pet her. After some quick observations — no collar, fleas, skinny, and a bad cut on her bottom lip — it was easy for us to conclude that she was abandoned, not lost.

As we stood on the court debating what to do next, we noticed a man approaching with his dog. When the dog noticed the cat, he immediately began to bark loudly as he pulled his owner toward the tennis-court fence.

"Excuse me! Do you know anyone who is missing a cat?" Rachael asked.

"I don't. Any collar?"

"No, we think she was abandoned."

"It looks like she's a Blue Russian. They're a popular breed. Someone was probably breeding them and dumped this one here because of the cut on her mouth. And it looks like her tail is bent."

We looked at her tail and realized he was right; her tail had a slight bend to the left.

"Do you know of any animal shelters in the area?" I asked.

The man shouted the name of one as his dog pulled him away from the tennis court. I pulled out my phone and Googled the number to call the shelter, but they were already closed, and their voicemail message said they were not accepting any new animals. We then discussed our options. At that point, we only had two: leave her on the court or take her home.

"If she follows us out of the park, we'll take her home," I said, knowing that she probably would.

Rachael agreed, and we began to make our way out of the tennis court. As predicted, there was a Blue Russian behind us. I picked up the small kitten and began to think of all the things we needed to do. The first thing we decided was to take her to the pet emergency clinic to have the cut on her lip examined. When we arrived and explained the situation to the front desk clerk, she asked if we were going to take ownership of the cat. When I replied that we weren't sure yet and just wanted to have the cat examined, she explained that they could not perform any treatment unless there was an owner.

They want to make sure they are going to get paid, I thought to myself.

I turned to Rachael, smiled, and said, "Well, it looks like we're officially cat owners now!"

After the clerk entered our information into her computer, she asked a question we were not prepared for: the name of the cat.

"Hmm… We don't even know if it's male or female," I said.

The clerk looked at her underside and told us we were the owners of a female cat.

"We'll call her Ana," Rachael informed the clerk.

As we waited in the exam room for the veterinarian, I asked Rachael how she picked the name Ana.

"It's short for Anastasia. We have to give her a Russian-sounding name since she's a Blue Russian," she replied with a smile and a small shrug.

The doctor informed us that Ana would need to have surgery to fix the cut on her lip but otherwise had a clean bill of health. After receiving a crash course in pet care, we went to the grocery store to pick up the essentials: cat food, food and water bowls, a litterbox, and a few toys. We finally made it back home around 10:00 P.M. and still had to give Ana a bath to make sure all the fleas were off of her.

After a few weeks, it was hard for us to imagine our house without Ana there. One morning as I looked around our house, I noticed the litterbox, a dozen-plus cat toys spread across the floor, and even one of those overpriced, wooden cat towers covered in shag carpet. Ana was perched on top of the couch looking out the living room window. I turned to Rachael and said with a smile, "Yep, we are definitely cat people now."

— Cory Conner —

Small But Mighty

12

The Alarm Cat

You are my cat, and I am your human.
~Hilaire Belloc

The phone rang, and I knew it was my routine morning call from my sister, Joan. "Good morning," I said. "How are you?"

"Tired," she replied. "This darned cat has rattled me out of bed at 2:30 A.M. three times this week! I don't know what on earth is wrong with her, but Kitty-Cat is driving me berserk! She's a hundred years old, and she's ornery as an old goat and absolutely lives to torment the dog. But she still knows exactly what she wants and has a ton of personality."

I laughed and said, "So, what does she want when she gets you up?"

"Tuna!" my sister huffed. "Ever since I had to start giving her arthritis medicine, I've had to hide it in tuna to get her to eat it. Now she wants her tuna for breakfast every single morning at 7:00 A.M. sharp. I wake up to her sitting by my bed meowing at the top of her lungs. And then this pitiful seventeen-year-old cat that cannot walk five steps without sitting down for a rest takes off to the kitchen like a cheetah on steroids!"

This was the cat my niece had brought home, against her mother's wishes. That cat had actually been a huge comfort to my sister shortly after she became part of the family because my brother-in-law died of a massive heart attack at only age fifty. The cat had started sleeping with her, sat with her in her recliner, and seldom left her side. They had been inseparable for several years. That is, until the day she remarried.

I was at her house one day and noticed that Kitty-Cat was not sitting with her. She reached down to pet her, and she hissed and swatted at her hand.

I said, "What on earth is wrong with Kitty-Cat? Did she just swat you? I thought you two were inseparable."

"Yeah, we were. She always loved me to pieces until I married Pat. She immediately threw me over, and now she's *his* cat and won't have anything at all to do with me!"

"So," I said, "if she gets her tuna at 7:00, why was she waking you at 2:30?"

"I don't know. That's the problem. But this past week, three days in a row, at exactly 2:30 she is sitting by my bed screaming like a banshee until I get up. I don't know what's up with her. Maybe daylight savings time has messed up her internal clock."

"Well," I said, "I sure know it has mine."

We chatted for a few more minutes and hung up to get on with our day.

A few minutes later, my phone rang again. It was Joan.

I picked up, curious as to why she was calling right back.

"Hey, what's up?"

"You know how I told you that Kitty-Cat woke me up at 2:30 for three nights this week?"

"Yes?"

"Do you remember me telling you that the doctor changed my diabetes medicine last week, and we were working to get the dosage adjusted? Well, it just occurred to me that each night when Kitty-Cat woke me, I got up feeling really weird. I checked my sugar each time, and it was drastically low. So, I had a glass of milk and a light snack and went back to bed. I've been a little concerned that it was dropping like that, so I adjusted my dosage down a bit yesterday."

"Did that help?"

"Well, yeah, it did. But I was sitting at the breakfast table just now thinking that if the cat had not woken me up when she did, I could have been in real trouble. And I realized that after I had adjusted my medicine yesterday, and my sugar appeared more stable this morning, that was the one night this week when Kitty-Cat did not wake me up. I know this sounds crazy, but I believe that cat was waking me up intentionally because she knew something was wrong. And I know, absolutely, that if it hadn't been for her waking me, we might not be having this conversation."

—Andrea Peebles—

13

S'more

I think having an animal in your life
makes you a better human.
~Rachael Ray

t had been a year since I resigned my first-grade position, and I was still struggling to find a routine and purpose. I had been in a classroom for the better part of ten years.

Why couldn't I just be content?

"Think of it this way," my husband reminded me. "If you were still teaching, you wouldn't be able to go on this choir trip with our daughters." At 4:00 in the morning I would be on a bus full of tweens.

Of course, he was right. I was grateful to be available to our family and our business.

When I woke up in the middle of the night to catch that bus I thought I was imagining the familiar meowing of our cat, S'more, at the back door. We had not seen our marshmallow, chocolate and graham cracker–colored kitty in over two months! She'd gone missing in January and we'd accepted that the cold Wyoming winter had been too much for her to survive.

S'more had come to us six years prior as an orphan kitten when her eyes were barely open. My husband had found her on the front lawn of our restaurant after closing. She was in a cardboard box, so small and alone. And so feisty! I had reached in the box to pick her up and jumped back in fear as she hissed and spit at me. I reminded myself that she was the size of a plum and was harmless. I snuggled her close as her little love motor started.

When we brought her home, she made it clear that she wanted to be outside and not trapped by the walls of our home. She came and went as she pleased, but always found herself most content in her cathouse on our back porch or curled up on our laps. We would pet her, and she would purr and drool to show her gratitude.

Now I raced to the back door. "Girls!" I yelled. "S'more is back!" She zipped in with the cold as I slid open the glass door. I noticed that she was skinny and had a little limp as she raced up the stairs and jumped up onto our daughter's bed. But she was alive!

It was a happy and tearful reunion. Unfortunately, it was crunch time, and we could not miss that bus.

Then I heard a call of panic and disbelief. "Mom! Get in here!" The girls' tears had gone from happy to frantic.

I raced down the hall. As they were petting her, they discovered that part of one of her front legs was missing. It was gone. Somehow, S'more had been in an accident that left her with only three legs. She didn't seem to be in a lot of pain, but we knew she needed a vet.

It was a difficult morning as we boarded the bus and left our kitty after such a short reunion.

"I promise I will take care of her while you are gone," my husband said.

And he did. My husband took S'more to the vet that morning. She had surgery to remove what was left of her front leg.

I called the vet later that day. "She may have got it caught in something. She will adapt quickly and know her limits. She is resilient. Even though she isn't going to be able to do everything she once did, she is still the same cat she was before her accident. She will probably be even more content to stay close to home."

The following fall, on a warm afternoon when school was about to start back up, I was once again struggling with my purpose and not being in the classroom. S'more rubbed against my legs.

I remembered what the vet had said. "S'more will adapt. She is resilient. She is still your cat."

S'more had adapted so quickly and effortlessly. She still chased after moths and found the best spots of sun to lie in. She was every bit as much our cat now as she was before and even more content to stay close to home.

I pulled S'more up onto my lap and let her drool on me. I was grateful that my three-legged cat was the teacher that day. She taught me to be content and grateful for all the blessings in my life, and that life a little closer to home was just where I should be.

—Leslie Colburn—

14

Friends for Life

The language of friendship is not words but meanings.
~Henry David Thoreau

Our tabby Abby was not happy when Mowgli showed up at her house. Abby was a rescue herself, and she had grown accustomed to being our only cat for the better part of a year. She did not welcome the tabby kitten who had brazenly invaded her realm.

In an effort to keep Mowgli out of harm's way, our response to Abby's aggression was to put him in a carrier so they could safely check each other out. And then we soon realized that fairness required that the two kitties would have to share the burden of captivity by taking turns in the carrier.

It only took a few days for things to improve. The turning point came when we walked into a room and witnessed Abby sleeping pressed up against the carrier, with Mowgli sleeping peacefully inside. The strategy had worked and their friendship blossomed.

Years passed, with Mowgli weighing in at about twelve pounds to Abby's eight. All the same, it was clear that Abby — never having fully given up her seniority — managed to occupy alpha-cat status. All she had to do was move in close with an air of calm detachment, and Mowgli yielded space.

It didn't really matter whether I understood all the mysteries of their kitty world. What mattered were their endless hours of grooming each other while awake, and how they curled up with each other while asleep.

Although Abby and Mowgli were free to go outside when they asked, they rarely did so except when some of their people were out. Even then, they seemed happy to stay close to the house, climbing and playing in the trees on our small but heavily wooded lot.

And so it was on a pleasant spring day when leaves and other debris were being cleaned up, and I was otherwise occupied inside. At some point, I noticed Abby following me around and nervously pacing. Distracted by my work, I didn't pay much attention. But when she frantically ran to the back slider door, began pacing in circles, and cried out in an uncharacteristically loud yowl, I knew something was amiss. I followed her as she darted to a bathroom, jumped on the sill of an open window, and resumed her bellowing. She looked at me beseechingly, with panic in her eyes, and then directed her attention back outside.

When I peered out the window, the pieces came together in a flash. Lying on the ground directly under the window was a black plastic yard-waste bag, filled up and tightly twisted closed. And where was Mowgli? I raced out the back door to where the bag lay. As I quickly yet carefully opened the bag, Mowgli popped out.

He didn't seem traumatized or hurt, just happy and grateful for the rescue, enthusiastically rubbing up against his people and Abby alike.

We're not sure exactly how long Mowgli was trapped. And we're not sure how Abby knew where he was. But we do know that the kitty who seemed ready to kill Mowgli at first meeting had now saved his life.

— Barbara Woods —

15

Claws for Concern

A beating heart and an angel's soul, covered in fur.
~Lexie Saige

My husband and I had just purchased our first house together, so we were eager to spend the weekend cleaning it out and fixing it up. The place was a tiny two-bedroom fixer-upper and we could hardly wait to make it into a cozy home.

My mother-in-law Denise had volunteered to do the heavy scrubbing indoors, leaving my father-in-law to do handyman repairs throughout the house. My husband and I would work on the fence and yard. We would be leaving our black rescue cat Squeakers indoors with them until she got used to the place. We didn't want the cat outdoors with us yet, possibly running away or accidentally sticking to the fresh coat of paint on the fence.

As we gathered our materials for the day ahead, we heard my mother-in-law grumbling that the upstairs bathtub had some water stains from a dripping tap that would be hard to get off. Since she was a fanatical cleaner, we were confident that she'd find a way. While we prepared to head out the door, she tied her trusty red bandana around her face to block out dust and fumes before marching upstairs to begin the hard work.

We began setting up for painting outside, while Squeakers peered out the upstairs window that had been left open to air the house. She mewed plaintively at us, letting us know she wanted to join us outdoors. She was going to have to grin and bear it for a few days before we let her outside.

From time to time, she would appear at the window with one of her toys. She was trying to entice us to come indoors to play with her. It was cute, but I hoped she would soon forget about us and tag along with my in-laws inside.

Our day progressed without too many cat interruptions until my father-in-law came out of the house a few hours later. He was heading to the hardware store to pick up some more supplies for the house renovation and asked for a list of anything else we might need. He would also pick up some sandwiches and cat food to feed us some lunch.

After he left, Squeakers came to the window more often, meowing more shrilly each time. We thought she must be getting bored now that she had one less person to stalk indoors. Like us, she was probably also wanting some lunch. We tried to ignore her as we kept our noses to the grindstone outside.

Then we heard her meows turn into muffled squeals as she returned to the window one more time. Looking up, we saw that she had something red and bulky in her mouth. It fluttered down to us when she let it go. Talk about a red flag! It was Denise's red bandana.

We stared at each other for a moment, and then we rushed inside to see if something had happened to Denise. Calling as we entered, we were greeted by a frantic Squeakers but no response from my mother-in-law. We found her passed out in the bathroom, surrounded by cleaning chemicals and sponges.

Two common household cleansers that should never be mixed are ammonia and bleach because they react together to form toxic vapors. Denise probably thought that if one product wasn't enough to handle the task of cleaning the stains from the bathtub enamel, mixing it with another would make it better. By the time we dragged her limp body out of there, the poisonous chemicals had eaten right through the enamel, creating a toxic mist that she had accidentally inhaled.

Our Red Cross training came in handy as we resuscitated her while we waited for the ambulance to arrive. The medical team took over immediately on arrival and then whisked her to the nearest hospital emergency ward. We followed them in our car, biting our nails while phoning my father-in-law.

After standing around the waiting room for what seemed like forever, a doctor arrived to let us know that my mother-in-law would recover relatively soon. They didn't think Denise had been exposed to the poisonous vapors long enough to do permanent damage.

We left Denise at the hospital with her husband at her side and headed back to our house project with the supplies, sandwiches and cat food that he had purchased. Once there, we feasted on lunch with Squeakers as we gave her extra attention and praise. Thanks to her, the day had not ended in tragedy.

—Donna L. Roberts—

16

Othello Revisited

While we are mourning the loss of our friend,
others are rejoicing to meet him behind the veil.
~John Taylor

We all know that some people become more famous after their deaths than they were while they were alive. Well, it seems this can sometimes be the case for cats, too.

Othello was a starving black cat who wandered into our garden in Derbyshire, England in 2015. He clearly didn't have a home, so eventually my partner and I adopted him. We nursed him back to health, and he grew into a good-looking and happy cat.

We used to go to cat shows in the past, so when Othello was healthy again, we decided to have a go at showing him. He did unbelievably well, ending up as an Imperial Grand Master Cat, which is the non-pedigree equivalent of an Imperial Grand Champion.

We then gave him his own Facebook page — Othello the Amazing Black Cat — and he had quite a following, though mainly among our own Facebook friends and cat-show acquaintances. But, soon afterward, Othello became ill, and eventually, in 2019, we had to say goodbye to him. As far as his Facebook page was concerned, I thought that would be the end of the interest. He had over 100 likes, which seemed pretty good to me at the time. It was obvious that people liked him. But his story seemed hardly likely to take off or go viral. Why would it? He was only a little black cat.

Soon after Othello's passing, I wrote a story about him that was published in *Chicken Soup for the Soul: The Magic of Cats* in 2020. I mentioned that Othello had a Facebook page but really just in passing, not expecting anyone to be very interested. So, what happened next left me utterly gobsmacked!

Soon after the book was published we started getting messages on Othello's page. These weren't from friends or even from anyone in England, the only country where Othello had been known when he was alive. No, they were from people I'd never heard of, from all over the world. They seemed to be cat lovers who had read about Othello in the *Chicken Soup for the Soul* book. We started getting messages on the page, slowly at first, and then more and more of them. Here are a few from the early days....

"I just read the story in the book and just had to look him up. Awesome kitty...."

"Just read about Othello in this book and wanted to look him up! He was very beautiful! I'm a cat lover/companion, too! I'm so glad you rescued him and gave him such a great life! Bless you!"

"Just finished his story in this book! What a Handsome Boy he was, and you were lucky he wandered into your garden and claimed you! He knew you would give him the right life!!! Thank you, Helen!"

"I just read his story and started to follow his page."

I was quite touched, and I replied to as many of these as I could. Still, I thought the interest in Othello would soon stop now that he was no longer with us. But it didn't. Indeed, it began to increase! By the end of 2020, even more people were finding Othello's Facebook page and leaving us messages....

"I just read the story to my daughter who is obsessed with cats and received the book for Christmas. She was thrilled when I looked up his FB page. Thank you for sharing his story."

"Othello the Amazing Black Cat is such a great story, definitely my favorite one."

"I just read Othello's story in the book. So excited to get to see the legendary cat. He must have been an incredible friend to you."

Then, things really began to snowball. By July 2021, Othello's page was up to 200 likes. It didn't stop there, as more and more people followed him, and I gave up attempting to reply to them all as there were just too many. By September, Othello had 300 likes, and in November it reached 400. In January 2022, we reached a milestone — 500 likes, and by October he had almost 700 likes. I can see it getting to 1,000 likes in the near future!

I must confess I don't quite understand what is happening or why. But it's good to know that during what for many of us has been a difficult couple of years, our much-loved cat Othello has touched the hearts of so many people, even long after his death. And perhaps I should leave the final words to one of those people writing very recently on Othello's page....

"Othello must have been an awesome little sweetheart.... You were certainly blessed to have such a friend and marvelous cat as Othello and his story will be one of my favorites. From a fellow cat lover."

Yes, we were indeed blessed to have him.

— Helen Krasner —

17

Where's the Demi Girl?

Where there is no imagination, there is no horror.
~Arthur Conan Doyle, Sr.

After a very unsatisfying experience sorting my old worn-out clothing I headed to the mall, leaving my cat Demi asleep on the back of the sofa by the living room window. Hours later, I lugged a huge shopping bag up to my bedroom and emptied it onto the bed. I started putting everything away when I heard a rustling sound behind me. Turning, I saw Demi stalking an intruder — the shopping bag I'd thrown onto the floor. I smiled and continued arranging my new socks and folding my new jeans.

Demi is actually my son's cat. When traveling for business, he leaves her with me. The first time she came, he told me that the quickest way to make friends with Demi was to give her "choo-choo rides" in a box. He even brought the one she loved most: a Fancy Feast cat-food box with easy-in, easy-out, low sides and no flaps. Each night after dinner, Demi would trot down the stairs to the family room, gracefully step into "her box," her head held high like a little princess, and then give me "the look" until the "trained engineer" — that would be me — motored her around the floor.

And she loved when a new bag came into the house, which was not very often, as shopping is definitely not "my bag." Well, this was Demi's lucky day. After much prowling around the gargantuan bag, she must have thought it would be a nice, quiet "kitty place" to sleep away the afternoon. But the bag collapsed around her like a Venus flytrap!

Jolted by an unrecognizable noise, I spun around. The bag was gone!

I ran to the bedroom door. It didn't register at first why a bag was moving at high speed down the hallway until I heard thundering paws frantically trying to flee the flying cape the cat was accidentally wearing!

Oh, my gosh. She's eighteen years old. I thought. *She's going to get hurt.* Racing down the hallway, I prayed the clattering would stop. I couldn't think what might happen if she turned left down the stairs to the safety of her choo-choo box.

Everything stilled as I entered the living room. "Demi?" I searched around. *Where the dickens did she go?* I spoke softly again. "Demi girl? Where are you?" Crouching low onto my knees, I looked into the dining room under the table. Nothing. I stood up. "Demi girl, come on, little girl. It's okay. Let's go."

With that, "the bag" came crashing from the kitchen into the dining room, finally resting in the corner on the other side of the dining table. Demi huddled beside it with the bag handle looped about her neck. There was a look of terror on her face, or maybe embarrassment. After all, she'd just been chased by a paper bag!

Not wanting to spook "the bag" and chance Demi taking off on another run, I approached cautiously. "Oh, Demi girl, what happened? Are you okay?" All I could think about was how frightened she must be, unable to free herself from the "monster."

Carefully, I lifted the bag handle from her neck and picked her up. I could feel her little heart racing. "Oh, God, don't let her have a heart attack," I prayed. "She's my son's life-long friend." I hugged and comforted her. "It's okay, Demi girl. You're okay." She gripped my arm between her front paws, snuggled her head beneath my elbow, and didn't try to escape.

After her heart settled, I gently placed her on the floor. She sat glued at my feet and watched as I picked up "the enemy." I figured the moment she heard the sound of rustling paper, she would bolt. But, to my surprise, she watched me fold up the bag and then bravely trotted behind me downstairs and watched from the garage door as I threw it into the trash. I think she wanted to make sure the evil thing was gone from the house.

She yowled triumphantly, pranced back up the stairs, curled into a ball on the sofa, and went to sleep.

— Margaret Rowan —

18

Cyrus, Defender of the Universe

When you touch a cat with your spirit, in return
they touch your soul with their heart.
~Author Unknown

As I pulled down my driveway with groceries rustling in the back seat, I saw a little white shape moving back and forth at the bay window like an anxious sentinel. I instinctively waved hello. It had been two years since my girlfriend and I had adopted little Cyrus, and he often sat vigil at the window until we returned from our sojourns.

This time, however, he wasn't sitting vigil. Seeing me, he stood on his hind legs, front paws pressed against the window.

Something's wrong, I thought, and my heart skipped a beat in fear.

I'd never seen him behave that way before, and yet it aligned with what I had come to learn about our home's newest inhabitant.

Something was wrong.

Cyrus was my first cat, and only through extreme reluctance had I consented to getting him at all. Two years earlier, my girlfriend had implored me to adopt him. I did not consider myself a cat person. In my admittedly limited encounters with the species over the years, I'd found them to be stereotypically aloof and unfriendly. My girlfriend Donna, however, had been asked by a cat-owning friend if she knew anyone interested in adopting from a new litter. I grudgingly agreed.

Cyrus was eight weeks old and about thirty ounces when we took him home, but it became evident that he disagreed with these vital stats. Right from the start, his behavior suggested that he believed himself to be appointed by ancient powers to be defender of his household domain. He needed to know where Donna and I were at all times, constantly padding alongside us wherever we went and dividing his time between us if we were in separate rooms.

Certainly, sometimes it was to play. Other times, it was to curl up on our shoulders. (He's a tree cat and insists on being atop the tallest point of any given environment, which more times than not is us.) Yet, overall, there was a protective quality to his antics. When Donna gardened in the back yard, Cyrus padded back and forth at the porch windows, insisting that she not leave his sight. He demonstrated an entire vocabulary of trills, chirps and chatters if other creatures came into the yard. We live in a very rural area, so there are enough birds, rabbits, foxes, deer, bear, voles, shrews, possums, and coyote to fill a medieval bestiary.

Most of these vocalizations were likely expressions of curiosity or that ingrained feline hunter's instinct. Some of them, however, were unquestionably the sounding of an alarm. I'd heard the "Cyrus alert" twice in two years, and both times it was to alert us to danger. The first time was when a bobcat came prowling around the house. Cyrus rushed from window to window to keep track of it while trilling anxiously, as if to say, "Brian! Donna! Something large has entered the domain and is circling the house!" The second time involved him trilling the "Cyrus alert" at one particular window in the den, exhibiting such worry that it brought me over to investigate from the other side of the house. I snapped up the curtain to discover wasps crawling between the panes of glass.

As a result, we had learned to pay attention to our guardian. It was clear that he had appointed himself as Keeper of the Realm. Whenever Donna and I went out, Cyrus's little white face was always at the window to watch us leave and always there when we returned.

Two years into having this peculiar bodyguard come into our lives, Donna was in a head-on car accident.

She spent a week in a coma and several weeks in the hospital. Being in the middle of Covid, visiting hours were strictly limited. When I wasn't by her hospital bedside, I was home, worriedly counting the hours until I could see her again, and constantly on the phone with doctors, surgeons and medical specialists of every stripe.

Cyrus knew something was wrong. There were undeniable empathic powers at work there. His shadowing of my every move took on an especially fanatical quality. He slept on my chest each night, practically clung to my ankles each morning, and draped himself like a living scarf over my shoulders as I went about my day. It was clear, too, that he was missing Donna. He recognized her absence, and many times I would catch him at the window like a fort sentry eager to catch a glimpse of his mommy in the yard.

When Donna was discharged from the hospital, Cyrus's attentiveness bordered on the obsessive. He flocked to her, grooming her, following her as she learned to use her cane, and curling up in her lap when she was on the couch. A few weeks into her homecoming, a plumber came to the house to work on our pipes, and Cyrus astonished everyone with his aggressive posturing, growling (and spitting!) if the guy came within a few meters of Donna. I couldn't believe what I was seeing. By this time, Cyrus had grown to about fourteen pounds, but his antics were akin to a Bengal tiger who is not to be trifled with. When the plumber left, Cyrus rushed to the window to watch his truck depart. When it was out of sight, he turned to me with an expression that said as plain as language: "He's gone now. We're safe."

Now I realized that Cyrus was alerting me again. Something was wrong. As I emerged from the car, his anxiety communicated across the distance like an electric current.

Since the accident, I had kept my time away from home to a minimum, leaving the house primarily to get groceries and other necessities. Donna had been making a slow but steady recovery. She'd even been able to discard her cane, although stairs were a challenge, and basic mobility required an exertion of strength that most of us took for granted.

I rushed into the house. Cyrus was already there as the door swung open.

"Donna!" I shouted, hurrying to the den where I had left her.

She wasn't there, but I heard her voice from another room, calling to me, "I'm here!"

She had fallen while navigating the rooms to get herself some tea. Mercifully, no physical damage had been incurred. But rising from a completely prone position is no simple thing for someone who is recovering from a major trauma like the car accident she had experienced, and so she had lain there in pain and fear. Cyrus had stayed by her side, knowing that something was wrong until he heard the crunch of gravel beneath my car tires on the driveway.

That was six months ago. Donna has recovered nicely. Cyrus persists in being our Defender of the Universe.

The plumber doesn't return my calls.

— Brian Trent —

19

A Fresh Start

What is a miracle if not the manifestation
of light where darkness is expected?
~Leigh Ann Henion, *Phenomenal*

We arrived at the cat shelter on the same day. I was a high-strung student who'd just moved to the other side of the country alone, leaving a troubled childhood and adolescence behind. There I was, living in a big city I'd never even visited before I made the move. I was painfully shy and needed something to keep me busy outside of school, so I decided to volunteer at the city's cat shelter.

The fresh arrivals that day, trying to make sense of the labyrinthine building just like me, were three female cats: a mother with two one-year-old daughters. They were beautiful tortoiseshells with big, distinct patches of white, black, and bright red with the subtlest hints of a herringbone pattern. They, too, were painfully shy. They'd lived for years locked in their owner's basement with no light or socialization, just an occasional bag of cat food thrown down to them when they complained too loudly from hunger. It was just one more tragic story in that place.

I started helping out two shifts per week — feeding, cleaning, showing visitors around, and facilitating adoptions. I loved all our cats, from the grumpiest, one-eyed, snaggletoothed old-timers to the zoomiest, needle-clawed, clumsiest kittens. I saw the repeating patterns: Red cats never stayed long. They had a tendency to be very sociable, eager to greet visitors and charm them with their antics. Black cats were harder to find owners for, either due to superstition or because people thought they looked boring. Purebreds, when we occasionally had them, were extremely popular no matter their behavior or health status. At one point, we had the castoffs from a breeder who had had an Oriental Shorthair sneak in and impregnate a prized purebred Persian. The litter all had long, gangly limbs and tiny, smooshed Persian faces.

As for the small family of torties, the mother was the first to find a new home. She had already been socialized before she was locked up in that basement, so she didn't need long to trust people again.

One of the sisters needed a few months of gentle encouragement to emerge from her shell. Although she was still a little shy, her beautiful coat and elegance won a visitor over.

The last one was Linni. In addition to being the most malnourished (her front legs were slightly crooked from cycles of starvation growing up), she was terrified of everything. She was always hiding somewhere when I arrived for work — inside the darkest recesses of the cat trees or under the furniture. When new volunteers came, they'd look at the board where each cat had a picture pinned up, and they'd point to the photo of Linni and ask, "That one's listed by mistake, right? She can't be in here. I've never seen her."

For a year, the only time I ever saw Linni move was when I or anyone else tried to pet her. She'd tear off, terrified, the moment any of us made an attempt. I realized that no one had ever petted her before. She didn't know that humans could ever be kind, that we didn't reach out to hurt her.

I'd routinely search for her at the start of my shift, leaving her food and sitting on the floor to talk to her, softly. After several months, she'd sometimes emerge slowly from her hiding place, looking at me with big yellow eyes as she carefully nibbled the pile of food I'd brought her. I didn't try petting her anymore. I knew that would only scare her away from her meal. Instead, I'd talk to her as she ate and watched me. I told her I could sympathize with her distrust, and that I knew that being mistreated was painful and confusing. I knew it was hard to see one's own trust as anything but a weakness or an invitation for bad people to hurt you more.

I discovered she adored soft fabrics. I'd offer her blankets and towels, carefully selected, and slowly presented them at her feet. She'd bury her head in them, work her paws against the fabric, and sometimes, very occasionally, be so blissed out that she'd purr. A mistreated child, raised starving in the dark, was learning there were soft and comforting things out there.

Winter came. I'd been working at the shelter for a year. I'd seen a hundred cats come and go in that time. I'd been overjoyed every time someone found a new family. I'd cried every time we had to do the final act of love for cats that were too sick or abused to go on. It had been a year since Linni was brought out of the dark. One day, when her head was buried in the folds of a soft, woolen blanket and her paws were kneading, I tried to pet her.

And she didn't run away.

She purred louder than I'd ever heard her, squirming happily, kneading faster, and rubbing her head deeper against the blanket folds. And, in that moment, I knew she wasn't too traumatized to accept kindness and affection. Maybe neither of us was.

I took her home to my small loft apartment. It was a nerve-wracking time for both of us — two aloof roommates figuring out how to share the same space. I started turning my back to her whenever I had to walk near her to show that I didn't mean her any harm. I spent days walking backward through my two-room flat. I covered the floor and my bed in the softest blankets I could find.

And, gradually, we learned to trust and love each other.

A decade later, I know when I open my front door, coming home from work at the veterinary clinic, that she'll be there to greet me. She'll circle my legs and then go back into the apartment, where she'll rush to open the bathroom door for me because she knows the first thing I do when I come home is wash my hands. She sleeps on my chest every night. She follows me around, complaining loudly if I go too long without petting her. She curls up in my lap when I read or watch movies, purring just as loudly as she did then.

Sure, she's still aloof with everyone else. I have friends who suspect

I'm suffering from some kind of delusion about owning a cat because they've been visiting for years without seeing her. The moment the doorbell rings, she's hiding under the bed.

I'm a certified veterinary nurse now. I specialize in cat behaviour and health. Every day at the clinic, I'm in demand as the residential "cat lady," the one who'll gladly handle the more challenging and scared cats we treat. I've read the textbooks; I've attended the lectures. But all my techniques, my patience, I learned from Linni.

She gave me a career. But, more than that, she taught me that no one is too broken by mistreatment to deserve love.

— Tilly Clark —

20

The Rescue Cat

When I look into the eyes of an animal, I do not see an
animal. I see a living being. I see a friend. I feel a soul.
~A.D. Williams

I n spite of failing eyesight and hearing, Taffy, our twelve-year-old
Cocker Spaniel, was the one that found the hours-old kitten.
For Taffy, going to the alley with me to dispose of the day's garbage was an exciting adventure. She'd follow me closely, carefully skirting the edge of the pool as she had been taught to do, and
then spring into the alley once the gate was open. Her sense of smell
was unaffected by age, and she dashed from one corner of the alley to
the other in olfactory paradise.

But not today.

I became concerned when I saw her hovering over something in
the weeds. And then I saw the something move.

It was a newborn kitten, wet, cold and barely alive. It mewed
like a squeak toy, and Taffy gazed up at me as if to ask, "Well, what
are you going to do?"

Cradling the fragile wisp of a creature in my hands, I brought the
kitten inside and began drying its fur. I knew there was little chance of
the kitten surviving but wanted to make it as comfortable as I could.

At least, that was my plan until my eight-year-old son, Miles,
walked into the room.

"Dad, it's a kitten!" he gleefully exclaimed. "Where did you find
him?"

"I didn't. Taffy did."

"Where's his mother?"

At this, I paused, unsure of how much Miles was ready to hear.

"Well, son, its mother is taking care of her other kittens."

The quizzical, hurt expression on Miles's face made me realize this wasn't going to be easy.

"You see, there's probably something wrong with this little guy, and his mom knew he wouldn't survive. Look…" I gently turned over the kitten. "See how his left front leg is shorter than the others?"

Miles peered silently at the kitten and said in a quiet voice, "When I was born, you said I had a heart problem. You and Mom took care of me."

"That's different, Miles."

"We need to save him," Miles insisted.

"I'm not sure we can."

Miles gently caressed the kitten with his finger and gazed up at me with tears in his eyes.

An hour later, after a call to Taffy's vet and a trip to the pet store for kitten-replacement formula (yes, there is such a thing), an eye dropper and a miniature squeeze bottle, Miles and I tried feeding the kitten.

Success! The kitten took five drops of formula and fell asleep.

"We'll have to feed the kitten every three or four hours," I informed Miles.

"His name is Lefty, Dad."

"Okay, we'll have to feed Lefty every three or four hours."

My wife, Miles and I went on a rotation system, making sure Lefty was comfortable, warm and fed. Taffy did her part as well, standing guard over Lefty, only leaving his side for the obligatory potty break or meal.

After a week of feedings with the eye dropper, Lefty opened his eyes. A profound joy swept over us. Lefty was going to make it.

And he grew. Like the proverbial ugly duckling, Lefty metamorphosed into a beautiful silky-gray longhaired cat. And while he had a discernable limp, Lefty pranced about the house, on couches, kitchen counters and dressers, like a well-heeled model, oblivious of his birth defect, behaving as if he was the most beautiful cat in the world. And, to us, he was.

Perhaps because Lefty didn't have any brothers or sisters, he looked up to Taffy, who taught him how to negotiate the doggy door, chase lizards in our back yard, and, on more than one occasion, tip over the kitchen garbage can to secure some bonus treats.

Descended from traditionally warring species, the two became inseparable buddies.

That was fortunate indeed when Taffy, whose eyesight had grown considerably worse, stumbled into the pool.

We were inside, unaware of the disaster unfolding outside until Lefty began yowling like a newborn calf. It was a sound that he had never made, and, up until then, none of us thought possible for a cat to make.

The three of us quickly converged on the scene to find Taffy flailing in the deep end of the pool, fighting to keep her head above water, alternately sinking and bobbing back up. Lefty was nervously pacing back and forth at the edge, her cry of despair unabated.

Sensing that Taffy was losing her battle to stay afloat, I jumped in. The shock of the mid-January water was immediate as I worked my way to the deep end and grabbed at Taffy's collar just as she dropped below the water line. In a few minutes, we were out of the pool, out of breath, shivering but safe.

Taffy recovered quickly, amused by all the attention, rolling and snorting in the cocoon of towels we wrapped her in. Lefty was still upset, circling around Taffy, voicing his concerns in repeated meows while licking Taffy's face.

"Isn't it funny?" Miles suddenly blurted.

"What's that, son?"

"Taffy saved Lefty, and now Lefty has saved Taffy."

"Sometimes, in life, things work out that way," I remarked, and then added, "I guess Lefty isn't just a rescue cat anymore. Now, he's a rescuing rescue cat."

— Dave Bachmann —

Chapter
3

You Just Have to Laugh

Half-Price Cats

Life constantly presents the greatest opportunity
brilliantly disguised as the biggest disaster.
~David Icke

t all started with my husband, who insisted we needed a mouser, a gopher getter, a critter exterminator. We have five acres, and he was getting tired of setting traps. Every morning, I would see him check the ten traps around the upper acreage.

"The gopher population is ridiculous!" he complained.

"You mean we need to get a cat," I replied.

"Probably more than one." He sighed loudly and looked up from setting the latest trap. He had a bucket full of traps and estimated that he had gotten about 100 gophers in the past year. At first, he was sort of like the angler who goes out fishing and has a really good day. As I drove into the garage coming home from work, he would hurry over to my car. "Today, I got three!" he'd brag. Not anymore. I could see the desperation in his eyes.

One day, my neighbor who rented the house next door was sitting outside on the porch smoking with a huge packing box next to her. When I took our Bulldog for a walk, she waved.

"Hi!" I waved back. "What's with the box?"

"We have to move. The owners are coming back. I thought I had another year here, but, well, you know the economy." She blew smoke upward and sideways. I used to do that when I smoked, and I thought I was being cool. Now, it just looked gross. "I am just so worried about what I will do with my cats," she added sadly as she looked into the distance and blew another puff of smoke.

Bingo! The answer to my husband's hopelessness was right next door. "What kind of cats?" This was almost too good to be true.

"Just two plain, shorthaired cats. One is sort of a scaredy cat, and the other one is a little standoffish sometimes, but they're great buddies. I have had them since my sons were little, and the place I found to move into does not allow animals." A tear trickled down her cheek.

"Do they hunt?" The neighbor had her memories. I had a mission.

"That's why we got them — to hunt mice. The big one caught bats."

"Bats?" I looked up into the trees apprehensively. "I haven't seen one of those. I guess I really do need cats now that you've added bats to the critter list," I said. "Let me see them."

"Really? I have to look for them." She stood up. "With all the moving men, they hid." So, she looked inside, outside, and all around. No cats.

"They're just frightened. Come back, and I will have them for you to meet. The big one is Bill, and the little one is Toby."

I should have had a premonition. Bill is my husband's name.

Mistake number one: Never tell a moving neighbor you will take her cats, especially if one has your husband's name. People are desperate when they're moving.

Two days later, the cats were still in hiding, although the neighbor assured me they were just worried about all the activity. I agreed to take the cats without seeing them because she was so grateful, and I really did need them.

Mistake number two: Remember mistake number one, especially with cats.

On moving day, her son and husband came over with two cats in crates. A tiny, gray one stuck to the back of his crate in fright. A larger white one hunkered down inside his crate, eyeing me worriedly.

I told the two men, "I'll wait until you're gone and then close the garage door, open the crates, and leave them in here for a couple of weeks to get used to us. Then, I'll move them to the barn for a week before I let them outside. That's what the vet suggested." They shrugged. Guys don't care, and even if they did, they don't usually show it, especially with cats. But I did have cats before, so I smugly thought I knew what I was doing.

Mistake number three: Cats have their own opinions. Cats do not care what vets say or what experience humans have with other cats.

After two weeks of feeding, watering and cleaning, Bill was getting friendly and purring when he saw me, but I had not yet seen Toby. My husband and I looked everywhere in the garage, but you know garages — virtual havens for cats that like to hide. Our garage could have won a medal. So, when I moved Bill to the barn that was to be their permanent home, there was still no little cat. For several days, I could tell Toby was eating, drinking and using his potty box. Bill (the cat) went into the barn but immediately hid behind horse jumps and wouldn't come out.

I finally realized these cats were not outside cats, not very friendly, and I had probably been had. Even when I called, "Bill, Bill," which was very weird to begin with, he never came to me again, although my husband yelled, "What? What?" several times.

I left the barn door open.

The renter from next door who had given me the cats moved away, and the owners of the house moved back. A month later, the couple waved at me from their porch when they saw me walking the dog. "Hey," said the man, "I think I saw Bill sitting by our glass door on the patio. He looked very confused."

Beyond doubt, if that cat came back, I would immediately change his name.

"Well, at least I know he is okay," I replied.

He continued, "I tried shoving him through the fence, but he came running back. What do you want to do? He's eating with our cats and going in and out of the garage."

"If he's okay, just feed him. Apparently, he didn't like us." Thank God, he did not ask me about the other one. Maybe he felt sorry for Bill. He and his wife already had three cats of their own. Maybe this was how people started cat collections. Neighborhood cats just kept arriving.

So it was on to the next idea — feral cats. After all, they needed homes, liked to hunt, and liked barns. They were the sort of cats that worked for dinner. We have a local rescue group that saves these felines, neuters or spays them, gives them shots, and then places them.

Mistake number four: Never work with people who have dedicated their lives to wild cats.

"Well, how about feral cats?" I suggested to my husband who was still setting traps.

"What are those?" he asked.

"Wild cats."

"Do they bite?" he asked, finally looking up from his golf magazine, intrigued.

"Well, you remember Sativa?" I asked. Our son had trapped a young cat in the forests of Carmel Valley and raised him. Sativa bit sometimes, but he was an awesome critter-removal specialist. But the problem was his name, Sativa, like cannabis sativa. For those of you who don't know a lot of Latin, that's marijuana. I would yell outside and around the neighborhood, "SATIVA!"

Finally, a neighbor asked, "Do you know what that means?"

"No," I answered.

"Well, look it up," he said.

I never liked that neighbor.

My son has an interesting sense of humor. But Sativa was the kind of cat we needed now.

"What about the dog?" My husband reached down to rub her ears. "Will they bother her?"

"She's an old person's dog. She just lies around inside the house."

I called the feral-cat project folks. The woman who called back had a nice, deceiving phone demeanor. She intensely interviewed me about my house and what the barn was made of, and then told me about the feral cats they had that were being spayed or neutered and would be up for adoption after the yearly fundraiser. She wanted to see my place. I was gratefully hopeful and a little impressed. I told her when I would be home. We made a date.

Of course, she made a surprise visit on a day when Bill (my

husband, not the cat) was painting the deck and I was at work. I guess getting feral cats is almost like adopting babies. I think social workers make surprise visits, too.

As soon as I got home, my husband met me in the garage and bellowed, "Those feral-cat people are weird!" My husband likes to speak loudly to make a point.

Oh, boy. This was not looking good. "Did she come today?" I asked.

"Did she come? As soon as she got out of the car, she told me the place was too sterile. What do you think of that? All day I work to make this place look good, and she said it's too sterile! She didn't even look behind the house and told me she was expecting a wooden barn."

"She must have had some picture in her mind of a dilapidated, falling-down, wooden structure with crates all over. That's silly. I told her we had a prefabricated barn with five stalls." My horses liked the barn. Even the Bulldog did when she made the decision to go outside. Bulldogs make their own choices, but that is another story.

I decided to go to the local SPCA to find a cat. They were even having a half-price sale that day because they had too many cats in residence, 200 of them. I called my friend who is almost a vet but without the degree, and she said she'd go along to help me pick out a cat.

Mistake number five: Always learn the proper wording to use with animal-shelter volunteers. Apparently, they have power.

On the way, my friend attempted to educate me on the proper verbiage. "Now, if they ask you if you want a male or female, never say you don't care. Say you have no preference. And, if they ask you where the cat is going to live, do not say in a barn. Say in a spare bedroom with its own bed, with lots of fluffy pillows."

"This is stupid. The cats are going to be indoor-outdoor cats. I can't lie."

"I am telling you to lie," she said, looking out the window, clearly disgusted.

When we arrived, there were lots of would-be adopters standing around with several volunteers. There was a volunteer supervising the other volunteers, who was also a sort of general information giver.

There was a volunteer for the dogs, a volunteer for the larger animals, a volunteer for the birds, and, of course, a volunteer for the cats.

The cat volunteer showed us into the small room with all the cats in wire cages. Some of them had signs that said "Not Adoptable," which made no sense since they were housed in a room with a sign that read "Cats for Adoption." Then, unfortunately for me, I told the truth.

"What kind of cat are you looking for?" she asked, all smiles.

"Well, I don't care if it's a boy or girl, but I hope it can catch mice because we have a barnfull."

My friend walked away.

The cat volunteer looked at me hard and quit smiling. Immediately, I knew my friend had been right. "Our cats need loving homes, not barns. Cats need to be inside, away from predators."

I thought a cat was a predator. That's why I wanted one.

"Where did you find this one?" I asked, pointing to a cat that had "stray" printed on the description card pasted to the front of its cage.

"Well, he was found on a rural road." Her hand lingered lovingly on the cage as if she was visualizing this poor creature wandering all alone on a busy highway.

"Look," I interrupted her reverie. "A road is outdoors. That is what I want, an outside cat."

Her beady eyes stared through me. "Maybe I could give you the name of the feral-cat organization."

I sighed. "No, I tried them. They said our barn was too sterile." About this time, a second SPCA volunteer came into the room with another customer, and she overheard my comment.

"Did you say that you already called them? Well, what happened? We are here to help people, so if something did not go well, we should be informed." And she smiled brightly as if she were on my side.

Now, I was finally wising up.

"Look, I don't really want to get into a discussion about another organization. I just want a cat." I was almost begging, and I had learned my lesson-lie.

I gave up. Maybe there was a cat or two out there for me, but apparently none of these people were going to help me find one. What a sad situation when a solid citizen cannot adopt a cat to run and frolic in a huge barn with lots of room to hunt and play.

But this story does have a happy ending. I did finally adopt two magnificent cats from a shelter far, far away, one that I won't name because, well, you can figure that out for yourself. I think their adoption was ordained because the volunteers at the faraway shelter said they had put the cats together one night, and they ended up being great friends. The volunteers always hoped they would both go to the same home. And the day I bought them was that shelter's half-price day! Maybe this was why everything happened. They love the barn, the house, and even the Bulldog. One or the other hits at her when she walks by and always just misses, but I think they intend to miss. They hunt together, and it's a joy to watch. We call them Smokey and the Bandit.

I adore them both.

— Carol Murphy —

22

A Taboo Thanksgiving

Laughter is a tranquilizer with no side effects.
~Arnold Glasow

The first family Thanksgiving after Jeff and I married was attended by Jeff, my three daughters, and my sister Kelly, who brought her beloved cat, Taboo. Taboo was a handsome cat. He was pure black with long hair and intense, emerald-green eyes. He was loved and pampered—a true member of our family.

While our turkey dinner roasted in the oven, my daughters decided to go for a bike ride. They left the door open by accident and we spotted Kelly's beautiful black cat outside. She ran into the street calling to him, but her panic scared him, and he ran in the opposite direction.

So began our two-hour cat chase. We ran across empty fields and up and down side streets, outsmarted at every turn by the crafty feline, who ducked into storm gutters on one side of the street, emerging moments later on the opposite side a block away.

At one point in our chase, I came close enough look into Taboo's emerald-green eyes. They were filled with fear. I ran back to Jeff and Kelly and announced that we would not catch the cat by chasing him. We needed to change our tactics. I suggested luring him to us instead. Kelly pulled her little car next to one storm gutter and opened the door so that if Taboo recognized it as his car, he could climb inside without fear. Jeff stationed himself next to a storm gutter nearby and across the street from her car. I dished up plates of turkey and side dishes and served Thanksgiving dinner to the two of them at their stations on the sidewalk.

While Kelly sat crying into her fruit salad, Jeff tore morsels from his turkey and laid them on the sidewalk near the gutter. The cat emerged, grabbed the turkey bits, and retreated back into the gutter. I returned home and plopped dejectedly into a chair in our front room close to the front door. I instructed my daughters to open the doors and windows so Taboo could come inside once he calmed down.

While I sat wearily in the chair, trying to figure out what else we could do to catch Taboo, the real Taboo strolled down the hallway toward me. He had been asleep the whole two hours in one of our guest bedrooms. Now, we were in danger of the real Taboo escaping! I sat very still and told my daughters to quickly and quietly close the doors and windows. I ran to the street where Jeff was still feeding the Taboo doppelgänger the remains of his turkey. Kelly dried her tears and drove her car back to the house. She was exhausted and decided to call it a day. She and Taboo went home.

Jeff discarded his plate of ruined food and started over with his turkey dinner. As he spooned turkey and dressing onto his plate, he looked at me and asked, "Can I please be bored now?"

— Judith Quan —

23

Unknown Number

Most of us rather like our cats to have a streak of wickedness.
I should not feel quite easy in the company of any cat that
walked about the house with a saintly expression.
~Beverly Nichols

My phone chimed a cheerful tune, and an unknown number flashed on the screen. I hesitated before pressing the answer button. "Hello?"

"Who is this? Why did you call me?" a voice laced with age demanded.

"I didn't call you," I stammered.

"Yes, you did," the woman insisted. "Your number came up on my phone."

"Ma'am, I didn't call you."

"Someone used your phone to call me. Who lives with you?"

I scanned the living room, wondering what to say next, when my eyes locked on a fuzzy face with bright green eyes.

"You know," I said brightly, "I do have a cat. Maybe she called you."

"A cat?" A snort came through the receiver.

"She's a very intelligent cat." I did my best to sound offended. "Should I ask her if she called you?"

The woman's voice softened a bit. "No." Then her tone sharpened. "Don't let her play with your phone anymore. I don't like phone calls from people I don't know."

"Yes, ma'am. I will talk to her about calling strangers."

The irate lady hung up.

Kit glared at me as I erupted in laughter and scooped her into my arms. "You really need to stop using my phone. Don't you have better things to do than annoy old ladies?"

—TaraMarie Dorsett—

24

Helen and Me

A cat will do what it wants when it wants,
and there's not a thing you can do about it.
~Frank Perkins

My cat Helen has gained five pounds since I got her last November, which makes her tip the scales at about seven pounds. I have also gained five pounds, which makes me weigh about as much as my college boyfriend did in his sophomore year. The added weight is not nearly as alluring on me as it is on Helen. This is something I have to accept.

My college boyfriend did not scratch the heck out of my dorm-room furniture. Helen, on the other hand, is destroying my couch and chair — one elegant stretch after another — where she sets her claws delicately into the upholstery and, closing her eyes in feline ecstasy, rips a collection of threads from the fabric.

I complain about this to my adult son who lives in California.

"Didn't you get her a scratching post?" he asks. He recently got a purebred cat, too. It is a British Shorthair named Wally who has a cat fountain, an automatic feeding station, a feather toy, catnip-stuffed mice, his own bed, and a nanny for when my son goes away on a business trip.

I have nothing to say. My cat has a bowl of water on the coffee table and a ball of tinfoil for a toy. I am a bad cat mother.

"I'll send you one," my son announces. "We have the best one!"

Days later, Amazon rings my doorbell, and I have a three-sided, vertical, quite tasteful scratching post that looks like a large cardboard musical triangle.

I set it on the floor.

Helen ignores it.

I tell my son.

"Have you shown her how to use it?" He sounds exasperated with me, like I am supposed to get down on the floor and demonstrate to my cat how to scratch this thing — which, I learn, is exactly what my son is telling me to do. "Get down on the floor," he tells me, "and show her by pulling your nails down the post. Then put her paws on it and pull them down so she can see how it feels."

I blink. Really? "Okay," I tell my son, and we hang up.

Helen sits regally next to the three-sided, vertical, quite tasteful scratching post, which matches the furniture that she is systematically destroying.

"Okay, Helen," I begin, getting down on my hands and knees. I crawl over to the scratching post and place both hands on the surface, drawing them down, making a gentle, rather soothing sound. "There. See?"

Helen watches with the same amount of interest she shows when she notices leaves on trees out the kitchen window.

I take one of her velvety paws and push it against the scratching post. She retracts her claws so when I draw her paw down the surface of the post, nothing connects. When I let go of her paw, she resumes her elegant, seated pose and flicks her tail once.

This scratching post is safe. It will look brand-new forever. I get a glass of wine and sit down, idly fingering the loose threads on the arm of the couch.

Days later, I find that Helen has discovered she can get her claws into hitherto unreachable parts of the armchair if she balances on top of the three-sided, vertical, quite tasteful scratching post.

She also likes to walk through it like a tunnel.

I decide that, after a year or so, I will just get new slipcovers to replace what will by then be unrecognizable hunks of torn fabric. It will cost me about one mortgage payment. Helen leaps into my lap, curls up into an irresistible ball of fur and purrs.

I consider calling Customer Service, but I suspect that whoever answers the phone will say something like, "Have you shown your cat how to use it?" So, I give up.

Just the other day, however, I heard the unmistakable sound of Helen's claws tearing into something. The sound is crisper than usual, more scratchy. When I peek into the living room, she is clawing the heck out of the three-sided, vertical, quite tasteful scratching post, and I rush to get my iPhone so I can take a picture to send to my son so he doesn't think I'm a moron.

Wait. Why do I think that my cat using a scratching post will make me look like a more intelligent person? This makes me question my intelligence and then my self-worth. And, eventually, I remember that I am fat.

Helen stretches languidly, claws latched onto the three-sided, vertical, quite tasteful scratching post. I have a glass of Chardonnay and watch her while thinking about my college boyfriend and wondering whether or not I outweigh him now.

— Sherri Daley —

25

Knocking on Heaven's Door

A well-balanced person is one who finds
both sides of an issue laughable.
~Herbert Procknow

Waldo was a personable fellow. Orange through and through, he pranced into our family one Christmas Day. We lived in the countryside back then, where most pet cats and dogs roamed freely. Waldo almost immediately established his territory by keeping both large and small animals at bay, and searched and destroyed almost anything else that looked fearsome within our property lines.

One day, he ate Freddy the tarantula.

When my former husband's beloved pet, Freddy, died, he paid a taxidermist to have it stuffed. The next year, Waldo discovered Freddy standing on our desk. One night after work, I discovered Waldo, still an adorable kitten, big-bellied and belching in the midst of a circle of crunchy tarantula legs.

Waldo always had a wound on his face and all the neighbors knew him. He visited places where he knew he'd find people: windows of TV rooms, sills over kitchen sinks, workshops, and stables. He was invited in most of the time, but especially when he'd knock on a door!

Waldo was clever. He'd rattle our aluminum kitchen door to let us know he was home from an outing, wanting a meal, a cuddle, or shelter from the cold. This delightful stunt of his, although appreciated by our neighbors and us, ended up contributing to one of the most embarrassing experiences of my life.

It was early one Saturday morning. I'd let Waldo out to do his business and was taking a quick shower before breakfast when the kitchen door rattled.

That was quick, I thought. Nonetheless, I grabbed a bath towel — a less-than-adequate covering — and dashed to open the door, where I expected to find Waldo.

Instead, my skimpy towel and I came face-to-face with… a little old man. I couldn't turn and run. I couldn't stand there half-naked. This was a pretty remote location. I'd never expected a visitor, let alone a strange visitor, this early in the day.

"I thought you were the cat," I said, slowly backing away from the door.

What cat? There was no cat in sight. The man looked at me disbelievingly, uncomfortably, and yet rather like he was expecting to be invited in!

"I've come to talk about Jesus," he said.

I could feel myself blushing from my temples to my toes.

Waldo continued knocking on doors for quite a few more years. He never ate another tarantula. Neither did he distribute Christian literature. He skipped over snakes, listened to phone calls and occasionally chatted back. He shared his outdoor food bowls with baby skunks each August. Approaching our kitchen stoop where Waldo had a rainy-day house and a kitty buffet, we'd see a row of tails up: black-and-white, black-and-white, orange, black-and-white, black-and-white, black-and-white.

When he finally passed away, we buried him in a flower garden, but we unearthed his bones and carried them with us in a cigar box when we moved. Even though we've had numerous pets since then, I never hear a back door rattle when I don't remember Waldo… and Jesus.

— Diane S. Bingham —

26

The Great Almost-Escape

Against the assault of laughter, nothing can stand.
~Mark Twain

"I'm stuck!" Wedged halfway under the porch, I wiggled frantically to free myself, my middle-aged backside waving like a flag. The feline responsible for the situation sat inches away, licking its paw. And smirking.

Earlier that day, I'd visited my friend Marge to help with her spring household purge. A sleek, black-and-white cat met me at the door and attempted to slip out. Marge quickly scooped him up. "This is Mr. Fluffykins. I'm watching him for Felicity, the new lady at church."

The animal twined around my ankles. He was beautiful and friendly. *Extra points to you, kitty.* Marge gave him a final pat, and we spent the afternoon sorting items for donation. When we finished, a towering pile of boxes lined the hallway.

Mr. Fluffykins strolled over. I lifted the languid sweetheart, and he rubbed his face against my cheek. "When's Felicity picking him up?"

"This afternoon, as soon as her plane arrives. I'll be glad when he's back home, safe and sound with his mama," Marge confessed.

I laughed and set Felicity's pet on the glossy hardwood floor. "Stop worrying. What could happen? C'mon, I'll help load these boxes in your car before I go."

We lifted three boxes each. Stacked past eye level, the cartons swayed in our shaking arms as we attempted to squeeze through the front door. At first, neither of us noticed Mr. Fluffykins ambling toward freedom. I felt something furry brush my ankle and saw him slide past with feline liquidity. I watched in horror as he pranced, seemingly in slow motion, down the front stairs.

A strangled "No!" burst from Marge's lips as the cat entered the semi-enclosed area under the front porch. "He's not allowed outside! He'll run away!" Marge cried. She dropped the boxes. "What'll Felicity do when she learns I lost her baby?"

"Calm down. I'll shimmy under the porch and get him."

Marge shot me an incredulous look. I dumped my boxes and hurried down the steps to the far side of the porch. "Look, there's only two places he can go — the back side where he went in and the front opening right by you. This lattice around your porch is the perfect cat trap. Don't worry. How hard can it be to rescue one kitty from a confined space?"

It turns out, pretty hard.

Dropping to my knees in the grass, I squeezed my upper body into the opening at the rear of the under-porch area. Mr. Fluffykins watched me inch toward him. He took a half-step toward me and then glided past my outstretched fingers. His purr sounded suspiciously like a snicker. "Come here, Mr. Fluffykins." I wiggled my fingers. He shifted closer and then sidled past, sat, and yawned.

No matter how I far I extended my arm, he'd casually move a bit farther away. Maddeningly close, but always out of reach.

We repeated the "yawn, stretch, purr, sidle closer, move back" routine for another ten minutes, which felt like hours to me.

"Marge, call him again. Maybe he'll come to you." I wiggled backward. Unfortunately, the porch opening's small size combined with the large number of cheesecakes I'd consumed over the years thwarted my extraction efforts. "Um, I'm stuck."

"Please tell me you're joking," Marge said.

"At least the cat can't get out this way. My rear's blocking the rear."

"I can't come over there and help you. Mr. Fluffykins might sneak out this exit." Marge squatted and coaxed, "Mr. Fluffykins, come here."

The cat eyed her with that special mixture of compassion and glee only attainable by felines. Marge tried again, "Come here, Mr. Fluffykins. Nice kitty. Here, Mister." He looked at Marge and then sat down comfortably in the magical center area unreachable by humans.

Unfortunately, with her concentration on the cat and her back toward the sidewalk, Marge didn't notice the tall man strolling past. In a cajoling tone, she called, "Come here, Mister."

Through the latticework, I saw the man on the sidewalk slow his steps.

"It's okay," Marge coaxed. "Come on."

The man looked at Marge's back and hesitated, clearly unsure if he should approach. Still oblivious to her sidewalk spectator, Marge crooned, "Come here, Sweetie."

Sidewalk Man took one hesitant step toward her. Marge waggled her fingers at the porch. "Good kitty. Sweet kitty. Come here."

The man must have finally realized Marge wasn't calling him because he sped off like a cheetah on a triple espresso.

It was then that Mr. Fluffyins flicked his tail and sauntered into Marge's outstretched arms. He purred with satisfaction as Marge rushed him into the house. After a great deal of effort, I extricated myself from my ignominious position under the porch. Marge locked her escape-artist houseguest in his carrier just in time because Felicity showed up soon after for her baby.

That afternoon, I learned to never underestimate a cat's ingenuity… or its sense of humor.

Marge and I never told Felicity about Mr. Fluffykin's great escape. And, as far as we know, neither did Mr. Fluffykins.

— Jeanie Jacobson —

Victoria's Secret

Some people have cats and go on to lead normal lives.
~Author Unknown

We had just returned to living in beautiful, sunny Italy when the unmentionable happened with the neighbor's unmentionables.

Moving our whole household from Germany to Italy was quite an undertaking, especially with a bunch of rescue cats and dogs in tow. We were also bringing my ninety-year-old mother-in-law, who had been living on her own in France until the pandemic struck.

We settled where we had been living once before, in the sleepy town of Aviano, Italy. I had been student teaching there years ago and was now returning as a psychology professor for an aeronautical university. We loved the town because it was like stepping back in time 100 years. Everything seemed quaintly old-fashioned.

Because it's a small town, everyone knows everyone, and gossip circulates at lightning speed. We knew we'd score good points for bringing an aging grandma with us since older people are still much respected and revered in Italy. However, we knew that we would have to be careful to ease our pets into the general population. Many people still kept gardens and didn't appreciate cats and dogs getting into their yards and digging up their vegetables.

We let our pets out a few hours at a time to get used to the area, but our cat Victoria was an immediate cause for concern. Vicky was attracted to human trinkets. She would pick up whatever she could carry and bring it home. Usually, it was just the flotsam and jetsam in people's yards, like a piece of string or a paper clip. But, once in a while she absconded with a piece of clothing, like a sock.

One fine, sunny morning, we got up and looked out our second-floor window to see our next-door neighbor hanging out her laundry. Lurking behind the bushes, waiting for her chance to steal something, was Victoria. As soon as the woman finished and went indoors, Vicky clambered up the steps to the clothesline and grabbed the only thing she could reach: the last piece of laundry on the line.

She trotted right home with her new item, proudly showing us her prize. It was a lovely, lacy pair of women's purple underwear. Sigh. What to do?

My husband took the undies from the cat and noted that she had been careful with them. Since they weren't torn or dirtied, he had the bright idea to sneak back to the neighbor's place and hang them right back up on the line. "No one will be the wiser," he confidently said.

When my husband gets an idea in his head, he can be a real Bulldog and not let it go. I tend to overanalyze things and could think of a dozen ways this could go wrong, but I have learned not to fight him over his strokes of genius. Sometimes, he's absolutely right.

But there are other times…

So, in stealth mode, my husband crept back to the neighbor's place to hang the unmentionables back on the line. I was to be the lookout, peeking from upstairs at our place and hissing at him if I saw any movement.

He crept toward the clothesline and up the step. Looking at me for approval, I gave him the thumbs up that all was clear.

Meanwhile, all our pets had lined up on the upstairs terrace to observe what he was up to. Since they were stuck indoors most of the time now, any outdoor action was fascinating to them.

Reaching upward, my husband managed to get one end of the undies pinned up. So far, so good.

But then the neighbor's curtains twitched, followed by the woman barreling through her door toward my husband. It all happened so fast that there was no way to warn him.

She came face-to-face with my shocked, red-faced husband, who sheepishly placed the second clothespin into her outstretched hand before turning around and heading back home.

As he entered our yard, he received admonishing looks from the amused cats on the terrace. They would never have been so clumsy as to be caught red-handed like that.

I stifled a grin as my mortified husband entered the house. We both knew that our neighbor would already have the phone lines blazing with the gossip about her new weird neighbor, the panty thief.

As I chuckled behind my hand, I offered condolences and managed not to say "I told you so" out loud. He may never live this down.

— Donna L. Roberts —

28

Chicken Soup for the Soul

Melina

I have studied many philosophers and many cats.
The wisdom of cats is infinitely superior.
~Hippolyte Taine

I run a small cat rescue. During kitten season, in addition to all the regular stuff, there are constant, frantic messages about pregnant cats, newborn kittens, stray mama cats with kittens, abandoned kittens, orphaned kittens, and kittens that were born because someone didn't get their cat fixed. On average, during kitten season, I am asked to take about a hundred every week. It is intense, insane and impossible.

About a month into kitten season last year, I got a message from one of my fosters. A stray cat had kittens at her sister-in-law's house. She asked if I could take them if she trapped them. Of course, I said yes.

A couple of days later, she texted to say she had the mama in a trap and the kittens in a box. Awesome! It is not always that easy. I went over to pick them up.

There were three kittens, about ten days old and totally adorable. Mama was a Russian Blue-type kitty. My first assessment was that she was skittish but not feral.

I took them home and set her up in a kennel with the kittens in a box. I named her Melina.

Melina was less than thrilled by this turn of events. She glared. She hissed. But she wasn't growling, and I wasn't bleeding, so I considered that a win.

Unfortunately, she was also terrified, huddling against the back of the kennel, and would not even get in the box with the babies. That was a problem.

For the next several days, I left her alone as much as I could, but when she continued to ignore the kittens, I had no choice but to bottle-feed them. And potty them. And listen to them purr. They were extremely sweet kittens! I was sad to see their mama so traumatized that she would totally neglect them. I hated it that humans had interfered in their lives to such an extent that her maternal instincts were completely disrupted. I especially hated that I was one of those humans — even though I knew it had been the best course of action for all of them.

I begged. I cajoled. I cussed. At one point, I sat on the floor and cried. I continued to take care of the babies while doing everything I could to convince their mama to do the same. It had no effect.

Five days into the saga, I told her, "If you aren't going to feed them and take care of them, I am going to take them away from you and get you spayed. I don't want to, but you aren't giving me any choice." She looked at me with full-blown disdain. Nobody does disdain like a cat.

I thought about it for the rest of the day and long into the evening. As she continued to act like the kittens did not exist, I made my decision. The next morning, I had a spay/neuter clinic scheduled, so I set the kittens up in a warm crate and took Melina to the clinic with me to get spayed. My brother would bottle-feed and potty the kittens while I was gone.

I talked to her while she was waiting. I apologized again for screwing up her life. She continued to glare at me and then pooped all over her crate so I would have no doubt about her feelings. I took her in the bathroom and cleaned her crate, her eyes glittering like green daggers the entire time. This girl had no appreciation for me at all!

That day, I was working second recovery, so the next time I saw Melina, she was already back in her crate and awake but groggy. Second recovery's job is to make sure the cats continue their wake-up process, keep an eye out for anyone starting to vomit, and transfer them to the racks when they are ready to go. Within a short time, Melina was standing up and bobbing her head, so I moved her over to the rack with my other cats and returned to the ones still needing my attention.

At the end of the day, when all the cats were done, and I was getting ready to load my group and head home, I checked them each one last time. I peered in at Melina, who was still too stoned from the anesthesia to remember that she hated me. I apologized once more for not being able to make her happy and then casually glanced at her paperwork.

I saw the word: NEUTER.

What?

My mouth dropped open. My eyelids twitched. I might have blinked a couple thousand times in the seconds it took my brain to process what that meant.

So… the entire time that this mama cat was showing no interest in her beautiful kittens, it was because (1) she was not their mama and (2) she was not even a SHE?

Well. Crap.

Rescue is full of "what the hell just happened" moments, but this was a first!

And then it became funny because this poor guy cat had just spent five days with me begging him to nurse those baby kittens. You know he thinks I am the dumbest human on the planet!

At that moment, I was not sure he was wrong.

So, Melina became known as Melvin. Melvin was allowed to recover from his surgery with no kittens clamoring for his attention and his nonexistent milk.

The other volunteers at the clinic had a good laugh at my expense (and shared stories of their similar experiences), and when I posted about it on my Facebook page, it garnered more laughs and more tales of mistaken identity. It's not uncommon to get the sex wrong, especially with a trapped cat. But giving kittens to a boy cat is a whole other level of goof!

I continued to bottle-feed the adorable kittens because, unfortunately, the real Melina was never trapped and reunited with them. I even took them on transport with me to Michigan and back! The leader of the little pack would march out of their crate every time I opened the door, stomping up to me with big eyes, big ears and a confident attitude that prompted me to name him Yoda. I could very clearly hear him saying, "Hungry I am. Feed me you will!"

A few weeks later, I posted a pic of a new litter of kittens on my Facebook page. Someone asked if one of the kittens was male or female and then added, "Or should I trust you with your recent track record?"

—Linda Sabourin—

29

9-1-1, What's Your Emergency?

*A cat is more intelligent than people believe
and can be taught any crime.*
~Mark Twain

As a military family, moving every few years had become commonplace. But for our newest feline family member, Tiki, the concept of moving was an adventure quickly turning sour.

At first, as the packers descended upon our house and left behind loads of empty cardboard boxes and crinkly wrapping paper, moving seemed fun. As a jet-black cat who loved nothing more than to play hide-and-seek in dark places, his hiding potential multiplied exponentially. But his time with the cardboard jungle was short-lived as we shuttled him into his cat carrier and transported him to the first of many hotel rooms in our trek from Germany to Alaska, where my husband had been reassigned.

Four flights and three hotel rooms in, Tiki was literally climbing the walls in a combination of boredom and anxiety. Our German home had two staircases, which Tiki had loved to race up and down. Our extended-stay hotel room, however, offered no such feline luxuries. So, Tiki did what cats do best: He got inventive.

Tiki tried to pick up one of his favorite games, but hide-and-seek quickly played out as there aren't too many places to successfully hide in a small hotel room. The cat-shaped lump behind the curtains was a dead giveaway and hiding behind the lamppost with one's head in the lampshade was an equally poor hiding spot.

Without stairs to climb, Tiki quickly scouted out new climbing opportunities. First, he leapt from the floor to the kitchenette countertop and then on top of the fridge. But that was too easy; any cat could do that. Tiki discovered that if he ran full-tilt at the six-panel bedroom door and jumped to the doorknob, the momentum would carry him just high enough where he could get his front paws on top of the door frame. From there, all he had to do was a Marine-style pull-up and, just like that, we found Tiki eight feet in the air, meowing at us in triumph upon learning how to scale doors.

We knew we'd be in the hotel for another three weeks waiting for our new rental home to vacate, so we did our best to keep Tiki entertained. I harnessed him on his cat leash to try and take him on walks, but he seemed to be afraid of the hotel's patterned carpet in the hallway and would race back to the door as soon as we stepped into the hall.

We remembered the adage that music soothes even the most savage beast, so we left the TV on for Tiki and played The Weather Channel, which always had upbeat, instrumental music on repeat. But the animated, red and blue arcs of cold and warm fronts moving across the screen were like catnip for Tiki. He jumped on the TV stand and attempted to swat the inbound weather systems into submission.

On our second week, Tiki learned how to flush the toilet and hold the lever down just enough to make the toilet run and make noise. That new talent was not welcome at 3:00 in the morning.

Tiki's last stand ended up being of all things… the telephone.

The telephone had gone unnoticed until Tiki stepped on it while trying to swat one of my books off the nightstand. At first, the dial tone sent him running to hide behind the shower curtain. But being an endlessly curious being, Tiki was soon back for another round of investigation. He realized the phone itself could be knocked out of its cradle or pulled off by its curly phone cord. After another round of scolding, Tiki ran into the small living area to see what my husband was doing before curiosity got the best of him.

I was standing at the window when Tiki raced back in and hurtled himself onto the nightstand. Before I could reach him, he stepped on the phone again—but this time he got more than a dial tone. Via speakerphone, I heard a string of staccato beeps followed by a sharp greeting, "9-1-1, what is your emergency?"

"Oh, sweet Jesus!" I said out loud and raced across the room to quickly hang up the phone. It immediately rang back. "Hello?" I answered.

"Ma'am, we just received an emergency call from this number. Is everything okay?"

I can only imagine the look on the operator's face as I tried to explain that our cat had called 9-1-1. "No, there's no emergency. My cat stepped on the phone and accidentally hit the one-push, emergency-services button," I offered.

"I see," she said in a tone that meant she didn't believe a word I'd said. Roughly ninety seconds later, there was a series of quick knocks at the door.

My husband looked at me, confused, as I rushed to the door where we were greeted by a manager holding a stack of bath towels. One of the hotel's security guards just happened to walk behind the manager in the hall and pause nonchalantly to look at his cellphone. "Ma'am, these are the towels you just called about?" the manager offered, trying to casually look around the room and assess the surroundings.

I explained to the manager that everything was fine and invited him to come in, an offer he warily accepted until I explained "who" had phoned in the emergency, and he spotted a tail swishing happily from under the curtains.

—Kristi Adams—

Lost and Found

30

A House Full of Cats

*If the Universe had a place for everything and
everything was in its place, there would
be little demand for humor.*
~Samuel McChord Crothers

t was a beautiful day in the country, just a little way outside
Knoxville, Tennessee. My husband, my stepsister, and I were on
a job at a new customer's house. We were installing luxury vinyl
plank flooring throughout some of the main living areas of their
home, which included installing some on the first floor and some
downstairs in the basement.

The customer let us know that he was leaving for work and that a
cat was hiding somewhere in the house and not to let him out.

After about an hour, my stepsister Candice went outside to get
more boxes of flooring. When she came back, I opened the door to let
her in since she had her hands full. As she walked through the door,
out ran the customer's cat who wasn't supposed to be let outside. So we
all dropped what we were doing and tried to round up this extremely
fast cat. We couldn't catch up with him, unfortunately.

After calling for the missing cat and pacing the long driveway frantically for twenty minutes without spotting him, we decided there was
nothing more we could do. We'd go back to working on the customer's
floor and surely the sly cat would come back eventually. Hopefully, the
customer would never even know he was gone! And, sure enough, after
thirty minutes or so, the cat scratched at the back door to be let in. We

put him in the basement where he couldn't get away again.

Then we heard another scratch at the back door. I peered outside, and it looked like the exact same cat, which puzzled me. I was almost certain that cat couldn't have gotten out again. But, against my better judgment, I figured that maybe someone had accidentally let him out again from the downstairs exterior door. And since both my husband and stepsister were now downstairs working on the basement floors, I couldn't ask them. So, I decided to let the cat in through the kitchen door so he could go back downstairs.

After about thirty more minutes, I switched out with my husband and stepsister and went downstairs to work on that floor as they came up to work on the first floor. While I was down there, the same thing that happened to me happened to them! A cat came scratching at the back door again, looking identical to the one we had captured and put downstairs before. Like me, they assumed it was the same cat and figured he had gotten out again. So, what did they do? Of course, they decided to put him back downstairs.

After a while, when we were all upstairs finishing the main level of the home, we heard a commotion in the basement. There was stuff falling everywhere along with a lot of hissing. We were completely puzzled as to what could be going on down there with one little cat. So, we hurried to install the last board and then rushed downstairs. To our dismay, we saw a huge mess and three indistinguishable black-and-white cats fighting with each other.

We managed to separate the three and grab the one who seemed to be the instigator. We escorted him outside and peace returned to the basement. But there were still two cats. Before we could sort that out, the homeowner arrived.

We quickly gathered our tools and cleaned up from the flooring work. Then, we told the homeowner what had happened while he was gone and that he now had two cats instead of one. We apologized for letting his cat out earlier and for bringing three separate cats into the home. And then we escaped, as quick as a cat.

— Skyler Burns-Cranfield —

31

Luck of the Irish

It is impossible to find a place in which a cat can't hide.
~Bill Carraro

The doorbell rang while I was cooking dinner one February evening. I was puzzled to see my cousin Micky standing at the front door because he had never stopped by for a visit before. *Something must be wrong with my car,* I presumed, remembering that Micky had serviced it at his automotive shop the previous day. Opening the door, I braced myself for bad news.

"Hey, where did you get this cat?" Micky asked, pointing at my calico cat on the front porch. He asked the question with urgency, without even saying hello.

"She just showed up here one day. Why? Do you want her?" I chuckled.

I loved Ireland, the affectionate kitty with emerald-green eyes that showed up at my doorstep approximately six months before, but I didn't feel like she was getting the attention she deserved at my house. My husband is extremely allergic to cats, so we didn't allow her indoors except when we confined her to the bathroom due to dangerously cold temperatures. We had recently experienced a few "arctic blasts" that, according to local news reporters, were potentially life-threatening for outdoor pets. Even though I knew we were doing what was best for Ireland by locking her in the bathroom, her meows of distress absolutely broke my heart. I wished we could find a better home for her. Therefore, Micky's next statement, although baffling, was good news:

"Well, that's my cat!"

Huh?!? I was speechless. "That's my cat, Bubbles," he declared with certainty. "I saw her when I came to pick up your car yesterday. I was pretty sure it was her because of the way she rolled over for a belly rub."

Like a light being flipped on, I suddenly understood this bizarre situation, and I figured Micky must be thinking the same thing I was. You see, for as long as I could remember, he had provided convenient automotive service for me and my family. His shop was close to my house, so if I needed an oil change, I simply called him a day or two in advance, and he would stop by to get my car on his way to work, leaving his truck in my driveway. When he finished with my car, he would return it and drive his truck back to work. So, even though it was almost unbelievable, there was a logical explanation as to how I ended up with my cousin's cat. Apparently, Miss Kitty had hitched a seven-mile ride in his truck one morning when he came to service my car.... In jumped Bubbles and out popped Ireland!

"How long have you had her?" Micky asked.

"Since last summer," I said, doing some math in my head. "So, maybe six months."

"Yep, that's about how long she's been gone," he said. "She just disappeared one day, and Carol was all torn up about it."

We both laughed, looking at the oblivious feline at our feet. I told Micky that my husband and I had named her Ireland because of her beautiful green eyes, which reminded us of our trip to the lovely Emerald Isle. Then he filled me in about her former life at his house, where she had free rein inside and was allowed to go outside as she pleased. He also informed me that she was the mother of one of their other cats. If only animals could talk!

"Well then, I guess I'll take her home," Micky finally said.

I felt a little jab in my heart. Even though I hadn't allowed myself to get too attached to Ireland, I was going to miss her. She always greeted me with purrs and "ankle hugs," and then she would roll over on her back, wanting a belly rub.

My sadness was quickly overshadowed by the excitement I felt for Ireland — or Bubbles, rather — as I imagined her having a joyous reunion with her daughter and her "real" mom in the home where she truly belonged. I was so glad she wouldn't have to endure another lonely night in our bathroom.

I bent down and rubbed the cat's belly for the final time. Then I picked her up, nuzzling her close as I stroked her fluffy spotted-white coat. She purred, and I felt like she was thanking me for caring for her and being her temporary mom. I handed her to Micky and watched them leave, with bittersweet tears stinging my eyes.

"You're not going to believe this," I laughed into the phone, sharing the news with my husband. Then, I called my mom, dad, and grandparents, anxious to hear their reactions to this crazy story. I was sure it would spread like wildfire throughout the Conrad family, generating tons of laughter.

I later heard that it took a while for Bubbles to get settled into her former home. Being an only kitty for several months, she didn't mesh too well with the other cats at Micky's house — not even with her daughter. However, Bubbles is now as happy as ever.

I'm so thankful that Bubbles' wild ride in my cousin's truck resulted in Ireland's safe landing at my house, and not some other destination. What a dangerous and scary ride that must have been for her. I believe she would agree that her temporary name suited her well because she had some luck of the Irish on her side.

— Mandy Lawrence —

The Miracle of Minde

It is in the nature of cats to do a certain amount
of unescorted roaming.
~Adlai Stevenson II

very year, my three best girlfriends and I have an annual girls' weekend to reconnect and recharge from our busy jobs. One particular June, we assembled at my brother's cottage on Manitoulin Island, the world's largest freshwater island, nestled in Lake Huron.

After a couple of days of laughing, crying, eating, drinking and communing by the campfire, we decided, for the first time ever, to take a walk.

We hadn't walked a mile down the country road when three little kittens ran out from a crack in a dilapidated red barn to greet us, mewing all the way. After much oohing and ahhing, we looked around for the kittens' mom but quickly came to the conclusion that someone had abandoned these precious babies in a cardboard box that we found.

We asked around, determined to reunite kittens with their mother, but it was not to be. We had to bring them back to the cottage.

They were hungry, barely five weeks old judging by the size of them. Two were pretty black females. The lone male, a tabby, was immediately christened Tigger.

We played with them until they fell into a heap, exhausted by the day's adventures.

Three of us girls decided to take a kitten each, and I got the sleek black girl with a little white blaze on her belly. I couldn't wait to take her home to meet my husband, Glenn.

It was love at first sight, and all we needed now was a name. She was quite the character, getting into all kinds of trouble from day one, so we settled on Mindemoya, after the lake we found her by, and Mischief, because she was full of it. Thus, Mindemoya Mischief (Minde) became part of our family.

Minde was a very lucky cat. Each winter, we would load her into her carrying case and take her to Arizona, where she would idle her days in the warmth rather than the northern Ontario snow. She stayed indoors, except for the odd foray onto the patio to snack on any stray cricket that had the misfortune to pass by.

One day, when Minde was almost nine, we moved from our old house in San Tan Valley to a new home in Florence, Arizona — a short move, maybe fifteen miles by road, ten or so across the desert landscape.

While in the process of moving, we took care to shut Minde in the master walk-in closet so she would stay calm and safe. Movers were coming in and out, and new neighbors were stopping by to say hello. It was chaotic. After a long day, we got Minde's supper out, but she wasn't in the closet. She was gone!

We set about searching every room, the yard, the neighbor's yard, everywhere, calling out the magic words, "Minde… treats." Still no Minde.

Glenn was devastated. We went door-to-door asking if anyone had seen our black cat, only to receive sad head shakes and the unwelcome words, "There are a lot of coyotes out here."

Day after day passed without our beloved girl, but we didn't stop looking. We went back to our old neighborhood, asking our friends to be on the lookout just in case. I felt in my heart that she wasn't dead, but maybe it was just hope.

One morning, Glenn and I were crying over Minde, and he looked at me and said, "I made a deal with God. If we get Minde back, I'll start going to church."

We settled into our new routine, getting to know our town and making friends, but the world was a bit grayer without the daily antics of Mindemoya Mischief.

Eight days after we had last seen Minde, I was scheduled to pick up my family at Sky Harbor Airport. They were coming in from Canada and had rented a place in Johnson Ranch, not far from where we used to live.

Glenn was still despondent and preferred to stay home. Since the flight was arriving at 10:00 P.M., I decided to spend the night so I could help them settle in and have a nice visit. It was exciting to see my family, and by the time we gathered at the rental, we were laughing and chattering like magpies. I decided to get rid of my overnight bag and was walking past the front door when I heard a noise. A meow? Without a second's thought, I opened the door. There was Minde, who practically leapt into my arms.

I started screaming with joy. "Minde, Minde! It's Minde." Everyone raced into the hall. I was crying and hugging her. None of us could believe it.

My sister Larraine, ever the pragmatist, said, "Are you sure it's her?"

Incredulous, I said yes, I would know her anywhere, and she still had on her collar and name tag. It was her. She had lost weight, and her poor little paws were scratched and bloody, but she looked pretty good for traveling eight days in the Valley of the Sun.

It was late, but I had to call Glenn. Without waiting for a hello, I shouted into the phone, "It's Minde! I found Minde."

"Who's this?" he slurred, voice heavy with sleep.

"It's me… your wife… Erin. I have Minde!"

"You better not be joking or I'll divorce you," he said. "Send proof of life."

Too elated to take offense, I gathered the group with our beautiful cat and e-mailed the photo to him. Not having the heart to make him wait to see his baby girl, I immediately went home.

What a reunion it was.

In the days that followed, everyone who knew of our story had a theory about how she found us. Some thought she was caught in the vehicle all along. Some thought someone had picked her up as a stray and brought her to Johnson Ranch where she got out.

However it happened, I knew it was a miracle. I believe that she was frightened by all the commotion and made the great escape as cats have been known to do. I don't know how, but she headed to the only home she had known back in San Tan Valley. Along the way, she crossed desert, washes, subdivisions and highways. How she avoided hawks and snakes, owls and coyotes, I don't know. I suspect that fate intervened, and she was close enough to the rental to recognize the sound of our truck and the familiar voices of family pouring from a strange house.

However it happened, our Minde found her way back home to us, and Glenn found his way back to church.

She was Mindemoya Mischief no longer. She is now and forever our Miracle Minde.

— Erin Downey —

33

A Burgled Cat

*Until one has loved an animal, a part
of one's soul remains unawakened.*
~Anatole France

I was twenty-eight years old, recently divorced, and recovering from a sexual assault at my workplace. I moved in with a friend temporarily for support and security. She and her husband lived in a spacious split-level home with a horse barn in western New York.

Shortly after I moved into their downstairs bedroom, my friend discovered a litter of kittens in the barn, premature and abandoned by the mom cat. We carried the sickly brood indoors to warm in her utility room. Soon, the forlorn kittens snoozed in a laundry basket, cozy on towels fresh from the dryer. My optimistic friend contrived a formula and nourished the orphans by bottle. Despite her efforts, each night one of the kittens died. By the end of the week only one lonely feline, looking more like a rat than a cat, remained.

A hapless survivor myself, I clung to the scrawny creature, each of us desperate for comfort. With bug eyes, oversized ears, a round belly, and patchy white fur, the malnourished animal resembled the ancient Jedi teacher, Yoda, from *Star Wars*.

After six weeks, resolved to make a new start, I packed Yoda in a box, and we drove from New York to our new home in California, "a galaxy far, far away." Together, we left our troubled past behind. Along the long trip, like the Ugly Duckling, Yoda magically transformed into a snow-white cat. Downy fur covered her bony legs and fluffed out her pink tail. Her ears were soft as velvet. Her bright eyes were green like lucky clover.

Yoda was a gorgeous cat stuck with a silly name. Although she appeared normal, she wasn't quite right due to her slow start. A scaredy cat, loud noises sent her into hiding. She was skittish with anyone but me. She shied from the outdoors. She never meowed. Perched prettily on a green pillow that accented her eyes, she chirped incessantly from behind the protective window at unruly squirrels, yard birds, and bugs. Yoda welcomed me home after work each day with twittering to rival any robin.

Yoda and I struggled over the rough road together. We were constant companions, riding tandem. Unfortunate like me, Yoda was my soul mate, my anchor, my reason to persevere. But, before long, bad news struck again.

One day, I returned from work to discover the back door of my duplex apartment in Oakland had been kicked in. Our safe home had been violated. Burglars had ransacked the place but failed to find much of value. At first glance, it appeared the thieves had made off only with a glass jar full of spare change and a plain gold ring—a reminder of my unfortunate first marriage. *No real loss,* I thought.

Then, I realized Yoda, my most priceless possession, was missing. I ravaged the apartment, more desperate than a robber searching for valuables. My slow-witted companion was gone. How many hours had passed since the kitchen door had been kicked in? The harsh banging would surely have sent Yoda scrambling for a hiding place. If she had bolted and was sheltering outside, chances weren't good that she could survive.

My landlady repaired the door. Two days passed. I dragged myself to work and home without purpose. I called her name again and again, but Yoda didn't appear. It seemed an impossible loss. Was I destined to encounter evil over and over?

On the third night, alone and fighting back tears, I detected faint scratching coming from under the couch. Could it be a rat? I froze, listening to the stirring. I was afraid to put my feet on the floor and look under the sofa. Where was the critter? The assault, burglary, Yoda's disappearance, and my solitude exaggerated my fear. Was it my imagination, or had the cushion under my bottom shifted? A prick to my rear compelled me to jump from the couch and scream. I kicked the cushion to expose the varmint. A sharp claw ripped the covering, and a bony leg with matted fur probed the air.

"Yoda?!" My burgled cat scrambled out from the springs. I scooped my hungry friend from her secret hidey-hole and showered her with water, food, and grateful tears.

Reunited, Yoda and I slowly recovered from yet another trauma. Over time, she grew fat and our luck improved. Through bad times and good, she remained my faithful friend, my fearless Jedi.

In the corner of the couch that had sheltered her as a kitten, sixteen years later, Yoda curled into a white ball. Her green eyes closed. Her velvet ears tucked in like little angel wings. She was transformed again from my swan-like cat into my guardian angel. Well done, my good and faithful Jedi.

—Marcia J. Wick—

34

Two Heads Are Better Than One

Motherhood: All love begins and ends there.
~Robert Browning

Goldie's belly was rotund so we knew that the kittens would arrive any day. Each day, my seven-year-old sister and I would tear down the driveway after school, and before even dropping our backpacks off in the house, we would run straight to Goldie to see if she was still round.

One day, my friend Tina came home with us, and we began our search for Goldie. We looked in all her normal favorite places, but she was mysteriously missing. We retrieved some flashlights from the house and continued our search in all the remote corners of the barn. At last, we located the new cat family deep in the rafters of the barn, right next to the sloping roof, in a tight little cranny obviously chosen to keep the babies safe.

There was no way that we would be able to get to the kittens. We could barely see them with the flashlight. But we desperately "needed" to see them. Our young brains worked to solve this dilemma. Looking back now, our chosen solution wasn't one of our better ideas.

We found a ladder and went outside the barn near where Goldie and her babies were located. We proceeded to pound on the tin roof directly above her nest. The theory was that she wouldn't like the noise, so she would bring her babies out so we could look at them.

When we tired of pounding, we went back to assess our progress. Goldie and her babies were still in their cozy, protected location... although Goldie had a more concerned look on her face. Our interest waned, and we headed to the house in search of a snack.

The next day after school, my sister and I returned to the barn to check on things, and we found Goldie anxiously walking along the top of a concrete wall. These walls had been partitions in the front section of our barn. They didn't go all the way to the ceiling but ended eight feet above the floor and four feet below the ceiling. Goldie was intensely trying to communicate something to us. We didn't know what to do, so we went in the house to enlist Dad's help.

Dad climbed the ladder and stood with his head next to Goldie's at the top of the wall. From there he could see that this wall was made with hollow concrete blocks, one stacked upon the other. He shined a flashlight down inside the wall. As he peered down through the hollow space nearest the nervous mom, she pushed her head against his forehead so they could both have a look. There, down at the bottom of the wall, they saw a little bit of movement. Goldie gave Dad a knowing look as if to say, "See? THAT is the problem we are trying to solve."

His first few attempts at a rescue plan failed. His lasso of twine and wire caught repeatedly on the mortar that was used between the blocks. When he finally was able to loop it around the baby's body and get her a few inches off the ground, she would twist or wiggle just a little and roll back out of the harness. Goldie was constantly watching this failing attempt from the top of the wall next to Dad, and my sister and I watched anxiously from below.

Dad knew he needed a new approach. He (and Goldie) moved to the bottom of the wall. They knew which hollow spot the kitten had fallen into, so he decided to cut a hole in the wall. Using a concrete drill bit, he began drilling holes in the wall just above the concrete block that the baby was in. After he made many holes in a circle, he tapped it gently with a hammer, being careful not to drop it on the baby below. It broke out easily, and the second the cat-head-sized hole was opened, Goldie stuck her head into the wall and lifted out the baby. Cheers erupted as Goldie ran off carrying the baby to her new nest in a stack of straw bales where the other babies were safely waiting for them.

Goldie didn't hold a grudge against us. We knew that we were the cause of her family's sudden relocation, but she allowed us to visit in the straw and pet the new babies. Obie (as we later named that lucky baby) ended up moving into our house when she was older. We figured she started out her life with serious trauma; she could spend the rest of her life relaxing, free from worry.

— Jesse Neve —

35

Catnapped

When you're used to hearing purring and suddenly it's gone,
it's hard to silence the blaring sound of sadness.
~Missy Altijd

Last Saturday afternoon, as I went out the front door to pick up the mail, my sister's tabby cat named Moses followed. Moses has beautiful orange stripes, clear green eyes, and tiny freckles on his nose. He's a good-looking cat, yet he has a couple of quirks. Moses is very afraid of strangers. He also doesn't like being held or petted — even by my sister Judy and me.

As I approached our mailbox that afternoon, a young woman whom I had never seen before was standing in front of it with her arms crossed. She seemed to be about twenty years old and had an angry expression on her face. "Hey, that's my cat!" the woman suddenly yelled when she noticed Moses behind me. Then she leaned over and tried to grab our very startled pet. Fortunately, Moses was able to escape by running to the driveway and hiding underneath my car.

"That is not your cat!" I loudly informed the woman. "His name is Moses, and he's my sister's cat. She's had him since he was a tiny kitten."

"No!" the woman angrily screamed. "His name is Casey, and he's my cat!" Then she bent down next to my car and tried to snatch Moses again.

Our very frightened cat shot out from his hiding place, ran to the six-foot-high backyard fence, and jumped on top of it. For a moment, he sat there, looking confused. But when the pushy woman approached

Moses again, he jumped off his perch and disappeared into the back yard.

"Come back, Casey!" the woman kept calling loudly. At that point, I went inside the house to get my sister. But when Judy and I walked over to where the young woman had been standing, there was no sign of her — and no sign of Moses either.

"I think that woman stole your cat!" I told my sister as I fought back tears. Judy and I carefully searched the back yard and the front yard, too. We also checked up and down the street.

"Don't worry, Carolyn," my sister tried to console me. "Lots of tabby cats look alike. That lady probably just made a mistake. I'm sure that Moses will be home soon. I'll put his favorite cat food on the front porch, and he'll be here in a minute or two. Just watch!" But, an hour later, there was still no sign of him.

I finally gave up waiting for Moses and headed back inside the house. I plopped down on the edge of the living room couch, put my head in my hands, and bit my bottom lip to keep from crying. *Why hadn't I watched that woman more closely?* I asked myself. *I should have kept an eye on her instead of going back inside the house to get my sister.*

Now, all I could do was apologize to Judy again and ask her to forgive me. Then, perhaps I should speak with all our neighbors to see if any of them knew who the mysterious woman was. I could also post a message and photo of Moses on the local Facebook page, describe what had happened, and ask residents to contact me if they spotted our lost cat. Or maybe one of our neighbors had a security camera that had caught some images of the alleged cat-napper.

But as I sat on the couch, wondering what to do first, I couldn't stop worrying about Moses. Perhaps he would never be found. Worse yet, I feared that the strange woman might not have just stolen our cat but had harmed him, too. That final thought was almost too much to consider, and I blinked back tears once more.

"Hey, what are you doing?" my sister asked as she came into the living room. "What's going on?"

"I'm so worried about Moses!" I quickly explained as the tears finally spilled down my cheeks. "What if we never find him?"

Judy gave me a puzzled look and then pointed to the front porch. "Moses came home ten minutes ago. He's still on the porch, licking his bowl!"

I bolted from the couch, ran outside, picked up a very surprised Moses, and held him close. Even though he squirmed a little, I could tell that our rambunctious tabby was delighted to see me.

"Carolyn, don't you know that cats have nine lives?" my sister asked, smiling.

"Of course, I do," I told her, smiling back. "But after what happened today, I think that poor Moses only has eight lives left!"

— Carolyn Bolz —

36

The Cat Came Back

The thrill of coming home has never changed.
~Guy Pearce

O ur Garfield became a mostly indoor cat under protest. He used to wander but we discovered he had a terrible sense of direction, so now he has to stay inside. He does not enjoy being on the inside looking out, but it's safer for him so that's how it has to be.

When Garfield isn't sleeping, he's either sitting on a windowsill or sitting with his wet nose pressed against our glass door overlooking the deck, like a prisoner behind bars. We have relented a bit though. As he aged, he earned back his outside privileges an hour per day because he showed us that he would stay close to the back deck.

When we let him out last week, a thunderstorm arose out of nowhere. By the time we heard the crack of lightning and remembered Garfield was outside, we opened the door to see nothing but howling wind and heavy rain. My daughter Janette put on her rubber boots and raincoat to check around the cul-de-sac, but Garfield was nowhere to be found. The thunderstorm obviously had scared him into a run in the wrong direction. Who knew where he would end up?

My husband Peter and I got in the car and drove around to scout the neighborhood. We spotted a few felines but none were our gorgeous orange cat with his white chest, white face and orange goatee.

It took me forever to fall asleep that night. I prayed God would protect him and help him find his way home. As I continued praying,

I realized that in my daily prayers of thanking God for my family, I rarely included Garf. Now that he was gone, maybe forever, I realized what an important part of our family he was. I thanked God for him and prayed for a safe return.

Peter was the first one up at 6:00 A.M. He checked the doorstep, but no Garfield was peeking in. I saw my neighbor Heidi taking her dog out for a walk, and I asked her to please keep her eyes open for our cat. Janette and her three brothers all walked around the house that day looking like they had lost their best friend. That evening, every time any one of us got up from a chair, we would automatically look out into the back yard hoping for a cat sighting. Janette printed up "lost posters" with Garf's photo and our phone number, and put them up around the neighborhood.

I looked online at Craigslist to see if anyone reported finding a lost cat. I clicked on the "Pets" section, and the first thing to come up was a disclaimer insisting that an adoption fee be charged for any pet exchange because people take advantage of helpless animals that they deem worthless and then abuse them. Feeling sick to my stomach, I forced myself to stop reading. Forget about Garf not being able to find his bearings and discover his way home again. What if foul play had befallen him? Or what if some crazy cat lady had scooped him up and thrown him into her basement full of cats? Garfield only knew how to be an only cat!

I posted my own lost-cat notice on Craigslist with a photo of my beautiful cat and our phone number. After another restless night and another empty doorstep in the morning, I thought sadly, *He's not an outdoor cat. He could not possibly survive two nights out there. We're never going to see him again.*

Never say never. At 10:00 A.M., Heidi called me at work.

"Hey, Jayne? I wanted to tell you that Garfield's on the doorstep, but he won't let me pick him up. I've got to go to work now, though."

I couldn't believe the prodigal had finally come home.

"Thanks! I'll call Craig to let him in."

The good news was that my son was home that morning, exempt from writing exams. The bad news was that he was sleeping in with his cellphone off.

My office is twenty minutes from home, and I worried that even if I rushed over, Garfield would have grown weary of waiting and gone elsewhere. I called Heidi back but got her voicemail.

"Heidi! I just remembered; didn't I loan you my house key last month? If you could please open the door for Garfield, he'll walk in on his own. Thanks!"

What if Heidi had already left? I called Craig again and, thankfully, he picked up.

"Craig! PLEASE go open the front door. Garfield is there."

"Really?" Craig said sleepily.

"Yes, Heidi saw him! Go let him in! I need to know he's okay!"

Through the phone, I could hear Craig running down the stairs and opening the door.

"He's not here."

My heart sank.

"Are you sure? Look around the front step! He was just there!"

After a brief pause, I heard Craig laugh.

"You're right. He's here. He's directly behind me."

I smiled with relief. Heidi must have gotten my message and let Garf into the house as I was trying to revive my son out of his sleep.

"Is he okay? Is he scratched up?"

"He's fine."

He was, and his feet never touched the ground that evening. We all took turns holding him and fussing over him as the long-lost friend that he was. The mystery of where he was for thirty-eight hours in the wild and how he found his way back will forever be known to him alone.

Garfield's still an indoor cat under protest. He's such an important part of our family that we can't have him out running the streets again. And I now thank God for all six of my fellow family members every night.

— Jayne Thurber-Smith —

The Great Disappearing Act

Cats are mysterious kind of folk — there is more
passing in their minds than we are aware of.
~Sir Walter Scott

nyone who has ever been owned by a cat can relate to the
experience of having the cat magically disappear, sometimes for hours, only to suddenly reappear as though it
never happened. A hunt always ensues, with us humans
calling the cat's name, looking high and low, worrying that the cat has
somehow gotten out.

Sometimes, we try opening a can of food to lure the creature from
its hiding place. We check the windows and doors to see if anything
is amiss. Eventually, we give up and wait, for the game is theirs, not
ours, and we simply must let them win. That is how it works.

Charlie once pulled a disappearing act on me for four days, which
aged me about ten years. But you have to understand Charlie. She was
an expert in all things cat-like and had no fear. She was one of those
nine-lives types, forever exploring the wonders of the world with no
concept of either her small size or the possibility of danger.

Charlie came to us by accident, and I should have known then
what we were in for. We had been married for just a short time and
were living in a second-floor apartment overlooking a busy street. One
afternoon, my husband glanced out the window and spotted something

in the street. He yelled to me, "There is a kitten in the middle of the street! It's going to get hit by a car!"

He raced to the street, scooped up the kitten, and was back in seconds. She cried loudly, demanding whatever it was that she had been seeking, probably her mother. How she got into the street, I do not know. There were no other cats around, and it would have been unusual to have cats in the apartments in town.

We checked her over and found that she was quite skinny and infested with hundreds of fleas. We gave her a gentle, warm bath, fed her, and named her Charlene — Charlie for short.

We had a cat already: Christine, whom we had inherited a year earlier from someone moving into a neighboring building. My husband knew our landlord and was able to convince him to let us keep the cat. It was a tiny apartment, and two cats were a bit much, but we showed the kitten to Christine, and she accepted her immediately.

The kitten thrived, and we were happy. Charlie took climbing and exploring to a new level. Nothing was off-limits. She climbed the covered garment rack that I had bought for lack of closet space and taught Christine to do the same. I would often find them napping together on the top of it. They enjoyed our big bay window the most, sunning themselves in the afternoons, watching the traffic below.

Charlie would get inside the furniture, climbing underneath the couch and up inside the springs. She did the same with the bed, and it became a habit to check her whereabouts before we sat on anything. She was very curious and always looking for something new to explore. I felt sorry that she had to lead an apartment life; she seemed to want to see the world. But she was safe and loved, and we planned to buy a house, so she would not be confined for long.

Charlie adjusted, and the days came and went. I guess I relaxed a little, thinking that she would never try to get out; I became a little less vigilant. That is how the terrible four days started.

The landlord was doing some construction in another apartment, so it was noisier than usual. We paid no attention and just tried to stay out of the way of the workers. The cats were nervous and clingy and stayed in the living room most of the time.

One evening, we prepared their supper, and only Christine came to the kitchen. We called for Charlie, but she did not come. We began the search, splitting up to save time. She was not in any of the rooms. She was not under any furniture. She was not in a window, cupboard, or drawer. She was not in the sink, nor in the tub. She did not meow when called. She was nowhere.

We expanded the search and went into the hall. The door to the apartment that was under construction was off its hinges but she was not in there. No one had seen her. We searched outside; she was not near the building, nor in the street. It was getting dark, and we would have to stop. She had probably found a magical hiding place inside and would come out later and surprise us.

But she did not. The next morning, she was still gone. By now, I had begun to panic. I walked around the neighborhood calling her name. I called the shelter. I put up posters offering a reward. I went as far as the river and searched the bowling-alley building and parking lot at the riverfront. I went into every business and talked to everyone I saw.

The next night I cried, lying awake and unable to sleep. I told my husband I was hearing her cries. He said I was imagining things.

We searched the building again. Another day passed. I kept hearing her cries. I could not eat. I could not sleep. Three days passed, and I was losing hope. I put up more posters and walked several blocks again, searching. I imagined that she was far away by now.

On the fourth day, I was convinced that our Charlie had disappeared as mysteriously as she had appeared on the day when she first presented herself to us. I told myself that she had found her way back to wherever she came from.

That evening, there was a knock on the door. One of the workmen had found a cat in the basement of our building. It had dropped out of the wall above his head. My heart sank to see that this cat was black, for Charlie was gray and white. It wasn't her. Then, to announce herself, she meowed in that sweet, familiar voice. It was Charlie! She was so covered in coal dust that I had not recognized her.

Somehow, she had gotten into the wall of the ancient building and worked her way to the damp stone basement, crawling through the darkness until she found an escape. I had been hearing her faint cries all along. I had not imagined it. We gave the man his reward and thanked him.

After a meal and a bath, she slept the deep sleep of one who has been lost and found again, purring contentedly. I took down the lost-cat posters.

I wish I could say that she learned from this experience, but Charlie was Charlie, and there were many more adventures in her nineteen years. Still, she never pulled another great disappearing act on us, for which I am grateful.

— Carol Gaido-Schmidt —

Princess Rumba Has Her Say

Of all God's creatures, there is only one that cannot
be made slave of the leash. That one is the cat.
~Mark Twain

know, I know — it sounds like the typical plea of a young child coming home with a tiny kitten in his hands. "Look, look what I found! Can we keep it?"

Except it wasn't a child.

It was my husband standing there, and he was asking my opinion because we already shared our small Florida apartment with Max, a German Shepherd, and an older cat, Melba.

"I think she's a Maine Coon cat," he said excitedly. "Look at those ears!"

He continued caressing the little bit of gray-and-black fluff that was mostly ears.

Of course, one look and I was smitten, too. Even Max and Melba quickly adopted her as a baby sister, with Melba grooming her with kisses.

We decided to name our new pet Rumbold after a favorite television character with large ears. But, over time, she grew into her ears and was so royal in appearance and movement that we affectionately called her Princess Rumba.

She had the characteristics of a ballet dancer, fashion model, and opera singer, exhibiting the poise and grace of one with royal blood and excellent breeding. When grown, Rumba remained petite, proper and well-mannered.

She could twirl and prance around the apartment like a graceful ballerina. While not a vegetarian, she preferred to smash green peas with her furry foot, scoop them up, eat them and, with a flourish, lick her lips like a connoisseur of fine food.

She had the power to twist her humans around her little paws.

Yes, she could do just about anything — anything, that is, except mew. She was the quietest of all cats. She never made a sound.

Rumba would often sit on a pillow-cushioned windowsill in a regal pose as if seated on a throne holding court. Sunbeams would shine through the window illuminating the jewels adorning her pink identification collar, as most befitting a princess. Still, no meows.

One afternoon as she stared out the window, she observed a bird perched upon a branch. Her whiskers started twitching, her eyes opened wide, and her bushy tail flicked to and fro. Suddenly, I heard it! It was a sound — not a proper meow, more like a squeak.

"Princess Rumba! You spoke! I mean — squeaked!" I cried out in surprise.

We were so proud of our kitty. After all, she had found her royal voice. Once our precious feline discovered she could sing, her songs sounded more like long purrs ending with a raspberry. She would honor us with purr-filled songs when greeting us at the door or when wearing her miniature football helmet as we watched a game on television or during dinner — especially when served green peas. But no meows.

The day came when we moved into a larger house because we had acquired more cats.

When we had our first overnight guest, we carefully gave him an orientation regarding proper house-cat rules — the most important being to keep the door shut and not let the cats out.

All was well until I awoke in the morning to feed my pets breakfast — and Rumba was missing.

"Rumba! Princess Rumba! Here kitty, kitty, kitty! Breakfast!" I called.

Our houseguest came in the kitchen, poured himself a cup of

coffee, sat down, and said in a sleepy voice, "Oh, by the way, Rumba ran out the door last night as I came in. She chased another cat down the street."

At that moment I felt as if my heart had bungee-jumped from my chest, crashed on the floor, and then been stepped on by my guest.

"What!" I yelled, and unlike me, added, "Why didn't you say something sooner? How could you be so stupid and inconsiderate?"

For weeks, I could not be comforted. We posted flyers in every neighborhood within a ten-mile radius of our home, knocked on doors begging neighbors to be on the lookout, and contacted animal shelters. I said prayers, asking God to bring my pet home. Still no news.

Where was my poor Rumba? What was she thinking? Was she okay? Although I was angry, I needed to forgive our friend. It was an accident. He'd meant no harm. He'd apologized. So did I.

Several weeks later, the telephone rang, and I heard my husband answer. "Yes. Yes. Really? How long? What's your address? We're in the same neighborhood. That's great. Thank you, we'll be there soon."

"What was that all about?" I asked.

"A lady who lives on the street directly behind us has Rumba!" he exclaimed.

"What?" I shouted. "Really? Is she okay? Let's go! No, I'll go!"

Snatching the address from his hand, I dashed to the van. Adrenaline rushed through my veins as I went around the block and located the house. The woman and her children met me at their door and led me inside to where Rumba was hiding under a bed.

"We've been leaving food out for weeks. I finally caught her this morning and noticed the phone number on her collar. Then she ran inside and under the bed," the woman explained. "She's been so quiet. Not a peep out of her."

"She doesn't meow or peep," I replied. "She just kind of squeaks."

Getting down on my hands and knees, I called out, "Rumba! Princess! Kitty! Momma's here!"

Within seconds, she leaped into my arms. As I kissed her head, nuzzled her ears, and stroked her soft fur, I could feel she was shaky and thin.

After much heartfelt thanks and appreciation, I drove my prize home, where fresh food and water were waiting. As we walked in the door, my husband kissed her, and the other cats gathered around to say hello.

Running straight for the food bowl, Rumba filled her belly for the next ten minutes.

Relieved and thankful that Rumba was safe with her family once again, we all sat and watched her.

"Well, Princess Rumba, we've been worried sick about you. And to think you were nearby the entire time. You've had yourself quite an adventure! What do you have to say for yourself?" I asked.

With that, she licked her lips, pranced around, shook her fluffy tail, and properly answered, "Meow, meow, meow, meow, meow, meow, meow, meow, meow, meow, meow, and meow!"

And she's never stopped since.

—Vickie Hano-Hawkins—

39

Houdini

Never try to out-stubborn a cat.
~Robert A. Heinlein

was house-sitting for my son and daughter-in-law while they attended an out-of-town psychological conference for work. They maintain a large group of rescue animals that need constant care and feeding. It was also time to do some of the brood's periodic inoculations, which they planned to begin on a rotational basis on their return home.

I got a call from a local friend of mine who mentioned that a new veterinary clinic had opened up in town. The veterinarian had hired a young, unseasoned staff with plenty of new interns and was offering a half-price deal on all services as an introductory offer to kick off the new business. I was already bored with being alone in the house, so I jumped at the chance to help inoculate the critters. I knew my son and his wife would be tired after their conference trip and would be delighted that I had begun their work for them, all at half-price.

My friend Jane would pick me up in a couple of hours, giving me enough time to have breakfast and select one of the cats for their shots. I decided to take Houdini because she was a tiny female tyke that didn't weigh very much. I'm ninety years old, so the thought of lifting a cat carrier with a big, heavy tomcat inside was immensely daunting, even though I had been working out a little lately.

Houdini was a dainty little thing, light as a feather. However, I had been warned about her. There was a reason she was called Houdini.

She managed to escape from just about anywhere she was confined. But, because of her small size, I figured that I could handle her weight along with the carrier, as long as I was careful not to open it outdoors.

Jane arrived, and I grabbed the carrier, marveling at how well I managed to maneuver it. The light weight-training and workouts my doctor had recommended were having great results. Even though Houdini was a light cat, I expected more trouble moving the carrier around than I was having. In a jiffy, I had loaded the carrier into Jane's car, and we were heading to the clinic.

Once there, we faced a long registration line and an even longer wait to get inside. Apparently, everyone in town had heard about the wonderful half-price discount on services. When our turn finally came, I heaved the carrier onto the examination table without help from anyone. I felt like Popeye after he slurped a can of spinach. Nothing could stop me now.

Imagine my surprise when I peeked into the depths of the kitty carrier to find it completely empty. "Houdini has disappeared!" I cried, to the amusement of everyone standing nearby. I couldn't for the life of me imagine how she had managed to escape.

Consoled by the staff, who helped me look around inside the clinic and surrounding area, I headed back home with Jane, but without Houdini. No wonder the cat carrier had been so manageable. There was no cat inside.

I trudged into the house feeling inconsolable, worried about where Houdini was and wondering how she had escaped.

And there she was, staring at me from the top of the stairs.

Apparently, in my rush to get ready for the trip to the clinic, I had forgotten to load her into the carrier. Sigh. The physical training I had been doing was great but not enough. It looked like I was going to have to start those mind-training exercises my psychologist daughter-in-law had been recommending.

Houdini was staring at me with a sly smirk on her furry face, knowing she had won the first round. I would not be mentioning any of this to my son and his wife when they returned home.

—Denise Del Bianco—

Meant to Be

40

I Do Not Like Cats

People who love cats have some
of the biggest hearts around.
~Susan Easterly

do not like cats. As a young boy, I kept an aviary filled with exotic birds from around the world. One by one, cats cleaned me out. First, when I was a child, then as a teenager, and finally as a university student.

"I'm done," I declared after my final loss. "I do not like cats."

Twenty years later, I met Suzi. As our relationship began to get serious, I needed to run through the checklist of deal breakers to make sure she was The One.

"I do not like cats."

She didn't flinch. She didn't argue. So, I thought I would go ahead and draw the line.

"We're never having cats," I announced.

Again, she didn't flinch. She didn't argue at my declaration. Suzi had owned cats since she was child, and somehow I had caught her "between cats" — that is, the period of time that occurs between having a cat and having another cat. It was not until about a year after we were married that she returned home one day with an anomaly.

"What is that?" I asked. "It looks like you've brought a cat into the house."

Suzi explained that while she was at a bakery, she heard the sound of an animal in distress. After a brief search, she recovered the animal from under the hood of her car.

"Clearly," she defended her actions, "I could not leave an animal, any animal, by the side of road after being in the engine bay. It could be injured."

Her point was valid. Although I do not like cats, I do not wish any animal, including a cat, harm or injury. We agreed that she would retain the cat overnight. She said we'd call this small black cat Jasper — only for identification purposes.

Jasper has been in the house twelve years now. He spends his days accompanying me as I care for Suzi's elderly mother. Jasper double-checks the medicine count, maintains the travel paths clear of obstacles, and rubs against the carpet to prevent undulations that may create a trip hazard. Thanks to Jasper's diligence, Suzi's mother has never had a fall on his watch.

About a year after Jasper arrived, Suzi returned home with another anomaly.

"What is that?" I asked. "It looks like you've brought a cat into the house. Again."

"Oh, no," she protested, fully knowing I do not like cats. "Someone who lives on a canyon heard the sound of kittens and found a litter. By the time they returned with a box to save them, the entire litter had been eaten by coyotes — except this one."

She placed the sole survivor in my hand: a black ball of fluff. The fluff was meowing and began suckling on one of my fingers.

"He's hungry," Suzi said. "I'll give him some of Jasper's food."

As she scrambled for emergency rations, I needed to validate her possession.

"How did *you* end up with this cat?"

"The person knew that you don't like cats and wouldn't allow it to stay in the house, so they gave it to us to get rid of."

There was sound logic in that reasoning.

Suzi said that we would call this cat Jacob — only for identification purposes.

"You can't very well be walking around and say, 'Where's the cat that's not Jasper?'"

Once again, there was sound logic in that reasoning.

Jacob has been in the house eleven years now. He spends his days adjacent to my laptop, putting his paw up occasionally to pause my typing to proofread. When it is time to retire for the evening, Jacob burrows under the covers until he reaches my midriff and then lies beside me until I fall asleep. Once I'm asleep, Jacob leaves the bed and, on his initiative, conducts internal security patrols of the house. Thanks to Jacob's diligence, we have never had an intruder in the house.

Not even a stray cat.

Which is just as well because… I do not like cats.

— Grant Madden —

41

The Cat in the Flowerpot

Cats are cats… the world over! These intelligent,
peace-loving, four-footed friends — who without
prejudice, without hate, without greed — may someday
teach us something.
~James Mackintosh Qwilleran

My husband Ralph and I were living in a house in Staten Island in a lovely country-lane area where we enjoyed taking walks. One evening, as we were passing the gardens of an ancient church, I saw through the hedge a gray cat being followed by a tiny black-and-white kitten. As I peered at them, the kitten stopped and looked at me with large golden eyes.

I called to Ralph, "Come and look at this beautiful kitten!"

He came to my side, but by then the kitten was gone, racing after its mother.

About a month later, as I was out walking alone in the early morning, I saw the kitten again. As I was passing a neighbor's porch, it sleepily lifted its head out of a large, ornate flowerpot. Clearly, this was now where it slept every night, and I told Ralph about it when I got home.

From then on, whenever we passed that house, we saw the tiny creature sitting in the flowerpot or sunbathing happily on the front-porch steps.

As the months passed, I often pointed out the cat to friends as he would almost always poke his head up out of his flowerpot abode when we walked by. He seemed a happy cat but a bit shy.

One morning, I met Jim, the owner of the house, and asked about the kitten and why it seemed to be living in the flowerpot.

He told me, "His name is Oreo, and he's the only one not adopted from a local feral cats' litter that I rescued. Actually, I'm glad he wasn't adopted because he's my favorite. He sits on my lap every morning when I have coffee on the porch."

"But why does he have to sleep in a flowerpot?" I asked.

"We tried taking him into the house, but my wife and I already have three very large older cats, and they were not nice to him. In fact, they tried to beat him up."

As we talked, Oreo went romping along the sidewalk, chasing leaves, and I saw that Jim was frowning.

He explained, "Oreo is getting bigger, and it worries me because he sometimes runs in the street."

That was the moment when I decided that perhaps Oreo would be a happy addition to our lives. So, the next time Ralph and I were walking by Oreo's home, I called to him.

"Oreo! Hey, Oreo!"

His head popped up from the flowerpot. Ralph was charmed, and he joined my chorus and called, "Oreo! Hey, Oreo!" To our delight, the little cat hurried down from the porch to greet us. However, as he limped down the steps, I noticed for the first time that he had a missing back leg.

So that was why no one wanted him.

Still, he looked healthy and full of affection as he rubbed our legs and purred loudly. "Let's adopt him!" I said eagerly.

But Ralph turned away. "We don't need a three-legged cat!" he said and walked on, leaving me alone with Oreo.

I felt sad, and as I sat on the bottom porch step petting Oreo, the front door opened, and Jim came out.

I asked him, "What happened to his missing leg? Was there an accident?"

Jim explained, "He was born that way. That's why nobody would adopt him. All the other kittens were taken right away. I kept the little guy because I didn't care about his missing leg."

I didn't care either, so I said to Jim firmly, "Well, I want him!"

"He's yours, if you're sure," said Jim. "I hate to give him up, but living outside like this isn't safe for a kitten, especially one as active as Oreo."

"Can I borrow a cat carrier?" I asked, an idea growing in my head.

Jim went inside and came out with a large carrier that had a tiny door in the front. He opened it and, holding Oreo, gently placed him inside and closed the door.

"If there's a problem, you can always bring him back," he said, as I started to walk away.

I was determined to face a problem if it arose. As if he sensed my mood, Oreo was silent and still in the carrier.

As soon as I arrived home, I placed the carrier in the front foyer. Opening the door into the house, I called to Ralph, "Honey, I'm back!" He appeared on the landing above and started down the steps.

"Darling," I said. "Come and see what's in the foyer!"

He came right down and, seeing the carrier there, leaned down and peered into the tiny door. A tiny black-and-white face with large golden eyes stared back at him.

"It's the little cat from the flowerpot!" Ralph exclaimed, and he reached down and opened the tiny door.

"Hello, Oreo!" he said.

In a second, Oreo jumped briskly out of the carrier, looked up at Ralph, and with a loud "Meow!" scrambled up into Ralph's arms.

That was seventeen years ago, and he has pretty much been in Ralph's arms ever since.

— Morna Murphy Martell —

42

Blood Is Thicker than Water

*Are we really sure the purring is coming from the kitty
and not from our very own hearts?*
~Emme Woodhull-Bäche

My husband and I crawled into bed on the Monday before Thanksgiving, exhausted. We'd sliced, diced, and prepared a multitude of appetizers that now resided in our spare refrigerator. We were hosting a dinner for twenty that holiday.

We lived on a quiet street and our nearest neighbor was a half-mile away. So, the sound of a car door slamming brought us both fully awake. We went to the window and watched the taillights of a car driving away.

We went downstairs to check the doors and windows. Our clowder of five rescue cats was on duty, each in his or her favorite sleeping spot. Starlight, our oldest, took the opportunity to grab a bit of water and jump on the kitchen windowsill. We returned to bed only to be awakened by the sounds of our gang racing around downstairs. When we went to check, all five of our cats were looking out the picture window in the living room. We spotted a ball of fur scoot across the front porch. In the moonlight, it wasn't too hard to identify the fur ball as a kitten — a very young kitten. An older cat and another kitten followed close behind.

I pulled on some clothes, grabbed a travel kennel, popped the top on a can of food, and filled a dish with water. I set up my kitten trap on the front porch near where I'd seen the cats disappear. Then I took a walk around the property line. I found a box lined with a towel in the corner of our driveway. It didn't take much imagination to figure out that the slamming car door was someone making an escape after they'd dumped a cat and kittens. When I got back to the front porch, a ginger kitten ran off the porch. I peeked inside the kennel. Sure enough, a brown tabby kitten was daintily munching food from the open can. I closed the door on the kitten and prepared a second trap. The larger cat was nowhere in sight, but I hoped the other kitten would come back.

When I got up in the morning, I peeked out my living room window. The ginger tabby was sleeping, his paw thrust through the grate on the kennel door as if holding hands with the brown tabby. I tried to sneak the front door open so I could catch him, but he scooted off at the first sound. The food in the second kennel was gone. Whether the kitten, the larger cat, or another animal ate it, I had no idea. I refilled the food and water and checked on the brown kitten. She was fine, so I moved her kennel to a shady area and waited. The ginger returned as soon as I closed the front door. Rather than heading for the food, he lay down and pushed his paw through the grate of the kennel. The brown tabby rested her chin on his paw.

Once again, he took off as soon as I opened the door. Resolved to spending my day on the porch, I sat in a quiet corner and waited. The ginger kitten returned. This time, he headed for the food, and I managed to close him in the kennel. I scooped up both kennels and took them to our garage where we set up two wire-mesh cages with litterboxes, food and drink. The ginger cat refused to be separated from the brown tabby. He screamed, bashed himself against the side of the cage, and tried to force his paw through the too-small space between the mesh.

Fearful that he would hurt himself, we decided to put the two kittens together. We had no way to know if they were littermates, but he definitely wanted to be with the other cat. We opened both kennel doors and braced to catch escaping kittens. Instead, the ginger ran into the tabby's cage, curled himself around her, and proceeded to groom her. There was no way he was leaving his sister. He panicked if we took her from the cage for any reason. It was clear that no matter where these kittens ended up, they needed to be together. The ginger made it clear. He was willing to risk his life, and his freedom, to be with his sister.

The larger cat stopped off at the porch for food. We managed to get close enough to see that she had been recently nursing. Mystery solved. She had to be the mama dumped with her kittens. She managed to elude capture, but she did come frequently to the garage for food and water. After a few days, she also used the litterbox we'd set up for her convenience. She was closer to feral than domesticated, and we set up a nest for her in the loft of the garage.

The kittens received a clean bill of health from the vet. We called The Humane Society, and they told us three things: 1) They had no room. 2) Other Humane Societies that might have room would not agree that brother and sister could not be separated. 3) Mama was too feral to be adoptable and would not be kept.

While we munched turkey on Thanksgiving Day, my husband and I considered our options. We already had five cats. Each of the five had found us. Three more wouldn't make that much of a difference. We moved Piper and Cub (the brown tabby and the ginger kitten) into a spare bathroom to begin the socialization process with the rest of the gang. Mama, now renamed Jenny, hadn't shown much interest in wandering out of the garage, so we redoubled our efforts to get her to the point where we could handle her. Once she decided she enjoyed human company, we had her spayed and then introduced her to the rest of the our cats, too.

Piper, Cub, and Jenny became an integral part of our household. Photos of all three regularly appear on my Facebook page. I'm writing this on March 15, the same day we celebrate Jenny's birthday. Piper still has Cub wrapped around her paw. All she has to do is mew, and he's at her side. Blood, for Cub, was definitely thicker than water.

— Kait Carson —

43

The Christmas Cats

Cats know how to obtain food without labor, shelter
without confinement, and love without penalties.
~W.L. George

olidays were the only time when pets were allowed in the living room, but this Christmas Eve there was a conspicuously empty space on the rug. It was the first Christmas after my little sister's cat had died, and we all knew there was only one thing she wanted.

It was a full house brimming with siblings, secrets, and holiday excitement. But, in a rare moment of opportunity, my teenaged brother discreetly pulled me aside. "Hey," he said with quiet urgency, "Pete says there's another litter."

He had my instant attention. Pete owned the farm up the road, and every winter his barn was a haven for dozens of feral cats hiding from the deep New England snow. Although the adult cats were tough customers — the unpredictably bad-tempered "junkyard dogs" of the feline world — Pete kept an eye out for new litters of kittens in the straw, and passed the news along in case anyone was able to offer homes before the newborns had grown too wild.

"We can go tonight," he continued, keeping his voice low and warily eyeing the room for eavesdroppers, "after everyone goes to bed." With the swift nonchalance only a sibling on Christmas Eve understands, he slipped away before anyone could question our conversation.

The rest of the day was a hum of suppressed excitement, and it was late when the last light finally clicked off in the house. We waited a few minutes to be certain the house was completely still before my two teenaged siblings and I assembled silently in the dark kitchen. Softly, we stole out into the snowy moonlit countryside without rousing a single sleeper.

We flicked on the lights in Pete's barn to the sleepy surprise of a few dozen black Angus cows munching hay in the dark. One chocolate-brown cat rose gracefully; we recognized Pete's adopted favorite by the crumpled ear and stood back respectfully to let it pass. Otherwise, the barn was empty with not a cat in sight.

"I don't see any kittens."

"He said they're in the hayloft."

We climbed the ladder and gasped in sudden shock.

There were cats everywhere. Black, tan, white, orange, calico, tiger—they were all colors and patterns and shapes and sizes, lounging around the hay, on the rafters, on the floor, everywhere. There had to be at least thirty of them, and each one stared at us suspiciously. These felines fully understood the concept of humans. Humans had food and shared it willingly. Many even understood the concept of warm houses and crackling fireplaces on a cold, wintry night. But these cats—the runaways, the strays, the ferals, and the lost-on-purpose—had chosen the freedom of the New England wilderness rather than the comfort of a fireplace and a Friskies can, and they weren't about to change their minds.

They stared at us. We stared back, hardly daring to breathe. Then every cat dove, and the next hour was complete mayhem. The loft was a blur of flying straw, fur, and teenagers. We were hampered by our inability to climb the walls; they were hampered by their reluctance to go out in the snow. We were hampered by our attempts to be oh-so-gentle; they were definitely not hampered by any such inhibitions. Around and back and up and down, we flew from one end of the loft to the other, trying to scoop up the littlest cats while dodging the largest hardcore felines whose claws could slice like chainsaws.

Finally, I did scoop one up—a yellow tiger kitten who looked vaguely reminiscent of the pet we'd mourned months earlier. With firm decisiveness, the kitten wheeled around and proceeded to tear my arm to shreds with razor-thin teeth and claws. I tried persuasion, soothing words—everything I could think of—but he was adamant: I had to let him go back to his gang.

We finally had to admit we were beaten. These cats didn't want to be rescued. They were feral-born, and feral they would stay. It had been an adventure, but our quest was clearly over. We turned off the lights, apologized to the cows, and trooped back out into the snowy night to slip back into our beds without anyone the wiser.

Although we didn't come home with a kitten that night, the visit started fate's ball rolling. Pete heard the story of our midnight adventure, and instead of calling a shelter a few months later, he called us with an urgent message. There had been a fight, and he'd found a newborn litter with only a single survivor, abandoned and literally starving. Our sister accepted the challenge, and for weeks she diligently fed and cleaned the tiny scrap of life every two hours until it grew fur, regulated its own temperature, and ate without assistance.

Having seen the best and worst of both worlds, that little rescue decided to stay rather than go back to the hardscrabble life of the feral-cat pack. He chose us. And in a way, I understand why the others didn't. They were sovereign beings who had deliberately chosen a life of independence. To them, our "gift" of a home was simply unwanted. But I will never forget that ethereal night, trying to rescue a barn full of unwilling cats on a snowy Christmas Eve.

—Krista Behr—

44

A Friend Is Never Far from the Front Door

*Animals are such agreeable friends — they ask no
questions; they pass no criticisms.*
~George Eliot

Ralph was up on his hind legs looking out the window next to the front door. His tail wagged enthusiastically as he whimpered with excitement. I peeked out to see a stray cat sitting on the front porch.

Although I'd noticed the cat out in the fields on occasion, I was surprised by her bravery at venturing to the front porch. Even more impressive was the fact that she remained on the porch despite Ralph's frenzy. But I supposed that she was accustomed to meeting up with critters much more threatening than Ralph.

We had a house cat of our own, but she was rather snooty and wouldn't give Ralph the time of day. It is no wonder he was excited at the possibility of meeting a new friend.

Our visitor was quite thin, and I was almost certain she didn't have a home. After finding a spare bowl in the cupboard, I scooped up some dry cat food and suggested to Ralph that we offer it to the kitty.

I knew I could trust the dog to be gentle because he loved every person and animal he met, but I wasn't sure what to expect when I opened the door. To my delight, Ralph and the cat met nose-to-nose, and the cat remained calm as Ralph nuzzled her face.

Little did we know at the time that greeting the little cat at the front door would soon become the favorite part of Ralph's regular morning routine. It's been six months since that first meeting, and Ralph runs to the front window every morning to greet his furry friend. And, without fail, she is always there to welcome him with her gentle meow and a sweet snuggle.

Of course, we feed her and give her fresh water, and Ralph hangs out in the front yard with her for a bit. The cat comes and goes as she pleases, spending much of her time on the front porch either in or, more often, on top of the little wooden house we built especially for her. The interior and the roof are each fitted with a comfy pillow — something she wouldn't find out in the nearby fields or woods.

There couldn't be a cuter sight than watching the cat stand on her hind legs from atop the roof to peek in the window, often finding herself face-to-face with the tail-wagging pooch!

We've invited her inside our house several times, but she is not interested in staying for more than a quick look around. She prefers living outdoors.

Maybe someday she will change her mind and decide to become an indoor member of our family. She is always welcome. Until then, she continues to be a blessing for Ralph, and he's extremely happy knowing he has a faithful friend who is never far from the front door.

— Connie Kaseweter Pullen —

45

Pirate Kitty

*No amount of time can erase
the memory of a good cat.*
~Leo Dworken

When you live way out in the country, you get used to having stray animals show up. Dogs. Chickens. The occasional rogue baby goat still small enough to squeeze under a fence.

The stray animals most likely to show up on a farm are — no surprise! — cats. Over the years, I've had cats of all ages, sizes, shapes, and colors show up in my barn, toolshed, woodshed and yard. Some are only passing through. Some take up permanent residence. And some aren't really strays at all — they just decide to hang out to see if what's on my menu is more appealing than what's being served at home.

That was the case with P.K., a mewling calico cat who appeared late one afternoon at my back door. I'm a sucker for a calico, and this one was a beauty. But the fascinating thing about her wasn't the random patches of black and tan that covered her mostly white body or her gray-striped tail. It was her eyes. One of them glowed eerily. The other was missing, its socket neatly hidden by what appeared to be a very professional sewing job.

Though she was silky soft and obviously well-fed, the cat meowed so pitifully that I couldn't help but pull a can of tuna from the cabinet and let her eat every bite. Afterward, she cleaned her face — eye socket included — and sauntered off into the dusk. Every couple of weeks or so, she would appear again, eat the tuna I offered her, and then leave.

While standing in the pet-food aisle of the farm-supply store heaving an economy-sized bag of cat food into my buggy, I noticed my neighbor Robin doing the same thing. "How many are you feeding?" I asked.

Robin laughed and shrugged. "Hard to say," she said. "You know how it is when you live on a farm. Cats are coming and going all the time."

I nodded. "But I've had a real interesting visitor lately." I proceeded to tell her about the one-eyed calico.

Robin grinned. "That's P.K.," she said. "Short for Pirate Kitty. I'm not surprised she found you. She travels far and wide."

"Is she yours?"

So, Robin told me the story of how P.K. came into her life. Robin is an artist. Late one cold autumn night, she was in her home studio painting when she heard a faint mewling. "I went out to check on it," she said, "and a slight movement caught my eye in the dark." A tiny calico kitten was frantically trying to crawl up and under the siding of the house. Robin carefully pulled the kitten from its hiding spot and placed it in a box on the porch. "I looked down and saw one glowing eye," she said. "It was really pretty creepy."

Job one was to provide the kitten, which looked far too young to be away from her mother, with food and water. The next job was to deal with the fleas and ticks that covered her scrawny body. Robin donned gloves to pull off the ticks. Then she gave the unhappy kitten a flea bath.

"I moved a litterbox into our powder room and made a bed of soft towels for the pitiful little thing," Robin told me. "Then I cleaned up my painting mess and went to bed."

In the clear light of morning, she discovered that the kitten's left eye was filthy and weeping. A visit to the vet was in order. Like Robin, he was surprised that a kitten so young could have survived away from her mother. And he discovered that the eye wasn't merely injured — the eyeball was missing entirely. He gently cleaned the socket and stitched the gaping hole closed.

Though the vet didn't provide the kitten with an eye patch, Robin knew immediately what her new pet's name would be: Pirate Kitty. P.K. for short.

It looked as though P.K. might be forever feral. Robin and her husband kept her close to them in a large wire dog crate during the day. "We thought that immersing her in the sights, sounds and smells of our house would settle her down," Robin told me, "but that didn't seem to be happening." P.K. stayed just as wild and skittish as ever. One day when Robin opened the crate door to feed the kitten, she escaped. "I thought, 'Oh no, this is it!'" Robin said. "'We're going to have a crazy, untouchable, one-eyed cat loose in this house for years!'"

Happily, things didn't turn out that way. After a couple of hours, P.K. came out from her hiding place and made friends with the dog. At naptime and bedtime, she lay curled between his front legs, purring. It wasn't long before Robin was able to stroke P.K.'s head while she slept and ate. When Robin decided the time had come to try and pick up the kitten, P.K. snuggled against her as though she'd been doing such a thing all her life.

"It was amazing," Robin told me. "She went from being terrified of me to acting like I was her beloved mother." Robin didn't try to keep close tabs on P.K., and she never worried about her. "When you live on a farm, you get used to letting cats wander around and do whatever they want," she told me. "I'm glad she's chosen to spend time with you. She rarely gets tuna at my house!"

Months passed during which P.K. visited me at dinnertime every couple of weeks. Then came the morning when I opened Facebook and saw Robin's post. There was a photo of P.K along with these words: GOODBYE, SWEET GIRL. YOU WERE ONE OF A KIND. I grabbed my phone and dialed her number.

"What happened?" I asked, not even trying to pretend I wasn't crying.

"I don't know," Robin said through her own tears. "I found her late yesterday afternoon, lying on the ground close to the spot where she tried to climb under the siding so many years ago. There was no blood. No sign of trauma. It was like she just curled up and died."

As animal lovers do whenever a beloved pet passes away, Robin tries to assuage her grief with memories of the good times. "P.K. had a rough start in life," she says. "But I know the rest of her time on earth was extraordinarily wonderful. I'm grateful I was able to play a part in that."

Me, too, Robin. Me, too.

—Jennie Ivey—

46

A Mother's Gift

Sometimes, the strength of motherhood
is greater than natural laws.
~Barbara Kingsolver

Leaning over my cold frame, focusing on the young plants I hoped would survive the forecasted early April snowstorm, I could easily have missed hearing the soft "meow" behind me. In fact, I have no idea how long she had been there, watching me, evaluating. When I heard the plaintive mew, I turned to find a thin, fearful calico cat staring at me from twenty feet away. As I squatted down, she approached tentatively.

"Wait. Don't leave. I will be right back," I said quietly, hoping she understood.

I headed toward my kitchen door, marveling at the timing of the cat's arrival. Just before heading out to check the plants, I had cooked and chopped chicken for chicken salad. There it sat in a bowl, cooling on my counter. I put a few small pieces in my hand and turned toward the door, fearing she had run away. But there she was, waiting for me and my offering.

She approached instantly and began to eat from my hand. I made more trips inside for additional chicken. After this encounter, the cat returned regularly to our covered front porch for the food and water I began leaving for her. I also made her a bed from a sturdy box and a towel. In the days that followed, I gradually gained her trust. She allowed me to stroke her back and scratch her head. She seemed to crave attention.

My husband and I live in a parsonage in rural Virginia's Shenandoah Valley where he pastors a small church. We had been cat people, but one of our last cats developed lung cancer and couldn't be saved despite the best efforts of the veterinarians at Virginia Tech. The loss was so heartbreaking that we decided to take a break from cats. That break turned, one day at a time, into twelve years. During those years, an occasional stray wandered through our yard, but none ever stayed or sought our friendship. I settled for feline fixes when visiting some of our parishioners.

But this stray, the one we started calling Ginger, had clearly chosen us. And in return, we became pretty attached to her. I regularly checked her food and water supply, making sure she wasn't on the porch waiting for me. Gradually, it became apparent that she was not just a stray cat; she was a mama cat, too. I often asked if her kittens were okay, telling her that she could bring them to our house, and we would help her.

A few weeks after her arrival, she came one day but wouldn't eat. She sat, and I petted her, but then she stood up and walked a few feet away. She stopped and looked at me. I walked toward her and stooped to pet her. Just as I reached for her, she moved away from me again. As this kept happening, I realized she wanted me to follow her, so I did, right up until she disappeared through the thick hedge at the edge of the property.

One Friday night, a month after Ginger had first appeared, we had terrible thunderstorms, complete with a tornado warning. Around 9:15, we heard a pitiful meowing and opened the door to find Ginger and three kittens, soaked to the skin. The skittish kittens bolted, running into the dark. Ginger let us dry her with a towel, but we were at a loss as to how to find the kittens hiding in the storm.

"Ginger, bring your kittens to the porch and put them in the box," I told her, sadly closing the door. Feeling helpless as the storm raged, I spent a sleepless night listening and praying, asking God to keep Ginger and her babies safe. During the storm, a huge tree limb crashed to the ground, landing a few feet from the front porch. If she had somehow managed to gather the kittens into the box, that would have been enough to terrify them and scare them away.

Saturday dawned with no sign of Ginger or her kittens. She came by later but showed no interest in eating. Again, she acted like she wanted me to follow her. This time, armed with pruners and wire cutters, I hacked my way through the hedge and the fence that had stopped me before. But by the time I got through, she had vanished.

Ginger didn't reappear until mid-afternoon on Mother's Day. She started her follow-me dance routine again. Despite the misty rain, I determined to follow her to the ends of the earth if need be. She led me past properties adorned with abandoned cars and campers, wonderful places to hide a litter of kittens. But we continued walking, with Ginger in front and me following. She led me through a field where the leftover cornstalks poking out of the ground made it difficult to walk. As we passed the last house on the street, she turned right and walked within five feet of it, prompting me to fear that someone might shout at me or, worse, shoot me for trespassing. We soldiered on through a gate in a fence and through another field until we reached a forlorn-looking shed. She led me inside.

Wading around junk tossed haphazardly, we found her family huddling inside a roll of window screening. I discovered an empty bucket, thinking this would work to transport the kittens to our home. The first one I managed to catch was the black one. He jumped out of the bucket as soon as I put him in. I found a cover for the bucket and started again, moving slowly, speaking softly, hoping I would be able to collect all three kittens before one of them escaped into some unreachable corner. It was a slow process. Ginger supervised.

"Ginger, I am taking your kittens home," I told her repeatedly, waiting for her to lead the way or follow. Instead, I made the half-mile trek alone with my bucket of kittens, feeling like a kidnapper. I kept expecting their mama to join us, but she never did. We fed the babies warm milk, settled them in a cozy box, repeatedly checked the porch, and then reluctantly went to bed.

On Monday morning as we sat down to breakfast, Ginger finally showed up. I spotted her sitting by the hedge.

"Ginger, come. I have your babies," I called as I opened the back door. She came running. I scooped her up and brought her into the house. She was thrilled to see her kittens, acting as if she almost couldn't believe they were really there. What a joyful reunion, full of meows and trills, rubs and cuddles!

—Deborah J. Bollinger—

47

My Lucky Charm

I think that cats are spirits incarnated on Earth.
A cat, I am sure, could walk on a cloud
without falling through it.
~Jules Verne

Not every eight-year-old would find it fascinating to be followed around the neighborhood by a huge black cat when trick-or-treating. But, then again, not every eight-year-old longs for companionship as I did. Though I was delighted to be making my rounds with my single mom and little brother, there was something about that cat's devotion to me that made me feel special beyond measure.

"I think he wants to come home with us," I said to my mom, who reminded me of our imminent move to an apartment that prohibited pets. Surely, such a friendly cat already had a home. I can still see it so clearly: how we left the cat behind in the darkness, me looking back at him apologetically over my shoulder, and him staring after me with unfathomable wisdom.

We moved. Then, within a matter of years, ironically, we moved back into the same house we had loved. I was eleven when I was playing in the back yard and found a huge black cat hiding in the honeysuckle shrub. I did not make the connection then that this could be the same cat who had followed me on Halloween years prior, even though the cat looked exactly the same as that one. It had the same hauntingly familiar look in his eyes that made me feel as if he was trying to tell me something, and—once I extended a hand for him to sniff and then rub against—he showed the same eagerness to join the family.

I bought him food and a collar, which he gratefully accepted, along with a warm blanket on the couch to curl up on. I had the impression of a weary creature who had been lost for far too long but knew he was finally home. There was no warming up to him; he came ready to be loved, and loved he was.

I named him Lucky because everyone else was calling his black fur unlucky. From the moment I welcomed him out from the honeysuckle shrub, I felt there was something truly special about him, magical almost. Something in his eyes was deeper than I had ever seen before in a cat—or since. *This cat has seen things,* I would always think. And I felt safe, being his special human whom he followed everywhere like a bodyguard.

Soon after my family welcomed Lucky into our home, he brought some of his neighborhood cat-friends along with him to the front door. One was a terrified young female who ravenously ate when I set a bowl of food before her. As it turned out, she was pregnant, and when the babies came (in a laundry basket in the living room, with my mom and me staying up all night to assist), it was obvious who the father was. In no time, the house was bustling with miniature Luckies. Another litter followed before we could spay the mother, and every kitten born was given a collar and the promise of being kept by us forever. We felt like we were living a feline version of *101 Dalmatians.* Such joy was given to our family by these kittens and their mysterious parents. I realize now that we had needed that joy for a long time.

Over the years, Lucky became like a guardian to me. Whenever I would climb the trees in my neighborhood, he would climb them and sit contentedly with me on a limb for hours. When I would jump the fence and pull myself on top of my roof to sit and watch the world go by, Lucky was right there beside me. He even appointed himself gargoyle of our home and sat proudly upon the banister of our porch, sometimes without moving for hours. His vigilance was admired by the neighbors.

When I would get off the bus from school, he was always there to walk me home. Whenever he was off on an adventure — somewhere in the neighborhood or beyond — and I wanted to see him, all I had to do was whistle, and I would see his rotund body galloping toward me from the end of the street in minutes.

When I was a teenager beginning to date, and my various boyfriends would come over, Lucky never seemed to approve of them. Once, my boyfriend and I were holding hands while watching a movie, and Lucky sat between us and put his paw over our hands. I never knew if it was intentional or not, but he let his claws come out a little and prick my boyfriend's skin, making him gasp and remove his hand from mine. Lucky was quick to put his paw in my boyfriend's place — claws retracted. Whenever a boy and I sat and talked in his car on the driveway, Lucky would jump on the windshield and watch us through the glass. Sometimes, I think he and my mom had arranged it.

Whenever I was sad, I would sit on the driveway and whistle for him. He appeared in no time at all, and I would take him onto my lap and hold his fluffy body between me and the world. Lucky was always there for me, even in the form of his children who tumbled and chased each other through the house. He was there for all of us.

I kept growing older, but Lucky never seemed to age. And we never knew how old he was when he came into our lives. My brother and I often joked that he was immortal.

Still, I wonder where he came from, and if he could have been the same cat who had followed me on Halloween night. Sometimes, it feels like a meteor crashed and delivered him right into our lives. Regardless of where Lucky had been before he came to us, he was just what my family needed, and he arrived right on time. I never would have guessed all those years ago that so much of my emptiness could be filled by a cat. Now, looking back, the very silhouette of what's been most memorable in my childhood — the very glue that bound my broken family together with laughter and smiles — is my Lucky charm.

— Stephanie Escobar —

48

When the Thief Doesn't Fall Far from the Tree

Since each of us is blessed with only one life,
why not live it with a cat?
~Robert Stearns

One summer, my ten-year-old son Keith was hired to pet-sit our neighbor's cat. Jazz was a gray shorthaired tabby who was aloof with everyone, even her own family. My son was excited to have his first job and walked over several times a day to check on the kitty. As instructed, he left their garage door open a crack to allow Jazz to come and go as she pleased. By the third day, Keith proposed that we leave our garage door open, too.

"That way," he explained, "Jazzy will come to our house, too, and you'll see me more often."

When the three weeks were up, the owners called to let us know they wouldn't be back until the end of the summer. Keith was thrilled, and by then Jazz was in the habit of waiting for him every morning on our porch.

Keith and Jazz became inseparable. That was made apparent the night I found her cuddled up next to him in his bed. He confessed he had cut a little kitty door in his window screen so she could "come in from the cold." (Remember, it was summer.) We then discussed the deeper meaning of the Bible verse, "Thou shalt not steal," and I assured him it applied to cats. I also reminded him that Jazz already belonged to a family, even though she wasn't all that excited about them. Prying her out of my child's arms, I escorted "Her Highness" back to her castle. It happened a few more times, but eventually the neighbors returned, and we resumed our cat-free lives — or so I thought.

The day we drove down our street and saw the for-sale sign planted in the cat owner's yard, Keith burst into tears. He confessed he had been sneaking Jazz into his room for the last few months and couldn't bear the thought of her moving away. He was heartbroken. That night, the neighbor called and asked me to come over. While sitting on her couch, she told me they had noticed Keith's "attachment" to Jazz. I quickly apologized for my son's behavior, babbling on about how I would do everything to make sure he didn't continue on his path of crime. She assured me they were not upset and were wondering if he would like to keep her. A couple of days later, on Christmas morning, Jazz was presented to my son wearing a big, red bow. She would be his official shadow and constant companion for the next fifteen years.

Recently, I shared this story with my eighty-three-year-old aunt. When I finished, she had a funny look on her face and casually said, "I stole my first cat from my neighbor, too! They had one of those Persian cats, all fluffy and white. I thought he was so beautiful, so I picked him up and brought him into our house. I think we had Mr. Kitty-Cat for a few months before he got out again. The next time I saw him, he was wearing a new collar with a bell attached. I guess the owners wanted everyone to know he had a home."

"Ce-ce, you stole your neighbor's cat? Are you kidding me?" I couldn't believe what I was hearing.

Without batting an eye, she replied, "I could tell he wanted to be in our family, so we figured out a way to get him back. One night, I peeked over the fence and saw him in their back yard. I had your uncle climb over and get him. When he handed me the kitty, I got so excited that I started to run into our house. Then I heard a whisper-shout, 'Hey! Help me get back over!' Eventually, we all made it back inside. I don't think they ever realized it was us because we were on our way by the next day."

"On your way where...?" I was afraid of the answer.

"To our new home up the coast. We had everything all packed up. Mr. Kitty-Cat was the best little traveler, too. Honey, don't worry too much about how Keith got his cat. He didn't really steal her. If anything, it's Jazzy's fault. She stole his heart. They do that, you know."

— Lorrie Osmonson —

Roommate Needed

No man or woman can be called friendless
who has the companionship of a cat.
~James Lautner

A post in my local online feed caught my eye: "Permanent homes are needed for three cats who were the beloved pets of my friend, who was brutally murdered in her apartment last month. Amos is a beautiful, black domestic longhair who may be part Maine Coon...."

How tragic! As I read it, I thought about my only cat, Pinkerton, with her long glossy black fur and big sad yellow eyes. My other two cats had recently died, and when I came home from work each day, I felt the loneliness in the house as only Pinkerton came to greet me. I imagined that she was lonely, too, and wondered if she would accept a roommate if he looked like her.

Pinkerton had never been an easy pet. Declawed, spayed, and possibly mistreated as a kitten, she was skittish and tended to bite, sometimes for no apparent reason. Still, I felt sorry for her — or was I just missing the company of the other cats myself? Intrigued by the story of Amos, I arranged to meet him.

The three abandoned cats described in the post were being fostered by a kind friend of the murdered woman. The kind friend must have loved cats because there were dozens of them in her cluttered apartment. She asked me why I was interested in adopting. I explained my wish to find Pinkerton a companion. I hoped the woman would appreciate my concern for my cat's wellbeing, but then I realized the other reason: I was lonely, too.

Hardly two minutes into my story, a large but skinny black cat jumped onto the sofa and curled up in my lap. Purring loudly, he rubbed his head against my thigh as if to say, "My savior! Get me out of here!" I needn't have worried whether I would be judged an acceptable "cat mother" when the woman observed, "I think Amos has adopted YOU!" I loaded this smelly yet very appealing cat into my car, and she handed me a file with Amos's papers in it. "Well, Amos," she said, "you're moving up in the world!"

Reading through his file, I learned more about Amos's history. His unfortunate murdered owner had adopted him from PAWS, an animal-welfare society. It showed that he was three years old, neutered and chipped. His name was Digit. Wait… I thought his name was Amos? How did he get from Digit to Amos? Was this some other cat's file? Curiosity may have killed a cat, but mine was certainly alerted!

The PAWS advertisement gave more information about his habits and sweet personality. There was even a picture of him rolling over on his back to get a belly rub! And there was this:

"Digit was once a beloved family pet until his family fell on hard times and lost their home. They had to live in their car, and they took Digit with them. They soon realized a car was no place for a cat to live, and with a very heavy heart, they surrendered Digit to PAWS."

So, Digit had once belonged to a family who loved him but had to give him up. His next owner apparently gave him a new home and a new name: Amos. But she soon gave him up too — by death, not by choice. How could I show him that mine would be his forever home, especially since moving in with a feline diva like Pinkerton would not be easy?

Despite Pinkerton being the older cat, Amos became the alpha cat as soon as he was released from temporary confinement in the guest room. He cleaned himself up a bit and greedily enjoyed his regular meals. This was no surprise, since he had recently shared his home and food with many other hungry cats. Unfortunately, while Pinkerton snacked, Amos gobbled. If she left food in her dish, he ate it. Hissing, yowling, and wary avoidance ensued.

After a few weeks, Amos and Pinkerton developed a grudging tolerance of each other. As they passed each other on their rounds, there might be sniffing, nose-nuzzling, or paw-boxing and, very occasionally, some cooperative lick-grooming. Most of the time, Pinkerton would settle into one of her favorite napping spots, and Amos would follow me around the house like a bored child, as if to say, "What are we gonna do now, Mom?"

In the past, other cats who lived with me had their own agenda and would squirm and protest if I picked them up. Not Amos. He comes looking for my affection. As soon as I get into "downward dog" pose on my yoga mat, he will flop down next to me on his back, legs splayed, for a belly rub. When I settle in to watch TV, he sits beside me, waiting to have his chin scratched, his ears twirled, or his fluffy tail stroked. Around 10:00 P.M., he wanders back in and meows a reminder that it's bedtime. When I snuggle into bed, he curls his body against mine until I fall asleep. If I'm not out of bed by 7:00 A.M., there he is, chirping and trilling, "Hey! It's time for breakfast! Are you getting up?" By 5:00 P.M., he appears, parks himself in front of me and stares until I feed him dinner. Words are unnecessary. We communicate in the language of "cat."

The kind friend was right: Amos adopted me. I've lived with many cats, each of them rescues with unique personalities and habits. None seemed as aware of my routines or as eager to be in my presence as Amos. In my effort to find Pinkerton a roommate, and perhaps do a good deed by rescuing an orphaned cat, I found an affectionate companion of my own. When Amos adopted me, we bonded in some strange way. Maybe somehow he knew he'd find his forever home... in my heart.

— Judy Bailey Sennett —

50

The Real Burger Kitty

Cats seem to go on the principle that it never does any
harm to ask for what you want.
~Joseph Wood Krutch

t's not often that you get a call from Burger King. And certainly
not at 6:00 in the morning.

"Hi," said a tentative voice on the other end of the phone.
"This is Delores from Burger King. You know, the one on Stockdale
Highway? My manager won't be happy I'm calling you, but someone
has to do something about that cat. Oh, I hope I have the right number.
Is this the cat-rescue organization?"

I struggled to get my eyes open. "Erk," I said. Then, "Um, well,
yes." Actually, it was my home number. Delores must have phoned our
office, gotten my number from the recording as an emergency contact,
and was therefore phoning me. I struggled to disentangle myself from
the sheets and put my feet on the floor. "How can we help you?"

"Well, there's this cat," she said. "She shows up a little later in the
day and hangs around in the bushes until just before noon. Then — you
know, it's the darndest thing — she waltzes into the drive-through. Even
puts her paws up on the speaker. It's as though she thinks the message
'Welcome to Burger King, can I take your order please?' is someone
talking to her, maybe inviting her to place an order. Anyhow, I'm afraid
she's going to get run over. So… I was thinking someone from your
group could come by. One of our customers leaves food for her in the
bushes. I'll show you where. Then she disappears until the next day."

"Sure," I said. "We can trap her and get her out of there. Why don't I come by tonight? I'll leave a trap in the bushes."

"Oh," she said in evident dismay. "I won't be here tonight. My shift will be over at 2:00. And I want to be sure I show you the right bushes and so on. I guess it's silly, but I feel…" she trailed off.

I got it. She felt responsible for this cat. *Bless you, Delores,* I thought. "No problem," I said. "See you about 2:00." I went to our office — a small space we rented in downtown Bakersfield — and talked with our volunteer phone answerer, returned some phone calls, opened the mail, and did some paperwork. Then it was time to go meet Delores.

Two o'clock found me parked in the Burger King lot, waiting for Delores to show me the bushes in which the kitty hung out. I guessed some kind person ordered a burger for themselves and left a piece of it under a bush for the kitty. That was kind, but as Delores remarked, risky. Sooner or later, the kitty was going to get hit in the drive-through. It was not a good situation for a cat. I sighed. I'd trap her, take her to our vet, get her checked out, and then find a foster home for her. No more mooching at Burger King.

A young woman with curly dark hair, dressed in a Burger King uniform, came outside just after 2:00 with a backpack slung over her shoulder. I got out of my car and went to greet her.

"Hi," I said. "I'm Linda. We talked on the phone. You must be Delores."

"Hi," she said, giving me a worried look. "I'm so glad someone is going to take care of that kitty. She's so sweet and pretty. A brown tabby with stripes, a white chin, and pretty eyes the color of green leaves. I figure she's someone's pet. Maybe she ran away? Or her people moved and left her? With a little TLC, she'd warm right up to you, I think. I'd take her in, but my boyfriend has two dogs, and, well, you know…"

If she couldn't take kitty in herself, the next best thing was to call a group that would. Her heart was in the right place.

"Over here," she said, pointing to a clump of bushes on a strip of grass beside the parking lot. They grew low to the ground, providing good cover for a small animal like a cat. "This is where she hangs out." We walked over, and Delores parted the bushes. "Here," she indicated.

I kneeled down. There, almost completely hidden, was a small blue plastic plate. On it was a mostly eaten piece of breaded fish. "It's our fish burger," she said, laughing. "She's fussy. Doesn't like hamburgers. When I see her in the drive-through, I tell myself, 'There's the kitty ordering a fish burger.' Of course, she isn't. Someone orders for her." She looked at me with concern in her eyes. "Some kind person is trying to take care of her. Kitty comes by later on to finish her meal. Then, she waits for the next day and the next meal."

"Don't worry," I said. "We've got this. I'll put my trap right here later on tonight when things are quiet. With any luck, she'll be in it tomorrow morning."

"I'll call you," Delores said.

I drove home, mentally high-fiving myself. This was an easy one. Mission almost accomplished. Tomorrow morning, Burger Kitty, as I'd started to call her, would be in the trap, and all would be well. Another poor pussycat in peril would be rescued from the streets.

Delores did indeed call me when her shift started the next morning right after 6:00, but it wasn't with good news.

"There's a cat in the trap!" she cried. "I went to take a look. But it's not the right cat!"

"Not Burger Kitty?" I said stupidly. I'm always stupid before my coffee. "Really? Are you sure?"

"I'm sure," Delores said. "It's a tabby, but…"

"It's not the right tabby." I groaned.

"Not the right tabby?" my roommate Martha asked from the kitchen where she was scrambling eggs for breakfast. I poured myself coffee and jammed my baseball cap on my head. "How many wandering tabbies can there be in that shopping center?" she asked. "So, the cat in the trap is, who, the False Burger Kitty? Here," she said, tossing me an old sheet to put over the trap.

I grabbed the sheet and dashed out the door.

At Burger King, I parked, hurried over to the bush where I'd set my trap, and looked inside. Yup, we'd caught a cat, and it was, well, kind of a tabby — light brown with barely discernable stripes and terrified pale-yellow eyes. This was definitely not the pretty green-eyed tabby

Delores had described. I draped my sheet over the trap and called our vet. In about fifteen minutes, I'd delivered the False Burger Kitty to the vet clinic where she was to be checked over, spayed, and vaccinated. *Now what?* I asked myself as I drove home. I hadn't a clue. Tired from two days of early morning emergencies, I fell into bed.

When the phone rang just after noon, interrupting my nap, I wasn't sure if I was alive or dead. "She's back," Delores said. "I saw her go into the bushes. She's probably having lunch."

"You didn't happen to see the good Samaritan who's ordering for her, did you?" I asked, thinking ahead. Maybe, just maybe, I could persuade the burger-buying cat lover to, well, adopt Burger Kitty after a trip to our vet. If, indeed, she was the Real Burger Kitty.

"I did," Delores said. "And I talked to her. I was hoping that, well, she'd take her home after you came back to trap her. But she said no. She couldn't. Her husband doesn't like cats."

"Okay, I'll bring my trap later on, and we'll hope for the best," I said.

Well, the best happened. I set the trap and, the next morning, Burger Kitty was in the trap. "Got you," I said to the prettiest little brown tabby I'd ever seen. Her stripes were dark and magnificent, her eyes were leaf-green, and she had a devastatingly cute white vest and chin. The only wrinkle was that we didn't have a foster home for her. I'd called around, and none of our foster families was available.

At the vet, I delivered Burger Kitty to be checked over and received the bad news about the False Burger Kitty. "She's a wild child," the vet's receptionist, Millie, said. I groaned. We'd been thinking about a barn-cat program for the ferals we rescued but hadn't gotten around to planning it yet. As if reading my mind, Millie said, "My husband and I have a horse-boarding business just outside town: Lost Creek Stables. We could use another rodent ranger, if you're interested."

Was I interested? You bet. "Millie, you've just saved our bacon," I said. "Thanks a million. Give me your business card. Our group will make a donation to Lost Creek Stables to help with kitty's expenses."

That left me with just one problem: What to do with Real Burger Kitty? When I inquired about her, Millie said, "Oh, that one? She's a doll. Just a scared pussycat. We spayed her and gave her all her shots.

She'll be ready to go tomorrow."

As I was driving home, thoughts of crawling into bed occupied my mind. Then, the answer came to me. One of our board members, Amy, had said that if we ever got jammed up and needed a foster home for a well-mannered adult cat, we could count on her and her husband, Jim. At home, I called Amy. To my amazed relief, she said yes.

I delivered Burger Kitty to Amy and Jim's spacious, quiet house the next day. Burgie, as Amy called her, was indeed a scared pussycat and spent her initial weeks in the closet of the spare bedroom. Amy, for her part, spent evenings on the bed in the spare room, reading, dangling one hand over the edge of the bed, and talking softly to Burgie. Her patience paid off because, according to Amy, one night Burgie just decided to come out and rub her head against Amy's hand. Not too long after that, she was on the bed with Amy, reading with her. Not too long after that, Burgie was out exploring the house.

I visited Amy one afternoon, and Burgie was on the back of the sofa behind Jim's head, looking out into the back yard, bird-watching. All was well. But it was now time to get Burgie adopted. When I mentioned this to Amy, she said, evidently shocked, "Adopted? Why, this is her home. We're adopting her, of course."

As I drove home, grinning, I said a prayer of thanks to whatever celestial being watches out for cats. This entity (The Great Cat?) couldn't have done better than to send one lost tabby to the local burger joint where Delores, plus a kind benefactor, and finally Amy and Jim, gave a fish sandwich–loving kitty a second chance.

— Linda J. Wright —

Chapter
6

My Very Good, Very Bad Cat

51

Socked

*One reason we admire cats is for their proficiency in
one-upmanship. They always seem to come out on top,
no matter what they are doing, or pretend they do.*
~Barbara Webster

Raisin, a beautiful longhaired chocolate-colored calico cat with a bushy tail, was thrilled to be an only cat in my parents' home. She held that privileged position for several years, and then my parents brought in Patches, a striking shorthaired calico, and Raisin grudgingly accepted her.

These two were a good match. Raisin had a vivacious personality and was always on the move. She raced around my parents' spacious house, dashing from room to room as if she were a busy executive going from one important meeting to another.

Patches was much more reserved. She rested most of the day. Basking in the sun in a large bay window, Patches would watch Raisin with a quizzical look, as if she were wondering why this fellow feline couldn't sit still.

The two of them got along well, but Raisin was clearly the top cat, and that was fine with Patches. Patches never wanted to be burdened with the pressures of leadership.

Life was pretty good for the two felines until, one day, the unthinkable happened. A dog came into their lives. Well, actually, two dogs came into their lives.

My parents had a friend with two well-trained Scottish Terriers.

But he could no longer take care of the dogs and asked my parents if they would adopt them. My parents knew the dogs and, after thinking about it for a few days, decided to give the two canines a home.

They were very well-behaved, mild-mannered, and affectionate pooches. My parents had a big back yard that the dogs loved. The two Scotties easily took to their new surroundings, and Patches maintained her philosophy, which simply came down to, "You mind your business, and I'll mind mine." The Scotties, named Mac and Duff, liked hanging out in the kitchen near the back door and sleeping in the dining room at night. Patches and Raisin, meanwhile, still had the run of the house.

Raisin, however, was having none of it. She didn't know what these intruders were doing in her home.

Raisin loved to sit in a particular kitchen window, right next to the back door. To get there, she had to walk past the dogs. But that was no problem for her. She was very self-assured and had a commanding walk and a "Don't mess with me" look in her eye. As she approached the dogs to make her way to the window, one hiss cleared the path. My folks used to think that Raisin walked to the window just to hiss at the dogs.

The dogs didn't mind that Raisin occupied the window, but the feisty cat still didn't want these interlopers around. The whole time she was sitting on her perch, she kept looking at these two cute dogs, and you could tell that she was plotting against them. When she exhausted her scheming for the day, she would jump off the window, hiss at the two dogs again—for no reason whatsoever—and take a slow, imperious walk past them.

Patches could see all this going on from her vantage point in the bay window in the dining room opposite the kitchen. Patches already knew to stay out of that kitchen window. Whenever Raisin was on the move, Patches, who was usually sound asleep, would wake up. Then, she'd open one eye to view the action. She would then yawn and stretch and go back to sleep. But she seemed amused by the drama, as if to say, "That's just Raisin being Raisin."

Even though they were well-trained, Mac and Duff still had to learn the rules of their new abode. Every once in a while they would jump on the furniture, pull out clean wash from the laundry basket and throw it around, or engage in other mischievous canine behavior that my parents had to correct. Every time something like that happened, the dogs got a stern talking-to from one of my parents, much to Raisin's delight. Raisin seemed to think that these scoldings would eventually lead to the two Scotties being banished from the premises for good.

Mac and Duff learned quickly, and they rarely had to be told things twice. They seemed to want to please my parents.

But there was one stubborn behavior my parents could not get the dogs to stop. Every night, or so it seemed, one of the dogs would take one of my father's socks from the side of my parents' bed and drag it into the dining room where the dogs often slept. It appeared as though whichever dog dragged the sock in would fall asleep next to it.

My father would go looking for the sock the next morning. He would usually find it next to one of the dogs and reprimand either Mac or Duff for taking the sock. The dogs always seemed bewildered by my father's annoyance. When my father came to retrieve the sock, either Mac or Duff would look at him in a daze, as if they didn't know what was going on. Raisin would watch the scolding from a nearby doorway.

The sock thievery went on for months, and my parents could not understand why these two obedient dogs didn't understand the "sock rules."

Late one night, when she couldn't sleep, my mother was sitting in the kitchen across from the dining room, and she happened to look up from the newspaper she was reading. Off in the distance, down the dark hallway, she saw Raisin drag a sock into the darkened dining room and leave it next to a sleeping dog. Once the dastardly deed was done, Raisin went back to her bed and waited for my father's predictable reaction the next morning. It appeared that Raisin had devised a plan to get these two irritating canines out of her life for good.

My mother told my father about Raisin's ingenious scheme. They both were amused by it and went along with it for a while.

My dad would leave a sock out just for Raisin to drag into the dining room on her nocturnal errand. Every so often, he would play-fully scold the dogs about the sock for Raisin's benefit. The longhaired calico worked her plot for about a year before she got tired of it and realized that the two Scotties weren't going anywhere.

The dogs never caught on that Raisin was behind the sock caper. Eventually, Raisin came to realize that you can rule two dogs just as easily as you can lord it over another cat, especially if none of them have any desire to be in charge. And they didn't.

Just like Patches, Mac and Duff knew that Raisin could only be in one place at one time, and if she wanted to commandeer a particular spot, why argue? There was plenty of room for everyone. They all eventually made peace with one another, although Raisin still got in an occasional hiss, just so nobody forgot who was boss.

— Robert Grayson —

52

Whose Chair Is It Anyway?

The cat is the only animal which accepts the comforts
but rejects the bondage of domesticity.
~Georges-Louis Leclerc de Buffon

When we brought Matsu home from the local animal shelter, we thought there might be a fight for dominance between the new cat and our old dog. After all, the dog had been around for years, and the cat was a newcomer.

The dog wasn't thrilled to have a feline sibling suddenly appear, but she saw no need to make a fuss. The two quickly formed a mutual non-aggression pact and agreed to live and let live.

Instead of a canine-versus-feline fight, the battle lines were drawn between man and cat. The father of the house versus the furry feline. The point of contention? A chair.

"The cat," the father announced upon Matsu's arrival, "can never sit in my chair. I don't want to sit down and end up with cat hair all over me."

The chair in question was a large, overstuffed wingchair sitting right next to the picture window. It had an excellent view of a back yard full of bunnies and squirrels.

"How do you expect to keep the cat out of your chair?" I asked.

"Simple," he replied. "I'll just put stuff on the seat when I'm not sitting there." He stood up, set down the stack of bills he had been working on, and headed off to get a snack. He returned to find the cat happily sitting on the crumpled papers, intently watching the birds at the birdfeeder.

Round one: Dad 0, Cat 1.

"Papers are too comfortable," he declared. He set down his closed laptop with the charger placed on top. Minutes later, Matsu was curled up, half on the laptop, half off, with his head nestled up next to the charger, purring happily.

Round two: Dad 0, Cat 2.

"More stuff," a determined dad declared. "I need more stuff." His next attempt featured the laptop, charger cord and block, piles of bills, and a Kleenex box. Matsu waited until he left the room and then jumped up on the chair. He gently rearranged the items until there was a perfectly formed cat space in the middle.

Round three: Dad 0, Cat 3.

"You aren't going to win this fight," we all told the human.

"I have a brilliant idea," he replied, undaunted. He took a barstool from the kitchen counter and placed it sideways on the chair. "That will stop him."

It did not. Matsu climbed up through the rungs and settled himself down comfortably. The barstool legs framed his triumphant grin as he surveyed his kingdom.

Round four: Dad 0, Cat 4.

There were no further rounds. Dad capitulated. The chair was no longer his alone but a shared property. Sometimes, he would sit in the prized window location, and sometimes the cat would take possession.

Occasionally, they would share the throne with one body filling the seat and another smaller but just as determined individual making his place on a lap already overflowing with paperwork.

All attempts to ban the cat from the chair ceased, and instead a lint roller was placed by the front door.

When you open your doors to abandoned animals from a shelter, they may claim more than just your favorite chair. They may conquer your heart.

— Mary DeVries —

53

Miss P. and the Turkey

To a cat, "No" means "Not while I'm looking."
~Author Unknown

I remember that Thanksgiving as though it was yesterday, even though it happened years ago. The china sparkled under the dining room chandelier. The handprinted dinner menu was proudly displayed on an easel. All my best serving dishes and Rosenthal china were strategically placed on a beautiful gold-threaded tablecloth. I believed even Martha Stewart would have approved.

This was the first holiday of my marriage and the first event for his family that I would be hosting in our home. Everything had to be perfect. My lofty and probably unattainable goal was to receive the approval of my extremely critical mother-in-law. She was a proper Southern lady, interested primarily in how things looked. As I put the finishing touches on the table scape, I turned to my curious cat, Miss P., who sat on one of the dining room chairs. She stared at my handiwork, carrying out her duties as feline snoopervisor. As she sat primly, with her silver-and-white tail wrapped around her feet and bright blue eyes blinking at me, I discussed my expectations for her.

"Okay, all I need for you to do is to stay out of trouble. Not everyone coming is a cat lover. Please don't jump on things. Stay off the fireplace mantel. And, for heaven's sake, don't jump into the fridge or freezer when someone opens the door."

She stared at me for a moment. I could almost see her brows knitting together, pushing the "Tabby M" a bit lower on her face. She then slow-blinked twice, stood up, and gracefully jumped down from the chair, tail high and waving as she left the room.

When you receive a slow blink from a relaxed, happy cat, it's a sure sign of affection. I was praying that this slow blink was also her way of saying, "I love you, and because I love you I agree to behave."

My optimism restored, I returned to the Thanksgiving chores at hand. I could hear the sound of the football game coming from the TV in the living room. No help would be forthcoming from my husband, but that wasn't necessarily a bad thing.

The thirty-pound turkey was ready for its place of honor on the antique platter. I checked my watch. The guests would be arriving soon, and I needed to finish the side dishes and arrange the food on the table. We didn't have enough space to seat everyone, so we would be eating buffet-style. I added cream and butter to the homemade mashed potatoes, and then I put sea salt, olive oil and pepper on the Brussels sprouts and slid the baking sheet under the broiler.

Getting the food on the table in time and making everything look elegant would be a delicate balance. I didn't see Miss P. anywhere and sighed in relief. Some of the tension left my body as I concluded the final preparations. I removed the vegetables from the broiler and reset the temperature for warming the other dishes.

I wrestled the turkey onto the serving platter, sliced some of the white and dark meat, and then carried it into the dining room, placing it in its prominent spot on the table.

I returned to the kitchen. While I was pouring the fresh cranberries from the pan into a bowl, my ears picked up the sound of slurping and smacking. Dread washed over me as I ran into the dining room. The sight that greeted me almost made my heart stop.

Miss P. reclined across the table, stretched to her full length, with a piece of the sliced turkey between her paws. She gnawed on the meat, leaving stains on the glittering table cover. In order to create a more comfortable attack on the bird, she'd "removed" a few things. A beautiful, antique bowl (given to me by my mother-in-law) lay in pieces on the floor with some other serving dishes. I saw all my dreams to be the acceptable daughter-in-law disappear as fast as those turkey slices.

The cat was so engrossed in her meal that she hadn't heard me walk in the room. Before I could grab her and begin to repair the damage she'd done, the loud "ding dong" of the doorbell startled both of us.

Miss P. believed that doorbells were invented for the sole purpose of torturing cats. She sprang up and started to jump off the table in terror but was stopped when she caught her claw in the tablecloth. I grabbed her around the middle, attempting to extricate her claw from the fabric. I shoved my hip against the edge of the table to stop the entire set-up from being pulled down onto the floor and deal with the now-squirming, howling feline. My husband walked into the room. While I grappled with Miss P., I yelled, "Stall and keep everyone in the living room!" He assessed the situation quickly, nodded and headed toward the door.

Fortunately, I was able to detach the claw from the fabric, and as soon as she was released, Miss P. made a beeline for the back of the house.

While my husband greeted his family, pouring wine and initiating small talk, I removed the tooth-marked turkey slices to the garbage, sliced more meat and rearranged everything on the platter. I reset the dishes on the table, strategically placing a bowl to cover the turkey stain, swept up the glass shards of the antique bowl, and quickly rolled the sticky pet-hair remover across the tablecloth.

I breathed deeply as I took one last look at the table. Deciding all was in place, I smoothed my hair, checked for any stains on my clothing, and went into the living room to greet the guests and calm my nerves with a glass of wine.

Dinner was a success. The family appreciated the homemade dishes and loved the turkey that now showed no signs of being previously mangled. My mother-in-law congratulated me on the beauty of the table. I relaxed in the knowledge that the table fiasco had gone unnoticed.

As we were enjoying our coffee and pumpkin pie, Miss P. sauntered into the living room to see what was going on.

"Oh, what a beautiful cat! She's so sweet!" The more compliments she heard, the more Miss P. played to her audience. Granted, she was beautiful. The blue-eyed "Applehead" (part tabby, part Siamese) with her silver-and-white coloring was gorgeous. When on her best behavior, Miss P.'s presence elicited much admiration. I decided not to mention how she'd earned the name "The Slasher" at our veterinary clinic.

I watched her as she moved from person to person receiving the petting and chin scratching she felt was her due. She saved me for last, purring and wrapping herself through my legs. When she jumped up onto my lap, my anger dissipated, and my sense of humor returned.

Over the years, whenever my mother-in-law found my attempts to be an acceptable daughter-in-law lacking and my social skills wanting, I would close my eyes, remember the near disaster on that Thanksgiving, and think, *Oh, if you only knew!*

— Anita Aurit —

54

Move Over, Rudolph

If you would know a man, observe how he treats a cat.
~Robert Heinlein

The snow was coming down steadily on that January night. I had worked later than I hoped, and it had taken me nearly an hour to drive what would normally take fifteen minutes. I was relieved when I finally pulled into the driveway. The snow was already up to my knees, so it was difficult to even make it to the front door. I looked forward to putting on my pajamas and getting in bed. Tomorrow would be a good day to sleep in.

The wonderful thing about snow is that it absorbs sound, so there was little noise from the nearby highway. But all of a sudden I did hear something. I was just about to put my key into the door when I heard it again, and it was getting louder. It was a cat meowing.

Who would leave their cat out on a night like this? I looked around the yard but didn't see anything. I figured the cat would find its way home.

When I walked into the house, I expected my own cat, Shadow, to greet me as he always did. But he wasn't around. I searched the house. I looked in all the closets and in the rafters in the basement where he sometimes liked to hide. That couldn't possibly have been Shadow outside meowing, could it?

I pulled my boots and coat back on and went out into the snow. I yelled out his name, and the meowing got louder. It definitely sounded like him, but where was he?

I trudged around the side of the house where the snow was even deeper. I could barely walk through the drifts that were almost up to my waist. I kept calling, "Shadow!" and he kept meowing back. I could hear him clear as day, but I didn't see him anywhere. It was baffling. I paced back and forth along the side of the house.

"Shadow!"

"Meow!"

"Shadow!"

"Meow!"

It was crazy. I was getting so frustrated. "Shadow! Where are you?" I yelled, spreading my arms and throwing my head back. And that's when I saw him.

He was perched on the edge of the roof, three stories up, looking like a vulture.

"How on earth did you get up there?" I said, as if I expected a response.

Shadow began pacing and meowing a mile a minute.

I had found him, but now what?

I tried to coax him down to the second-story eave, but he wouldn't move that far.

Okay, I thought. *Time to get some back-up.* I went inside and woke up my husband. "Should I call the fire department?" I asked.

"I don't think they're going to come out for something like that," he said, still half-asleep.

At this point, my son woke up and came into our room to see what was going on.

"Shadow is on the roof," I said. Of course, my son thought this was both hysterical and frightening.

"We have to get him off!" he said.

"I know, but how?" I asked.

"The attic room!" my son replied.

Oh, the attic room. I hadn't even thought of that. In the back of our attic, we have a "secret room" that is lined with windows. It's a small space that I occasionally used as an art studio, but it was always too cold to use in the winter. We ran up the stairs and opened one of the windows. We could see (and hear!) Shadow, but he was still afraid to move.

"Come on, Shadow! Come here!" my son tried to coax him.

"He's not going to come. What are we going to do?" It was more of a rhetorical question, but my husband answered, "Hold on."

He disappeared and then returned a minute later wearing his coat and boots. "I can't believe I'm doing this," he said.

He removed one of the window screens and crawled out onto the snow-covered roof.

"Shadow, come here!" he said, holding out his hand. Shadow took a few timid steps forward. We called out to him, and he very slowly made his way over to my husband.

"Be careful!" I pleaded. The snow was coming down so heavily that it was hard to see what was happening. A few seconds later, my husband was able to grab Shadow and hand him over to my son. The late-night snow rescue was a success, and now our cat had a new nickname: Roofcat.

— Patti Woods —

55

A Little Too Well-Trained

The cat is, above all things, a dramatist.
~Margaret Benson

I often sit at my dining room table eating supper in relative silence. Then a knock or a thump occurs just outside the sliding glass door to the patio, and I look over, fully expecting to see my cat Lucky hunched in the doorway, desperate to come in.

My shoulders sag a little every time I turn my head and see nothing through the glass. It must have been a moth or a bird making a minor sound, I reason. With disappointment, I resume my meal.

It used to be Lucky making the ruckus outside. And it used to drive me crazy. You see, my cat Lucky was a little too litter-trained. He liked to go outside, but at least once a week (if not once a day), Lucky would run up to the sliding glass door and launch himself against it, meowing his head off. I couldn't actually hear him through the glass, but the frenzied expression on his face let me know that he was screaming to be let in.

He used to prance and spin on the narrow doorstep like a break dancer, frantically performing stunts to get my attention. His eyes darted around, his ears slanted back, and he hopped from foot to foot.

Silly me. I always gave in to his antics. I'd get up and open the door. Lucky raced in as though his tail were on fire and ran pell-mell down the stairs, through the family room, and into the laundry room where he slid into his litterbox like it was home plate.

I would still be standing at the sliding door when I'd hear the bulldozer-ish scratch of litter being scraped up from the bottom of the box and landing like pebbles on the floor.

"Lucky!" I used to yell in disgust.

Just as I'd grunt my annoyance and head down the stairs, Lucky would race past me again in his hurry to get back to the sliding door. He'd put his litterbox-stained paws on the glass and scratch to get out as if demons were about to get him. I might have worried about it if I wasn't privy to these same hysterics time and time again.

Foolishly, I chided him even while I opened the door, and he zoomed out into freedom again.

Unbelievable. Lucky had simply come in to use the litterbox. He'd spend the whole day outside if he could, but nature called him back to the house, and he did it as eagerly and spastically as a little boy who had to run in the house for the same purpose.

It was exasperating. That rotten cat.

We'd do this ridiculous routine again and again, and I always fell for it. He was probably outside entertaining his friends, saying, "Watch this. I'm going to run up to the door and act all panicky, and she'll let me in to use the litterbox. I'll meet you back out here in five minutes."

But now I missed it.

Lucky didn't wait at the sliding door for me anymore. There was no frantic pawing or blur of orange fur running past. There wasn't even a litterbox anymore. How I missed him and his annoying, little game. It drove me crazy while he was alive. But I'll say one thing: Lucky had me well-trained. And he always used his litterbox.

—Juliann Wetz—

A Cat Named Cat

Even if you have just destroyed a Ming vase,
purr. Usually all will be forgiven.
~Lenny Rubenstein

When my husband and I owned a pub in New York City's Financial District, we had a house cat we rescued from a shelter. At first, he seemed a little anti-social. He hid in the kitchen, and I didn't see him for two whole days. Neither did the cook or dishwasher. His food bowl was empty every morning, so I knew he wasn't starving, and his litterbox had to be cleaned every day — another reassuring sign that he was still with us.

On the third day, I decided that the transition from the shelter to the pub had lasted long enough. I went into the empty kitchen that late afternoon (we only served food at lunch), filled his food and water bowls, sat next to them on the floor, legs crossed, and waited for him to make an appearance. I kept talking to my invisible friend, assuring him that all was well and I would really like to see him again.

It took a while, but I was eventually rewarded. He cautiously stuck his head out from under the sink. I watched and never moved, just spoke to him in a soft voice. Minutes ticked by. Inch by inch, he crept over to the fresh food and then gobbled it down.

I wondered if this meant he was ready for his debut in the pub. I got my answer as soon as he finished his dinner when he jumped into my lap and curled up in a ball. I was thrilled, but it also meant I was trapped in the kitchen. Rubbing his back and head, I could feel and hear a soft purring sound.

Maybe he trusts me now, I thought.

"Well, Cat," I said. "Time to stop being a hermit and come outside to meet your public."

He looked at me and listened intently, but I had no idea whether or not he understood. Deciding to take a chance, I moved him off my lap, stood, and walked into the mostly empty dining room. And Cat followed.

He looked around at the customers and decided he would have a seat on one of the banquettes. He chose a spot next to a woman who stopped in every evening for a cocktail before heading home. She had told me she enjoyed this quiet time when she could sip a cold drink and read her book after a hectic day of trading stocks.

But that night, Cat decided to invade her private space. I apologized for the intrusion and reached over to shoo him away. But she told me not to do that. She loved cats and started rubbing his head behind his ears. Before I knew it, Cat had climbed into her lap and settled in for the evening. That became their daily routine. She and he enjoyed their quiet time together every day.

However, Cat's involvement with our customers didn't end there. He overcame his reluctance to socialize and became a regular fixture in the dining room. In fact, customers began asking me where Cat was sitting so they could join him.

One customer, Nick, had a regular table every day for lunch. And Cat knew it. Nick would sit down and, within minutes, Cat would jump onto the banquette and sit next to him. And I soon discovered why. Nick was sharing his meal. As much as I pleaded with Nick not to, he insisted that Cat was the most delightful lunch companion he could wish for, and it didn't do any harm to give him little bites of his lunch. When Nick finished his lunch and left to go back to work, Cat curled up in Nick's spot and napped. And no wonder with a belly full of food.

But Nick wasn't the only customer whose heart Cat won. Two other gentlemen who often stopped in for lunch also enjoyed Cat's attention. In fact, they began to ask for a table for three so Cat could join them on his own chair instead of having to sit next to one of them on the banquette. As they discussed the various bonds and their benefits, or lack thereof, Cat followed their conversation, his head turning back and forth between the two as if he were at a tennis match. One day, I watched this phenomenon and shook my head.

"Eileen," Jim called over to me. "Want to see me put Cat to sleep?"

"And how do you think you're going to do that?" I asked.

"Watch." He looked Cat straight in the eyes and said, "Zero coupon bonds."

It was as if Jim had cast a spell on Cat. He curled up on his chair, closed his eyes, and went to sleep.

"Works every time," Jim said. "Even Cat's smart enough to know how boring they are."

Another day, the dining room was full. The only empty seat was being held by friends for a late arrival. I didn't see Cat anywhere but figured he had retreated to the kitchen where he could find a cozy place to curl up. A few minutes later, Chuck, the late arrival, strode into the dining room and pulled out the one empty chair to join his friends. And there was Cat, perfectly happy, taking an early nap. Chuck was a regular customer and knew Cat, so he felt comfortable pushing him off the chair and onto the floor. But Cat didn't want to go onto the floor. Since the chairs were upholstered, Cat dug his claws into the fabric and glared at Chuck as if to say, "This is my chair. Find someplace else to sit."

As I said, there were no other chairs available, so Chuck picked up the chair and shook it to dislodge Cat. Cat just dug in harder.

"Eileen, help!" Chuck yelled over to me. "Cat won't get down, and there's no place else to sit. And I'm starving."

By this time, half the dining room and the bar were laughing and following Chuck and Cat's war. I walked over to the table and looked at Cat, who was trying his best to ignore me.

I stood next to the chair, hands on hips, with a deep frown creasing my forehead. "Cat," I said, "you have to get down. There're no other chairs, and Chuckie's hungry. So, get down now."

Cat looked at me and, I swear, gave a sigh, jumped down and

strutted off to the kitchen where he could rest undisturbed by these pesky customers.

Chuck, with a face as red as a furnace, thanked me and sat down to enjoy his well-earned lunch.

Over the years, Cat became a real personality in the pub, and I sometimes wondered how many customers came for lunch simply to spend time with him.

— Eileen Joyce Donovan —

The Cat Burglar

Cats are only human; they have their faults.
~Kingsley Amis

In our college years, my husband and I lived with several other students in a big old house. One consistent roommate was a guy named Bob who brought with him a black cat named Miss Kitty. It was a time when cats could roam freely in the city and were usually safe to do so. That's how Miss Kitty came to be pregnant, and how she was subsequently renamed Mrs. Kitty to show her proper decorum.

We had made arrangements for good homes for each of the five kittens as soon as they were born. We had a couple of months to wait for them to be ready to go to their new homes, so we made Mrs. Kitty and her family comfortable during what was one of the hottest summers on record up to that time.

We figured that's how the popular pizza parlor just two doors down on the corner of our street came to have the window of their kitchen open nearly all the time. The hot pizza ovens, the scorching days, the weary chefs working inside — it was at least an attempt for a bit of fresh air, if nothing else.

The neighborhood and house were busy at night, but during the day everyone was at work or school. I was alone at home one afternoon when I noticed Mrs. Kitty scurrying through the yard with a mouthful of what looked like meat. *Ugh, she's caught a bird*, I thought, as I ran into the yard to try and free it. But it was a piece of chicken that Mrs.

Kitty carried — a fully cooked, seasoned chicken breast. She carried it through the back door with a triumphant gleam in her eyes.

Very strange, I thought briefly, before sitting back down to my schoolwork at the table near the window. I figured she must have fished it out of a garbage bin or something and didn't give it another thought… until the next day when I arrived home to find a hunk of white cheese sitting on the floor in the middle of the kitchen. Parmesan, I surmised, as I plunked the gnarled block into the garbage. It must have fallen from the fridge when one of the roommates was making a sandwich for lunch.

But the next morning it was a full-sized meat-lovers pizza. It was a Saturday, so most of the household was home, although many were still asleep. One of the guys who lived in the upstairs suite saw it first: the strange sight of Mrs. Kitty half-rolling, half-pulling a freshly baked pizza along the grass in the back yard. We all watched, dumbfounded, discussing what she might be up to and where she could possibly be getting the food. We compared notes on what we had seen her with over the past few days, with the others adding slices of meat and crusts of home-baked bread to my own list of items.

We watched as she hauled that day's catch up the back stairs and into the alcove of the entryway where we had placed blankets and water dishes — and what we thought was enough food to see her through the nursing stage with her kittens. We determined that we weren't feeding her enough and poured more food into the saucers of the temporary kitten hutch.

But, the next morning, we found most of the kibble still in the saucer. We figured that Mrs. Kitty, who was clearly not interested in mere dry food, was already out on the prowl for tastier morsels. The few of us who were up that early quickly raced from the house, ready to catch the thief in action. The nearest route from the back door was into the back lane, which is where we headed.

It didn't take long to reach the pizza shop on the corner, where we could easily spot Mrs. Kitty sitting on the open windowsill, working an entire prime-rib roast over the ledge. Her haunches were braced, and her whole body was heaving. Before we could even yell, "Stop thief!" the massive roast gave way and fell to the ground.

I'm sure there were three mouths agape as we watched her begin to haul the roast into the lane without missing a beat. She dragged it behind her, and the fresh meat left a streak of bright red along the ground in her wake. It had to be because she was nursing, we surmised, some sort of primal need for a whole lot more protein than the dry bulk food we had been giving her.

Before long, the discussion turned to what should be done to set this right. Meat was expensive, after all, and these innocent people were just trying to run a business. But, really, one of us muttered, why would they leave fresh meat to sit out in such heat? And in an open window to boot? Not very hygienic, to be sure. Looking at that cut of beef, we realized it could feed the whole house of broke college students, even if we would need to wash off a bit of road grime before popping it into the oven. It was tempting, but it felt like we were conspiring to join the thieving ranks of Mrs. Kitty.

After further consultation, we stepped forward with a plan. First step was to take the roast away from Mrs. Kitty—an act that caused us some guilt after all her efforts. Then, all three of us carried it back to the restaurant, where we had to knock on the door since it was still too early to be open for business. After some sheepish explanations and apologies, followed by our plans to make amends, we walked back home with the roast.

We rinsed the whole thing at the kitchen sink, freeing the dirt and pebbles while Mrs. Kitty watched. Then, we cut a generous slice for her, peppered and seasoned the rest, and popped it into the oven before placing our call to the hardware store. From then on, even after her kittens were in their new homes, Mrs. Kitty got ample servings of meaty food along with her kibble. And the pizza parlor went on working their magic for many more years—behind the safety of their newly installed window screen.

—Sandy Kelly Bexon—

Status Report

The cat is domestic only as far as suits its own ends.
~Saki

Project: Cat on a Diet

Problem summary:

Approximately two years ago, the Feline was poked and prodded by a certified veterinarian and determined to fall under the classification of Fat Cat.

Fat Cat was placed on a diet consisting of smaller portions of food consisting solely of diet kibble. Fat Cat has lost almost four pounds.

Follow-on problem summary:

Fat Cat has reached the end of her sense of humor about the diet food. Daily full assaults have begun at 4:30 A.M. with objective to obtain Early Breakfast.

Boy Human is the main target of the attacks.

Since Boy Human is the kind of person who can't go back to sleep easily after being awakened, this 4:30 A.M. assault strategy is resulting in severe sleep deprivation.

Sleep deprivation means a very cranky Boy Human.

Proposed solution:

In order to alleviate general crankiness issues, Girl Human sought corrective action.

Research was conducted via Google and a determination made that a timer food dish might provide relief.

A simple, one-meal device with timer was procured and received from the online supplier known as Amazon.

Field trials:

On Saturday, December 3, the timer food dish was fully locked and loaded around 11:30 P.M. before Boy Human retired for the night.

As expected, at 4:30 A.M., the timer dish lid properly deployed, and food was made available.

Fat Cat easily discovered this bounty and dined appropriately. Upon full consumption of morning kibble, Fat Cat then retired to the heater vent and returned to sleep.

Around 7:00 A.M., Fat Cat roused and then entered the bedroom of Boy & Girl Human.

Operating under the "That earlier meal was a gift from the Kibble Gods, and since human hands did not dispense it, it didn't count" mode, Fat Cat initiated usual morning aggressive tactics upon the Boy Human, including loud protesting, sharp paw to the forehead, knocking possessions off the bedside table, and biting errant limbs hanging over the side of the mattress.

Girl Human groggily commented, "This wasn't covered in the Amazon reviews."

Boy Human was again forced to rise from said mattress and delivered a second breakfast to Fat Cat.

Upon consumption of second breakfast, Fat Cat brought her now roly-poly, stuffed tummy back to the bedroom of Boy & Girl Human and tucked herself in under the covers for the day.

Rating of outcome:

Moderate success.

7:00 A.M. is a more decent hour than 4:30 A.M., so Boy Human was, in fact, less cranky.

However, Fat Cat ate twice, meaning kibble ration was exceeded for the day.

Full reporting must be delivered to veterinarian upon next review.

Next steps:

Food dish armed with a small excess of kibble rationing was locked by Girl Human on or about 10:00 P.M. on Sunday, December 4.

At 4:30 A.M. Monday, lid properly deployed, and food was consumed.

Soon after, a sated Fat Cat re-entered bedroom of Boy & Girl Human, climbed into the bed and fell asleep.

Boy Human slept until 7:30 A.M. when Monday morning alarm went off.

Boy Human awoke feeling more rested than he has in months.

Conclusion:

Field trials of timer food dish continue. Team is cautiously optimistic.

— Karen Fayeth —

59

Meow Visits the Vet

Intelligence in the cat is underrated.
~Louis Wain

My cat is such a sweet, gentle girl,
The most darling in all the world,
So soft and cuddly all the time,
I'm truly glad that she is mine.
Yet, when I take her to the vet,
I want to scream, "That's not my pet!"
Who hissed, snarled and showed her teeth,
Who wound herself around his feet,
Who bit the sleeve of her vet's coat,
Who wrapped her claws around his throat,
Who coughed up fur balls in his face,
Who ripped his trousers into lace.
When she grew tired from her attack,
She sat alone and turned her back.
My cat's insane, I began to weep.
She'll surely kill me in my sleep.
The doc bandaged his bloody wounds,
Then grabbed a syringe like a whaler's harpoon.
My furry feline turned to react,
Round two began with the vet and my cat.
She used his arm as a scratching post.
He grabbed for her but caught a ghost.

She pulled his hair like spools of thread,
Then carved an "X" on his balding head.
But then the tide began to turn,
The nice doc's eyes teared and burned.
He grabbed a towel and wrapped her tight.
Now restrained, she couldn't fight.
Doc examined her eyes and ears.
He checked her nose, and it was clear.
He pried her jaws and looked inside,
"Her teeth are strong and sharp," he sighed.
He gave her shots, examined her nails.
She lay quiet without a wail.
So, he released her from constraint.
Squeezed her belly without complaint.
But when he lifted up her tail,
Round three scored an epic fail.
She growled at him then blocked the door.
I clenched my teeth and yelled, "No more!"
Her arms rotated like a fan.
I reached for her, nearly lost a hand
My knees buckled in my distress,
"Is this the cat that I've caressed?"
Then I fell down to fake my death.
When she came by to check my breath,
I stuffed her in her carrier cage,
And left her to her feline rage.
The vet choked down a couple of pills.
He gave me his inflated bill.
Said future visits would be banned.
My cat smiled — her brilliant plan.

— Sheila Valesano —

Chapter 7

Miracles Happen

60

Keeping the Faith

The cat has nine lives: three for playing,
three for straying, three for staying.
~English Proverb

He was a tiny, orphaned kitten when he found me at a church bake sale. This four-week-old orange tabby came across the room and climbed up my jeans and sweater. He nestled into my neck. I already knew he was special, so I left the church bake sale with a cake and a kitten.

Snickers grew into a beautiful orange tabby with a fluffy tail, like a raccoon, ringed with orange and black. He followed me everywhere and he also loved our little dog, Soffi. They would sleep together and play in our yard. And while Snickers loved to lie out in the sun by our pool, he never ventured out of the yard.

That was until the tree service came to the house behind us. They were chipping the trees or limbs they'd taken down and it was very loud. I didn't realize Snickers was outside while this was happening and later, when I couldn't find him in the house, I went outside and called his name over and over, to no avail.

I searched the neighborhood for hours. Some friends came to help. It was dark by then, and I came home disheartened and afraid for him. Snickers hated thunderstorms, and the clouds were gathering. He was out there somewhere, all alone.

I put Snickers' pictures on social-media sites and printed 325 colored flyers. I went out every day to put the flyers on trees, telephone poles, businesses, and anywhere that people would notice. I went from door to door to every house in our neighborhood and beyond.

Snickers' photograph was in the newspaper every week. He became well-known in our small town and our county.

I sometimes had a friend help me hunt for him at night, crawling around people's houses, in their bushes, under porches, and checking culverts. It was dangerous to be on other people's property at night.

I hung clothes in my yard with my scent on them. "A little crazy," my husband said. I even contacted a psychic. She said, "He's in the woods, and he is being fed, but it's not enough." My heart dropped.

I hired a tracker whose dog searched the neighborhood and alerted me when she found Snickers' scent. I kept going back to the horse farm where the dog had tracked him. Every night, I went out to search for him. I felt he knew I was searching, and he was waiting for me to find him.

The police officers in our neighborhood even went into vacant houses to search for him, saying it wasn't safe for me to go in alone.

Four months passed. We offered a reward for anyone who found him. I went on so many wild-goose calls. One night, at 2:00 A.M., I was so distraught that I even brought a cat home thinking it was Snickers. He looked so much like Snickers. Soffi took one sniff and got back up on the bed. She knew it was not our Snickers. I took the cat back to where I found him. My husband said, "You need to let this go." I couldn't.

Then one night, I got a call from a woman who said she'd seen one of my flyers. She lived across the field from the horse farm where the dog had tracked Snickers. She said, "We feed a feral colony, and a cat that looks like yours showed up three months ago. He's not a part of the feral colony, and they often don't let him near the food. He lives in the woods behind us."

She said she couldn't get near him. I told her that if he was my Snickers, he would come right to me.

I went to the woods that night and called him. I heard the rustle of the brush and saw a small trail in the beam of my flashlight. Snickers came down the path and jumped into my arms, wrapped his paws around my neck, and pressed against my chest. I felt myself getting dizzy as if the area around me was twirling. Snickers would not let go, and neither would I.

We sat there in the dark, and I rocked him back and forth. He knew I would never give up. He knew I would find him. He was pitifully thin, but he was clean.

The couple later came and helped me up and to my car. Snickers clung to me, and I held him tightly. We drove the two miles back to our home. That night, I posted on Facebook that Snickers was home. The phone rang late into the night. Neighbors popped in.

Snickers and I sat up late with him in my lap, just looking at each other. He did not have any fleas or ticks despite having lived in the wild for four months. He always loved me to wash him down with a wet washcloth. So, I did that before we went to bed. Snickers sat in his usual place on my pillow.

I told the couple I would bring the reward money to them, and they declined, saying, "We had our reward tonight." I gave them a gift certificate for a lovely dinner at one of the finest restaurants in our town. They were very happy for me and Snickers.

When I called the newspaper, the employee shouted out, "It's Snickers! Snickers is home!" I could hear loud cheering in the background. The newspaper did not send a bill for the lost-cat ad that week but ran a Snickers picture with FOUND stamped across it in bold letters.

One day, the doorbell rang. It was our mail carrier. She had mail for Snickers and asked to meet this famous cat. Of course, he was happy to oblige. We received many notes and calls from our friends all over the United States. They said, "It's a miracle."

Yes, a true miracle. For four months and two days, I searched. I knew he was out there. My intuition was right.

—Zoa Ann Beasley—

61

How My Cat Found Me a Husband

Cats are smart and know they are.
~Tomi Ungerer

My cat, Lady Puff, was behaving very strangely — even more than usual. Alternately scratching the open kitchen door and glancing back at me, it seemed as if she wanted to romp about in the garden.

"Well, go on," I said as I indicated she should go out. "It's not like you to be so meek."

However, as her green eyes kept fixing me with a compelling stare, I sighed and poked my head out the door.

"Oh!" I exclaimed as I simultaneously banged my head against the thick French door and realized that my handsome neighbor, Ned, was strolling out for his newspaper. As I quickly retreated inside, I silently thanked the blooming magnolia tree for shading me from view.

"Look at my hair! You spend hours preening yourself, but you can't empathize with another female?" I admonished my white Shirazi companion.

Lady Puff looked down her haughty nose at me and bolted out across the lawn. I mused about Ned, who had moved into the house next door a few days earlier. However, I immediately shrugged off the thought — he already had a partner, judging by the lovely woman who lived with him.

Sipping my holy basil infusion, I stretched luxuriously like my cat and looked forward to catching up on my meditation practice this Saturday. As a junior partner in a law firm, I had been busy welcoming entertainment-law associates to our Santa Barbara office and shamefully neglected my spiritual schedule.

Suddenly, I cocked my head as I heard the gate open, and I rushed to the window, wondering who was calling at this ungodly hour. I froze when I spied Ned crossing my lawn, with Lady Puff cradled contently in his arms. Swinging my head frantically in all directions, I searched for a hiding place as I remembered that my meditation T-shirt oozed needy vibes with "So Ready for Love" emblazoned across my chest. With only a few seconds to spare, I dived headfirst into the walk-in pantry and quietly closed the door behind me.

"Hello? Anybody home?" Ned called out.

To my horror, I heard Lady Puff purring and scratching against the pantry door. I sent telepathic messages to my feline companion, urging her not to disclose my hiding place. But it became swiftly apparent to me that my cat, who had the treacherous soul of a sorority sister during hazing ceremonies, was bent on humiliating me.

"Is anybody in there? Please shout if you're in trouble!" Ned insisted.

With the approaching steps of my neighbor, I promptly decided that breathing was not essential and closed my eyes in dismay.

"Are you all right?" Ned asked in consternation as he wrenched open the pantry door.

"Oh, the door got stuck. Thank God my cat found you!" I mustered enthusiastically.

By his quizzical gaze, I knew he sensed that something was amiss. Luckily, he was too polite to probe further.

As we greeted each other, I could not help noting how Lady Puff was being uncharacteristically warm to Ned — rubbing her head against his calf. When Ned started to inch toward the door, Lady Puff became somewhat demented and started pulling at his pants, making it obvious that she wanted him to stay. I watched in mounting incredulity as Lady Puff became more desperate in her antics: jumping up and down, twisting herself around Ned's ankles, and jumping back and forth between us. With a murmur of apology, I picked up the snowy white cat, and Ned was finally free to leave my kitchen.

"Look, I understand that you don't believe in monogamy," I lectured righteously to Lady Puff after Ned's departure, "but I do. Ned is obviously in a relationship, and that's that."

With a pitiful glance at single me, Lady Puff turned her back on me and gracefully walked away in the garden. I stuck out my tongue at her satiny white back and retreated to my small, east-facing meditation room — hoping to seek divine answers about my feline housemate's intent to embarrass me.

More than an hour later, I emerged feeling happier, grounded and grateful; I could face anything, like a true warrior queen. As I hummed and skipped to the kitchen for more tea, I was dumbfounded. Right in the middle of the kitchen, I encountered a bundle of unknown clothes, still damp from the laundry and smelling of lavender fabric softener. Upon further scrutiny, I realized with consternation that it was a pile of male underwear! With a wave of intuition (most likely induced by the meditation), it dawned on me that Lady Puff had stolen Ned's clothes! I wondered how soon I could sell my house and move to another area.

Moaning in dismay, I gingerly placed the clothes in a clean jute bag while contemplating that it was the first time Lady Puff had stolen a neighbor's belongings. Still, it would be socially excruciating to be known as the single, desperate woman who resorted to dubious magic to secure a partner. In that line of thought, Lady Puff made her entrance, regally nonchalant, and observed me lazily. Feeling the need to display a semblance of dominance and discipline, I scolded her firmly.

"Lady Puff, this is very bad. You're not to do this again."

In response, she ran back outside and brought back a photo frame, which she laid at my feet. It was a picture of Ned and his female partner.

"Did my mum delegate her matchmaking efforts to you?" I queried wearily. "Look, he seems very nice, but he is already coupled up."

However, Lady Puff frantically picked up the photo frame and thrust it at me repeatedly. Sighing, I glanced at the picture half-heartedly and did a double take. I took a closer look and broke into a smile. The photo frame was embellished with sparkly letters that said, "Best siblings ever"! Incidentally, I could now perceive some common facial traits between Ned and the woman, whom I had thought was his significant other.

"Oh, Lady Puff! You do have moral standards after all!"

With that praise, Lady Puff basked in delight and rubbed her soft head against my ankle.

It turned out that photo had been outside because the sister had reglued a few of the letters and left the frame out to dry in the sun. And sixteen years later, I'm still happily married to Ned — the man vetted and chosen by my incredibly intuitive cat.

— Poppy Tillbury —

62

The Mooch

*My cat came out of nowhere and
became my everything.*
~Author Unknown

O kay, don't hate me, but I've never really been a cat person. My mom was one of those crazy cat ladies, and we always had an aloof Siamese or psychotic calico wandering around the house, sucking up to her and hissing at "the competition," namely me.

That was until I was sixteen, and Moochie came into my life.

The Mooch was everything I wanted in a dog, without actually being of the canine persuasion. (In today's vernacular, I believe he "identified" as a Basset Hound.)

I was a poor kid with few friends who couldn't have a dog; God gave me The Mooch to make up for it.

I found this scrawny, rain-soaked tabby huddling in the bushes outside our apartment complex, looking as hopeless and desperate as I, a single-parent welfare kid, felt. Like me, he had trust issues, and it took several days of leaving him the small fish that I caught in our local pond before he finally allowed me to pick him up.

It was an instant bond of friendship. Two loners, surviving on the edges of society, found a brother in one another. I can still feel his gravely baritone purr of gratitude reverberating against my chest as I tucked him under my coat.

Bringing Mooch home was a bit like a life-long convict suddenly being introduced into polite society.

I remember my mom's haughty calico, who despised me (and everyone else besides my mom), encountering Mooch for the first time and deciding to show this street urchin who was in charge. She hissed, slapping at him with the vainglory of royalty, at which point Moochie, the street-smart survivor, sealed his place in my heart (and our home) by slapping the stuffing out of the spoiled, elitist feline.

I'm not saying that I approve of violence as a response to the oligarchy, but... power to the people, baby!

The family hierarchy was never questioned again, and Mooch, being a man of honor, forgave and forgot. The two of them eventually became, if not fast friends, at least polite roommates.

What followed was a long three years of The Mooch sleeping at the foot of my bed, snarfing up the smaller rewards of my fishing expeditions, spending long hours happily lounging in front of the wall heater, and generally enjoying and appreciating the good life.

If I was cooking breakfast for Mom, Mooch was there at my feet, always happy to test the quality of the bacon.

If I was lounging on the couch playing Donkey Kong (yes, I'm old), he was right next to me, sitting up like a little person, critiquing my gameplay and happily accepting a share of my delivery pizza.

There wasn't an aloof bone in this cat's body. Like a young Oliver Twist, he knew what he'd escaped from, living on the streets, and was happy to show his gratitude for a bowlful of food and a little affection.

He was mellow, easy-going, and fun to hang with— The Big Lebowski of the feline world.

And man did I love him!

My mother died when I was seventeen, leaving me solely responsible for selling off our meager belongings and finding a place for myself to live. Luckily, I had an amazing pastor who didn't hesitate to take me in. Unfortunately, his wife and daughters were severely allergic to cats.

Like the classy guy he was, The Mooch seemed to understand the situation. Not wanting to make his best friend face a heartbreaking decision, shortly before the move, he just... wasn't there.

I searched the neighborhood, calling his name. I set out his favorite foods and even (with great foreboding) crawled under the house with a flashlight, but he was gone without a trace.

Me? I choose to believe that my pal, who always seemed to be a little more than "just a cat," sensed (in a Mary Poppins kind of way) that his work with me was done, and there were other families who needed him.

I choose to believe that my friend moved on to share love and pizza with the next lonely kid. I still miss him, and I hope with all my heart that, in true Moochie style, he lived out his life somewhere with a sunny beach, a soft couch, plenty of fish, and the occasional slice of pepperoni. He was the best friend a lonely kid like me could have asked for.

— Perry P. Perkins —

63

Moving On with Moxie

*Looking at cats, like looking at clouds, stars or the ocean,
makes it difficult to believe there is nothing
miraculous in this world.*
~Leonard Michaels

"One quick peek," I promised myself as I drove to the shelter. Though two months had passed, I still reeled from the death of my best buddy, Clouseau. The silver tabby Persian had succumbed to cardiomyopathy. His heart was just too big, in more ways than one.

Losing him had knocked the emotional wind out of me after a brutal divorce, and I was living solo for the first time ever. The lunch-hour jaunt to the SPCA was just a diversion, a bit of wistful kitty window shopping. I wasn't ready for a new friend yet.

I quickly toured the kitten room, watching the tiny fur balls romp and wrestle, climbing and leaping to and fro. Adorable, but not one of them truly touched my heart. So, I made my way into the adult cat area and paused in front of a cage holding two felines. The fluffy tabby with big ears, white boots and plush tail came right up to the front of the cage and locked eyes with me. When I opened the door and scooped him up, he kissed me on the nose. My fate was sealed.

Good thing my boss loves animals as much as me, I thought. I wouldn't have too much trouble justifying my extended lunch hour. I filled out the necessary forms and placed the kitty "on hold." Then, I sped to the pet store and purchased some necessary supplies. Back in the office, I made a halfhearted stab at working for a few hours until my boss laughingly urged, "Go on, get out of here!"

When I returned to the shelter, I found the adolescent cat posed calmly near the front of the cage, as if to say, "I'm still here. What took you so long?" I christened him Moxie.

As I stumbled through the next few months, trying my unfamiliar single life on for size, Moxie showered me with rainbows of kitty love. When I parked myself at the computer, he curled up on my lap. When a bout of loneliness struck, he proceeded to snuggle and purr it away. At night, he crept up onto the bed and planted reassuring kisses on my face.

Outdoors, Moxie amused me by racing up trees and leaping at butterflies. He put his whole heart into whatever he did. I remember the time I was strolling around the apartment complex in an effort to round him up for dinner, and I happened to glance into a nearby window. There was Moxie, perched on a dining room table, looking back at me. I knocked and rang the doorbell. No one answered. Evidently, my neighbors had left Moxie to hold down the fort! No doubt, that cat got around.

One day, I was out shopping when my cellphone rang. A neighbor had found Moxie lying in the road. He had been hit by a car and was severely injured. My friend had rushed him to the nearest vet before calling. The familiar feeling of grief threatened to overwhelm me. "Please, God, not Moxie," I said aloud.

I hurried to the veterinarian's office and found Moxie listless in a cage, unable to move from the waist down. His pelvis had been broken. His sad, puzzled look ripped through me. At that moment, I couldn't bear to give approval to end his sweet life. Instead, I went home to mourn what I was going to face the following day. I jumped on my bike and went on a long, tearful ride, praying for guidance and bracing myself for what I might have to do.

The next day, I dragged myself into the vet's office to share my terrible decision. This time, a different doctor greeted me. And he had a different point of view. "I've seen young cats like Moxie make a full recovery from a broken pelvis," he said kindly, sending hope zinging through my veins. "Because of his youth, the bones may mend themselves by growing back together."

If I was willing, he was willing to keep Moxie for a week to give him a chance to heal. The staff would administer any necessary meds and help him use a litterbox. When the week was up, we would see if a miracle had occurred.

I visited Moxie almost every day. My prayers were soon answered. After seven days, he could feel sensation in his lovely white boots as he tottered like a newborn colt. The X-ray showed a healed pelvis, and I was able to take him home. The added hitch in his gait just upped his cute factor.

We celebrated our reunion with an abundance of fake furry mice and extra cuddles. Moxie also resumed his mission of helping me cope with change. We agreed that he should stay indoors until I could move to a safer area. We substituted a cat tree for the real thing and augmented his play time with lasers, feathers, shoelaces, and other crazy items he hauled into the living room. Over time, Moxie's resilience induced me to embrace my single status. If he could make such a remarkable recovery, then so could I.

That was a number of years ago. I am remarried to a wonderful man, and I have taught him to love cats almost as much as I do. Now, when my memory lingers on Moxie, I can't help but smile. He was a survivor, and I got to enjoy him while he purred and kissed his way through his eight remaining lives.

I'll always thank him for inspiring me and showing me the true meaning of moxie.

— Kim Johnson McGuire —

The Message

Somewhere along the way, we must learn that there is
nothing greater than to do something for others.
~Martin Luther King, Jr.

Though I'd had many pets throughout my life and volunteered in animal rescue for years, I'd never met a cat as unique as Lucy. Feisty without being mean, as demanding as she was loving, blessed with a depth of loyalty unmatched by most people, Lucy was a friend to the end. When Lu passed away, I decided to give up working in animal rescue. It would be too painful to be around other cats. They would just remind me of her and the wonderful eighteen years we spent in each other's company.

Then, just a week after she passed, I had a dream. I had settled down on the sofa that Sunday afternoon, exhausted by my grief, and fell asleep almost at once.

And there she was, sitting on my chest as though she was still alive. I remember being astonished in the dream, unable to stop my heart from leaping beneath her little feet, hoping that it really was her. The weight of her paws hurt a bit, digging into my ribs as they did, and I could feel her soft tail brushing against my arm. The dream was so intensely real, so filled with everyday sensations, that I forgot my sorrow and just reveled in seeing Lucy again.

Before she passed, Lucy had gone completely blind, her once-brilliant eyes turned milky, with a vague searching expression that broke my heart. She had been so frightened. It had happened quite quickly as a result of her illness. To comfort her, I kept her in my lap for hours a day and carried her to the litterbox. Eventually, she did learn to make her way around the house, but it had been hard for her.

In the dream, her eyes were just as unsighted and unfocused as the day she died, just as heartbreakingly blank. Then suddenly, with no warning or any indication that something was about to change, a black mist began to seep from her pupils and rose from her face like smoke from a fire. For a second, I was horrified, wondering if I was having a nightmare when, just as suddenly as it had come, the mist was gone, leaving Lucy's eyes a vivid emerald green. With astonished delight, I realized that the darkness had left them, and Lucy could see me as she hadn't since months before she passed away.

The moment her eyes locked with mine, Lu burst into purrs so loud and strong that I could feel the vibration through my entire rib cage. Her body had changed, too. Instead of the drawn, emaciated look of an elderly, sick cat, Lucy was plump and healthy like when she was a kitten. Her fur was sleek and shining, her expression filled with playful happiness.

"Sweetie?" I asked in wonder, lifting my hand to stroke her face. But just as my fingers touched the dark fur, I woke up.

There was confusion for a moment as my surroundings went from nighttime in the dream to daytime in real life, leaving me disoriented and uncertain as to what had just happened. Blinking away the sleepy bewilderment, I realized that Lucy was still gone, yet I felt curiously lighter and more energized than before. It was as if a little of my old self had returned when Lu crept into my sleeping mind to bear a message I needed to hear.

"Here I am," she seemed to say, perched on my breastbone. "I haven't gone anywhere."

Sitting up on the sofa, I felt a few tears course down my cheeks, but strangely a large part of my sorrow was gone, like a weight had been lifted from my chest.

It took a few months, but after my dream I felt the urge to return to animal rescue, and my interaction with cats went from strained and painful to cautiously friendly. Though they reminded me of my Lu, it didn't hurt so much to look at them, and I found it easy to give them the care they needed. Eventually, I even took on two foster cats who desperately needed socialization and watched them sleep in Lucy's old chair without resentment.

Others might dismiss my dream as wish fulfillment or the product of a grieving mind, but I know, without any doubt at all, that it was more than that. It was much more special. It was something I thought I would never have again—a visit with an old friend, a moment with my lost girl, a reminder of our time together that didn't cause me pain.

But, more importantly, it was a message of encouragement, exactly when I needed it most. "Go on," Lucy seemed to say. "Go on. Help others just like me."

It still hurts to think of her. It still hurts to see her empty chair; there is no use denying that. There are days when I see another cat scamper across the floor with a toy in her mouth, and my heart falls because it isn't my Lu. Yet, that dream comes back to me in those moments, and I smile.

Now, I know that friends don't leave us altogether. Whether two- or four-legged, they never really do. We lose them in the most immediate way, we miss them terribly, we ache to hug and touch them, but when it comes right down to it, they are really quite close.

They are just a dream away, waiting in our hearts.

—Alex Lester—

65

Changing Places

Way down deep, we're all motivated by the same
urges. Cats have the courage to live by them.
~Jim Davis

Five years ago, we adopted two cats, sisters. The tortie cat was healthy. The gray cat was sick.

The healthy cat could leap to the top of the refrigerator in a single bound. She would slip into the rafters through the utility closet and walk like a ghost over our ceiling. She stalked socks and toy mice. When our puppy arrived, she swiped at his nose, only to snuggle with him days later. She loved people, greeting our guests with loud purrs and cuddling into our laps at night.

The sick cat couldn't jump at all. She had one eye that was badly scarred. She struggled to digest food and was often sick. She rarely played and shied away from strangers. She had nothing to do with the dog and slightly less to do with us. The only living creature she cuddled with was her sister.

One night, the healthy cat died unexpectedly. The sick cat was lost. She spent weeks calling at the base of the refrigerator or the utility closet, places where her sister could leap, but she could not.

It broke my heart — not just for the sister left behind, but for me, too. I missed our tortie cat.

One day, the gray cat leaped to the top of the cat tree we had in the living room. It was something only her sister could do, and it shocked me. I looked at her, seeing an unmistakable patch of brown on her otherwise gray chest.

That patch hadn't been there before.

Things continued to change. The gray cat no longer needed medication and could eat regular cat food. She started hanging out near the dog, even drinking from his water bowl. She found the stuffed mice and started stalking them. She still hid when strangers came but cuddled in our laps every night.

I joked that she had absorbed her sister's soul.

Lately, her stuffed-mice battles have become louder and more action-packed, causing her to slide into walls and tumble off tables. Her battle meows are shrill enough to make at least one of us shout, "Gray Cat! Honestly!"

I'll hear her fighting her toys at night. I'll often step on whichever plaything she has left outside my door, like a grubby package from Amazon. It's weird.

Recently, Gray Cat was violently and verbally wrestling her stuffed mouse while my daughter and I had lunch. My daughter told me that Gray Cat was meowing outside her bedroom door at 3:00 that morning. When she went to see what the fuss was about, she found Gray Cat standing stoically over a stuffed mouse. My daughter thanked the crazy feline for her "sacrifice," and the cat jumped into my daughter's bed and fell asleep.

At that moment, the meows stopped. Gray Cat appeared, stuffed mouse in her mouth, and dropped it at my feet, assuming a stoic pose. My daughter squealed with delight.

"Say 'thank you,' Mom! She's giving you a gift."

I looked at Gray Cat and her one eye and her brown patch over her heart. I looked at the bedraggled mouse sitting at her feet. For a moment, I felt both sisters looking back at me, which did silly things to my heart.

Thank you, Gray Cat.

— Nicole L.V. Mullis —

66

A Miracle of Hope

When gratitude becomes an essential foundation in our
lives, miracles start to appear everywhere.
~Emmanuel Dagher

We decided that a picket fence would be the perfect do-it-yourself summer project for my husband, Rob. It would add some cottage charm to our house in the coastal town of Santa Cruz, California, and would make the front yard more secure for our elderly calico, Tiki.

One afternoon, while Rob was working on the fence, we noticed a large gray cat hiding under our truck in the driveway. It seemed very shy. When we tried to approach, it backed deeper under the Toyota. We couldn't get a good look at it.

The kitty appeared under the truck again the next day. We weren't concerned, figuring it must belong to new residents in the area. After all, it wasn't likely that a cat could be homeless in a neighborhood of caring pet owners like our neighbor Rose, who strolled by to inspect Rob's handiwork.

As I brought her a cup of coffee, she pointed to the driveway and asked, "So, how are you getting along with the big stray? I've watched him making the rounds of the neighborhood, but nobody seems interested." From her house, Rose had a good view of the whole street. Giving us a knowing look, she added, "I've been putting food out for him, but he seems to fancy *you*."

That was an eye-opener for us. We shouldn't assume that a visiting cat is just out for a walk. It might be a cat in need. Now, we dared to pay attention. Shining a flashlight under the truck, we made out the kitty's large, flat head, tomcat jowls, and hefty frame. And though he was built like a little tank, he was thin, his ribs visible beneath his scruffy tabby coat.

"Watch out, honey. He looks big enough to do some damage," Rob cautioned me. But the kitty just looked at us with sweet, pale-jade eyes that reflected tentative hope and lots of fear. My heart started to melt.

I set up a little camp under some bushes along the driveway, complete with water, food, and a cat bed. When I backed far enough away, the kitty came out and ate ravenously. He showed up again in the days that followed. We called him Harry.

Rob and I talked about where all this was heading. Our beloved Tiki was seventeen now. Could we possibly expect her to accept a newcomer at this late stage of her life? No, we realized. It would be unfair, and possibly harmful, to stress her like that. She was already becoming frail. The best thing to do would be to find Harry a good home.

We had our work cut out for us. Adoption or not, Harry would need to be taken to the vet to be examined, neutered, and vaccinated. In other words, he would need to trust us enough to come out from under the truck.

As Rob added pickets to the fence under Harry's supervision from the shadows, Harry bulked up on his healthy diet, his coat taking on a lovely silver sheen. With a little help from catnip, we could sometimes entice him out into the sunlight, where he would purr and roll for a brief minute before slinking nervously back under the truck.

Three weeks went by before Harry finally allowed us to touch him. Not long after that, I was washing the dinner dishes and glimpsed something like nirvana through the kitchen window. There, in the driveway, were Harry and Rob. Harry was sprawled in the raptures of a belly rub, and Rob was grinning ear to ear. The frightened, scruffy stray had become a handsome, gentle giant. By the time the fence was finished in late summer, we were able to get all sixteen-and-a-half pounds of him to our veterinarian, where he was the heartthrob of the office.

I put a red collar around his neck with "Harry" embroidered in white.

Meanwhile, I had conducted the groundwork for his adoption. It was ironic that Harry had become a fine candidate for adoption now that he had won *us* over. Of the people we interviewed, a retired couple, the Millers, seemed especially sincere. They missed the presence of a kitty in their lives and could provide Harry with a loving home across town, a few blocks from the beach.

And so it was that, numb with heartbreak, we relinquished Harry to the Millers' care. The bewildered look in his eyes as we handed him over has left an indelible scar in my memory. We missed him so much it hurt.

Little did we know that our pain was just beginning.

We learned that Tiki had cancer. She soon died peacefully, but anyone who has loved, and been loved by, a cat knows how hard it is to say goodbye.

In the midst of our grief, we received a phone call from the Millers. In subdued tones, they informed us that Harry had run away. They promised to watch for him.

It was all Rob and I could do to even breathe. That both cats were lost to us was a reality I found unbearable. And so, with Rob's help in the kitchen most nights, and his arms enfolding me when I needed to cry, I set out to manifest a miracle: to find Harry and bring him home.

With every fiber of my being, I concentrated on Harry's return. I pushed away scary thoughts of him out on the streets, frightened and hungry, injured or even dead, and instead held only positive images of him safe at home with us. I made regular trips to the Millers' neighborhood, where I called out his name, scattered cat treats, posted flyers, and made inquiries. I kept in touch with the county animal shelter and placed ads in the newspaper. Weeks passed. No one claimed to have seen him.

Winter came. Near despair, I consulted a reputable pet psychic. She felt, to my tremendous relief, that Harry was alive. Curiously, she saw the word "ocean" again and again but couldn't interpret it. What did it signify?

The ocean was three blocks from the Millers' house. I could only guess that I should focus my search along the waterfront.

Two weeks of beachcombing followed. I was scouring the sands in the midst of a downpour when my cellphone rang. The manager of the Ocean Mobile Home Park had seen one of my flyers. "There's a scruffy, gray cat under an awning outside my office," he said. "It's got a frayed, red collar."

Rushing to the park, I read with joyful new clarity the entrance sign that I had passed so many times before. This "Ocean" was located right next door to the Millers'.

Minutes later, weeping with gratitude, I placed Harry, wet and pitifully thin, in his carrier and brought him home. It had been four long months. This special kitty, who inspired me to believe in the miracle of hope, lived happily with us for eight years in his forever home — the one with the picket fence.

— Gina du Bois —

67

The Cat Gods Have Spoken

*How you behave toward cats here below determines
your status in Heaven.*
~Robert A. Heinlein

My mother has a saying: When a cat finds you, or vice versa, the cat gods have spoken. In my small Idaho hometown, my mother took in stray cats that she found and those that found her. And many did find her — two from a local Chinese restaurant and some from local citizens who knew my mom would provide a good home. Through the years, there's been a menagerie of felines — as many as six at a time. But none had quite the story of Jenny.

Jenny was a mostly black-haired tortoiseshell cat. As a small kitten, she was found on a rooftop, crying helplessly. Of course, my mother took her in. Jenny was skittish, and she took a while to warm up to you. Inexplicably, she took a shine to my father, who tolerated my mom's cat obsession but maintained a staunch "I'm not a cat person" stance. Jenny would jump up on my dad's lap while he was reading or working, and I would hear an "Oh, Jenny!" bellowing through the house. It took months, maybe even years, but Jenny persisted, and the "Oh, Jenny!" eventually disappeared. When Jenny passed away, my father mourned just as much as my mom. But I'm getting ahead of myself.

My parents went through what you might describe as a mid-life crisis a couple of years after I left for college, and four or five years after they adopted Jenny. My parents were both dissatisfied with their jobs, and in an act of spontaneity that was very unlike them, they quit their jobs and found jobs in Madison, Wisconsin. They sold the house, found a moving company and began looking forward to their new life.

When the big day came, they loaded up the car, put Jenny and one other cat whose name escapes me into separate cat carriers, and began the long drive to Madison. Their first night was spent at a hotel in Rapid City, South Dakota. My parents took both cats into the hotel room and let them out to explore their surroundings. Disaster struck, though, when my parents opened the door to go out to dinner, and Jenny bolted out of the hotel into a nearby field. Distraught, my parents spent hours going through the field, calling Jenny's name. They repeated their search the next morning, but it was futile — Jenny was gone. Heartbroken, my parents resumed their journey to Madison without Jenny.

It was a different time when all this occurred. There was no Internet or cellphones. Hoping for a miracle, my mother took out a classified ad in the local newspaper. In the ad, she described Jenny, where she was last seen, and provided contact information where my parents could be reached in Wisconsin. The ad ran for several weeks, but it was radio silence. Jenny really did seem to be gone.

Just about when my parents were about to give up hope, they received a phone call from a woman in Rapid City who thought she found Jenny. The description matched Jenny. My mom was a little apprehensive. What if it wasn't Jenny? What if it was another cat that resembled Jenny? In the end, my mom decided the cat gods were again working their magic, and she would adopt this cat, whether it was Jenny or not. She told the nice lady to ship the cat by plane to Wisconsin.

My mom went to the airport, driven as much by curiosity about what would be in the carrier as hope that it would be Jenny. The plane arrived, and the luggage began rolling out. The cat carrier came into view, and my mom grabbed it and looked inside. There, a skinny, disheveled and frightened Jenny peered up. My mom couldn't believe her eyes — it really was Jenny. She took Jenny home and began brushing her, and Jenny literally melted into her arms, happy to be home and safe.

Jenny lived for several more years after her adventure. Things didn't work out in Wisconsin, and my parents moved again, to Louisville, Kentucky. When I would visit, I would see a mischievous gleam in Jenny's eye when she jumped on my dad's lap, like she knew she had vanquished my dad into being a cat guy. Above all, Jenny was a survivor. The timid personality on the surface obscured a fierce desire to live and thrive. And once Jenny decided you were not a threat, she stuck to you like glue.

Jenny is long gone, as is my dad. When he was diagnosed with prostate cancer, he and my mom decided to move once again, back to the same Idaho town where I grew up and that my parents called home for many years before they embarked on their own adventure. My mom is still around but is becoming old and frail, and her memory isn't what it used to be. She remembers Jenny, though. I mentioned Jenny during a recent video call, and Mom's face lit up like a Christmas tree. A good pet can leave quite a mark on you, and Jenny certainly did that. I picture Jenny up in some form of cat heaven, jumping up on my dad's lap, and my dad once again bellowing "Oh, Jenny!" to an audience of bemused angels.

— Kevin Porter —

68

That's What You Think

It's difficult to understand why people don't realize that
pets are gifts to mankind.
~Linda Blair

t was one of the worst days of my life. My thirteen-year-old, Mason, had been bullied in school, and I guess he felt like he couldn't take it anymore. So, one day, after what seemed to me to be just like any other day, he took the ultimate action to ensure that no one would ever make fun of his insulin pump again.

I was the one who found him. He was lying on his bed, fully dressed all the way down to his shoes, and he was unresponsive. Somehow, I instinctively knew what had happened. He had decided to give himself a lethal dose of insulin.

My husband and I were able to bring him back to consciousness, but several days in the hospital followed. It was a dark time, and I tried my best to find something, anything, that would bring joy back into my son's life.

So, it may come as a surprise that, when Mason asked for a cat, I said, "No." Years earlier, I had been allergy tested, and my allergy tests actually shocked the doctor, who informed me that he rarely saw anyone as allergic to anything as I was to cats.

However, every time Mason mentioned his desire for a cat, my heart broke. I would have done just about anything to comfort my son, but I didn't think he would want to gain a cat and lose a mom. The rest of that summer, Mason pleaded to get a feline companion. Each time it was mentioned, I tearfully explained that I could be nowhere near the allergy-inducing beasts.

It was the night before the first day of Mason's eighth-grade year. My husband and I had put the kids to bed and retired to the porch before the craziness of another school year began. Our summer porch time usually consisted of relaxing to the music of crickets, but the crickets had a competitor on this night. Intermittently, our insect therapists would be interrupted by a faint meow.

Craig, my husband, decided to investigate. A few minutes later, he came back with a scrawny, malnourished but fully grown cat in his arms. While Craig comforted the cat, I scrambled to find some food and water for him. He greedily ate and drank, and then jumped back into my husband's lap for more affection.

It made for an interesting night, but I honestly thought that we would never see the furry interloper again. After about an hour passed, we simply told the cat goodbye and went to bed thinking that we had done our good deed for the day.

Monday morning came. The kids went to school, and I went to work. Craig works from home, so he went to his home office and logged onto his computer. Then, he heard a familiar sound from the night before. He turned to face the noise and saw the cat outside his office window. Craig did his best to ignore his persistent friend and was able to do so for several hours — until our dog indicated that he needed to make use of our lawn.

When Craig opened the door, one animal went out, but another dashed in. Craig patiently caught the intruder and escorted him outside. When it was time to let our dog Flax back in, he was accompanied by the trespasser. Again, Craig reminded the uninvited guest that his place was outside. This went on long after Craig had logged off his computer. In fact, this ruckus lasted for several days. Anytime the door would open, the cat dashed in. We kept reminding the invader, "You don't live here." But his actions seemed to say, "That's what you think."

As you can imagine, Mason's pleas to keep this cat added to our challenge. Eventually, instead of simply responding "No," I decided to take a different approach. "Mason," I softly asked, "have you been praying for a cat?" Mason's head slowly dropped, and he quietly and almost ashamedly answered, "Yes."

At that moment, I knew that we would be adopting a new pet. Mason had put his request in God's hands, so who was I to question it? We shopped for the necessary cat supplies and then, for the first time, opened the door and invited our new four-legged friend inside.

Several years have passed, and Rags has been such a blessing that I have no doubt that he was sent to us as an answer to Mason's prayers. Rags and Mason are roommates, and we have had no more suicidal scares. But here is the strangest part: Before Rags came into our lives, I would have an asthma attack if I even walked into a home with a cat. Since Rags has become a part of our family, I have had none. I know that God works in mysterious ways; I just never knew that He worked through cats.

— Misty May —

69

The Miracle of Miracle

Miracles come in moments. Be ready and willing.
~Wayne Dyer

t was the Fourth of July in a small Arkansas town called Ozark. A woman and her teenage daughter were driving down the busy main street. They stopped at a light, and the daughter suddenly tore off her seatbelt, threw open her door, and leaped out of the car! The woman quickly found a place to park and went running down the street after her daughter, who was running down the street after a tiny kitten, who was running down the street dragging her broken hind leg behind her.

They scooped up the baby and took her home. She was weak. She was terribly injured. She really did not look like she would survive. It was Sunday, a holiday, and they did not have the money for a big vet bill, so they searched for local rescues on Facebook.

Eventually, they contacted me, and I said I would take the kitten. By then, it was already late evening. Ozark is thirty miles from me, so we agreed to meet early the next morning. I gave them instructions to keep the kitten warm and give her water and Karo syrup with a syringe if she would not eat or drink. I hoped the poor little thing would make it through the night.

She did, and shortly before 8:00 A.M. she was handed over to me. They had named her Miracle. To be honest, I felt like we needed one. My plan was to take her directly to my vet, but when I got there, I discovered they were closed for the holiday. I needed a Plan B!

I was volunteering at a spay/neuter clinic that day, so I took her with me. The vet there gave her pain meds and antibiotics. She looked doubtful about Miracle's chances, and I understood why. The tiny tuxedo girl was about six weeks old and only weighed a pound and a half. She might have been healthy before the accident, but she was not in very good shape now.

Her leg was not only broken but also laid open with a lot of the skin missing. Her rescuers had assumed she had been hit by a car, but I thought otherwise. I recognized this kind of injury and knew that most likely she had been under the hood of a car and fallen out, grazing the fan belt on her way down. She was lucky to have survived that and even luckier she had not been hit by another car after she landed. Hopefully, she had a little more good fortune in her stockpile; she was going to need it.

That night, I could see she was getting weaker. I gave her more pain meds and tried to persuade her to eat some high-calorie "recovery food." She was not interested, but I was able to get a couple of full syringes down her, one tiny bit at a time.

By the next morning, I was horrified to see that the rest of the skin had sloughed off her broken leg, leaving it bare to the bone. I wrapped her gently in a soft blanket and took her to my vet. I could see that he had his doubts, too. She was so small!

I have a great vet. They have done surgery on other kittens that small, but it is never easy and only when it can't wait. This could not wait. Removing that leg was this baby girl's only chance of survival. But could she even survive the surgery?

That day, I waited for a phone call I was hoping would not come. I am an experienced rescuer, but some things never get easier. Situations like this always make you feel like David going up against Goliath. Several times that day, I found myself crying, thinking about the tiny kitten that might not ever grow up to be a cat.

The phone call did not come. She made it through the surgery. And, by the end of the day, she was eating on her own! Two days later, I was able to pick her up and transfer her to a foster experienced with medical cases.

Her recovery was nothing short of amazing. Her surgery site looked great from the start. Two weeks later, the staples were removed and there was only a thin scar. I think it helped that she was much more sedate than most kittens. She seemed like an old soul, preferring to serenely watch her surroundings.

Her medical foster was going on vacation, so I arranged for Miracle to stay with another foster for the duration. That led to another crisis two days later when one of the foster's other cats fell ill. She rushed the cat to the vet and was told it was panleukopenia — the feline version of parvo, highly contagious and often fatal!

I immediately picked up Miracle and took her to my vet. I explained that she might have been exposed to panleuk and that I wanted them to keep her there. If she had caught it, being at the vet was her best chance to beat it. They agreed it was a wise course of action.

The next week was tense, waiting for the other shoe to drop, terrified she would get sick, hopeful they could save her if she did, and angry that this sweet little girl had had so many strikes so early in her life.

When I went to visit her at the vet, she was always calm and tranquil. They had her in quarantine in a kennel in a room by herself, but she did not seem to mind at all. She was pleased to see me but not excited. As for me, I was excited enough for both of us every time because she wasn't sick!

When the vet gave her the all-clear, she returned to her original medical foster. She continued to heal and thrive, becoming mobile, nimble and quick on her three remaining legs. She was still very quiet for a kitten her age, but that seemed to simply be her personality. Sometimes, she almost appeared to be waiting for something, but mostly she just seemed content with the status quo.

Little Miracle used up at least one of her nine lives and barely blinked an eye. When she was ready to start a new chapter in her life, her new chapter was waiting for her. Exactly one month after her tragic accident, she got to go home to the very people who had rescued her that horrible day. A connection was forged during that traumatic time, and her rescuers had checked on her frequently. They asked to adopt her, and I was thrilled to hand her back to them — happy, healthy and ready for her future.

A few days later, her new mama sent me a video of Miracle running around, jumping and playing like a kitten should. I guess she was just waiting until she got to her real home!

—Linda Sabourin—

Perks & Quirks

70

The Cone and the Cat

An animal's eyes have the power to speak
a great language.
~Martin Buber

Our family pet is a furry ball of cat known as Aggie. He is big, a bit scruffy, and intimidating. But he's really a cuddle monster with a mighty purr.

He's also an outdoor cat during the daytime. For the most part, this works fine, but recently he ran afoul of a hawk that tried to pick him up and make off with him. Since Aggie weighs a whopping thirteen pounds, the hawk failed. But it did leave several gouges in Aggie's side.

We rushed our beloved pet to the veterinarian to find that, thankfully, the gashes were superficial. Cleaned up, Aggie was ready to go home, but he would have to wear the infamous Cone of Shame to ensure he'd leave the cuts alone while they healed.

After several days, we felt confident enough to leave a recuperating Aggie home alone — inside, of course. Since we live in a rural area, we get a lot of bugs in the house — spiders, crickets, ants, leaf bugs, beetles, and even a small scorpion once. We leave flat, sticky, pest-catching mats underneath a large piece of furniture in each room to take care of business. This includes underneath the bed where — only the Lord knows why — our giant fluffy cat decided to insert himself and his big round cone.

We arrived home from our errands and found Aggie with all four legs spread stiffly out and his tail bushed straight up in the center of the hallway outside the bedroom. This seemed to be as far as he was able to get before being frozen in horror. At first, I had no idea what had happened, but the facts of the case were clear and didn't need much detective work. He had gone underneath the bed for the first time in the ten years we've had him and somehow managed to get the bug mat stuck right across his cone.

His wide yellow eyes stayed fixed on several dead spiders caught forever on the trap, which was now glued bug-side-up (also possibly forever) to the rim of Aggie's cone. No amount of petting or sweet words would get him to look away from those bugs or un-fluff his tail.

Some scientists think cats only see shades of blue and gray. Others think cats can also see yellow. This particular cat probably saw colors scientists have never thought of that day, outlined in pure fear. All his fur stayed fluffed, and his back was arched, but he stood as still as black ice. Obviously, he couldn't decide whether to fight or flee and went with the third option — to stand in the center of the carpet until either the bugs fell off or his head did. Whichever came first.

I have never seen a feline so obviously regretful of a decision in my entire life.

In the end, the bug mat refused to come wholly unstuck from the Cone of Shame. It turned into the Cone of Fear of Dead Insects. We took the entire thing off Aggie, who didn't appear to miss it in the slightest or worry about his healing cuts. We gave him lots of hugs, love, and as much reassurance as we could pack into our petting.

The gluey bug trap was never replaced in that particular location, just in case. But Aggie still refuses to go under the bed.

— SE White —

71

The Everything of Nothing

Time spent with a cat is never wasted.
~Sigmund Freud

Guinness's favorite perch is our bedroom window, which opens upon a mature cedar hedge that's about twenty feet tall. The hedge is overgrown, and some of its branches are just over a foot away from the house. When Guinness is there, my favorite perch is often the corner of our bed, which is about two feet away from the window.

I suppose it's part meditation and part fascination that keeps me there, observing him. Guinness sits, silent and tall, with only his darting black head to indicate he's anything but a statue. He is still but micro-aware of every movement in the hedge. I want to reach out and kiss the back of his head, to breathe him in. But I am still. I don't want to distract his focus.

His head bobs and shudders, and how I wish I could be him for just one moment. To see what he sees. To experience what makes his heart flutter. I've learned the art of doing nothing and doing everything from my cat.

What is it that commands his attention?

The hedge is home to countless birds. We often spot cardinals, blue jays and smaller birds that nest there. It is also a popular spot for the neighborhood squirrels — black, gray, and red. The greenery is a micro-community, a secret townhouse for feathered and furry creatures.

I continue my watch. I'm doing nothing and everything at once. That cat has captured my full awareness. It is a moment or two of joy and wonder in a regular day that is often bereft of such simple pleasures.

Guinness crouches, his front paws prepared to leap, and then he sits back. False alarm? The realization of a screen between him and his intended prey? Or simply a flyby?

His head jerks and twitches as something new grabs his attention. A chirpy, little mew. It's the sound he makes when he spots a cardinal. It's always for a cardinal, that sweet little shout-out.

Then, he suddenly turns to me and stares. His bright chartreuse eyes beckon me to join him in his pursuits. And suddenly he bounces onto the bed, rubs up and back against me, scrutinizes my facial expression, and jumps back onto his window perch. He turns to look at me again.

I can't help but think he's expressing his joy for this moment. To him, there is no other moment. He is not thinking about his dinner or wondering what the dog is doing downstairs. He is doing nothing except everything. He is living in this very singular moment.

But, somehow, it feels to me like:

"This is cool, right Mom? Right. Whoa, can you believe it?"

"It's the bird that smells red! That one you call Cardi B!"

"Can you smell them? Did you see them? This is good, huh?"

I notice his whiskers and nostrils going full tilt, working overtime to digest the sensory feast.

I smile and think to myself, *I can neither smell nor see them. You are a cat. That is a gift you've been given. I'm a mere human. That commotion in the hedge is apparent only to you, my feline friend.*

But you're right, Guinness. Taking a moment to do nothing and everything is a gift that's available to all of us. What a wonderful teacher creature you are. Imagine being fully in the moment, not thinking about cooking dinner or worrying about rising mortgage rates, or even wondering what the dog is doing downstairs. *Thank you for sharing your gift, my sweet boy.*

— Catherine Kenwell —

72

The Backpack Cat

*It is impossible to keep a straight face in the presence
of one or more kittens.*
~Cynthia E. Varnado

When I first picked up my cat from the farm, she was tiny, the runt of the litter. She could easily curl up in my hands. I had picked out the name Aurora even before meeting her. I knew that needed to be her name as soon as I saw her photos online.

I was shocked when I finally met her for the first time and got to take her home. One, because she was such a tiny thing, and two, because she was the most adorable and precious creature I had ever laid eyes on. I took her from the arms of the farm owners, handed them the cash, and placed her in the cat-carrying backpack I had ordered especially for her.

It wasn't hard at all to get her in the backpack. I placed her in like a rubber duck in a bathtub. The backpack seemed outrageously large compared to the tiny kitten it now held. Aurora fell asleep on the ride home.

In my apartment, she had the choice to lie on her kitty bed, a comfy chair, a couch with blankets, or my bed. All good places for a cat to hang out. During her first days with me, she would rotate among them.

I used the backpack for transport, but otherwise it was put away in a closet. I only brought it out if I had to take Aurora somewhere.

I would just plop her in and zip it up, and we were good to go! She was fine with it. Never had a complaint about going in there. Didn't struggle or meow, just let me put her in and zip it. I was grateful I got a cat that was so easy to travel with! I had heard stories of other cat owners not being so lucky.

Aurora had to get up to date with her shots, and I used the backpack to bring her to the vet and then back home. When we got home, I didn't put the backpack in the closet right away like usual. I left it near the closet and told myself I'd put it away later. It wasn't doing any harm lying out in the hallway for a bit.

And that's how I learned that Aurora's favourite place was in that backpack.

I started leaving it out and would find her in it quite frequently! She had the couch, the chair, her bed and everywhere else in my apartment, but she would choose her backpack. I put in a cat-sized afghan and some soft toys. It became a safe place and cozy cove for little Aurora. She took naps in it. She relaxed in it while I worked at my computer. She threw her jingly balls in it and played by herself in it.

It was official. I had a backpack cat.

Since she liked going inside her backpack so much, it was never a struggle to get her in it when I needed to travel with her.

And it was never a struggle to take her out for walks.

I'd wear the backpack backwards so Aurora was on my front. It was like I was a mother with my baby. I guess in some ways I was a mother, but I was a mother to a cat rather than a human.

We'd stroll around the neighbourhood. The neighbours enjoyed this. I could see them sometimes out of the corner of my eye, straining to look past the mesh and see what I was carrying inside there. As soon as they realized it was a cat, their faces would light up.

The backpack was now left out 24/7. It was never put away. Her fondness for it made things so much easier on me. I could zip her in there while I worked or cleaned, and she would cuddle up in her mini afghan and just observe. I could bring her in the car, and she would sit quietly in her safe place.

I signed up later for a gift exchange that had the theme "presents for pets." I had no idea who I would get or what kind of pet they would have. When I was matched with my giftee, I read that they had two cats and a small dog.

And I knew just what to get them.

I bought the exact same backpack.

I added a note to the gift to say that it was highly recommended by my own cat. My very own backpack cat.

— Gillian A. Corsiatto —

73

Jump at the Chance

*There's no need for a piece of sculpture
in a home that has a cat.*
~Wesley Bates

flipped on the light in my bedroom to carry the clean laundry to my dresser and stopped in my tracks. Once again, there she was. I called in my son from the other room. "She's doing it again," I said when he arrived, pointing at our big, beautiful gray-and-white tabby. Oddly, she didn't even acknowledge our presence as she sat there, frozen.

He shook his head and shrugged. "That is so weird! And you still can't figure out what she's doing?" he asked.

"Nope, no clue."

This had been going on for weeks. The first time I discovered her there, sitting completely still just inches in front of my dresser, I thought she must be watching a ladybug. But I never actually saw a ladybug, then or the next five times I found Nellie staring at nothing.

It continued. Every single day, early in the morning and night, I walked into my bedroom and turned on the light, only to find her sitting at the foot of my dresser staring at… nothing. She sat there sometimes for hours. Each time, we investigated, dug through drawers, tapped on walls, listened, watched, and waited for the great reveal, but found no explanation. We started to worry.

Nellie was getting older. We started talking about her mind slipping. My son brought up the often-talked-about animal intuition about such things as weather, earthquakes and spirits, speculating she was just seeing something we couldn't see.

The inexplicable behavior continued for months. It became an ongoing conversation in our house. Poor Nellie had lost her mind. I continued to pursue an explanation for her behavior. I decided to use my social-worker skills to produce an answer to this great mystery; I would sit by Nellie's side and stare.

So, for the next three days, any time I saw her poised in front of the dresser in her motionless trance, I would get down there with her, eye level, and watch for whatever she was captivated by. On day three, at the end of my fifth fifteen-minute Nellie watch of the day, I gave up. I flipped off the light and walked out of my room. And then I froze. The lightbulb went on. I suddenly realized that every time I had seen her positioned on guard, when I walked into the room, I had turned on the light. It had been dark outside.

I had no clue what it meant but knew it had to mean something. I rushed back into my room, leaving the light off this time, and crawled beside her, watching to see what she saw. Another fifteen minutes. Nothing.

I went on about my evening, but I still thought I was on to something. The next morning before daybreak, there she was once again, eyes glued to my dresser. I sat on the bed and watched. Five minutes later, my frozen baby came to life and jumped, swatting at my dresser! The excitement of this new piece of information ran through me. I scurried to her side, got eye level beside her, and waited. Finally, with a bit more patience, a little light was shed on the subject.

Literally.

I watched in jubilation as she jumped and swatted at a small flash of light that quickly flashed across my dresser. It was so fast that it was easy to miss if you were not looking for it. I followed the path to the source as she returned to her post. There, at her level, I was able to see the tiny gap in the curtain that covered the window facing the road in front of the house. She was chasing headlights.

I was thrilled that I had solved the cat mystery that had perplexed us for months. At the same time, I was relieved that my sweet girl had not gone crazy. She was just doing what cats do. She was hunting. Hunting light. Since we had always turned on the light when we came in the room, we eliminated the opportunity to see the light she was waiting for.

Waiting for being the key words there. The amazing Nellie never waited for anything. She was, at best, impatient and bossy. When she wanted something there was never any hesitation in her letting you know it. But, for this light, she was different. She was beyond patient — determined even — to catch a glimpse of the rare flash of headlights from our sparsely traveled rural road. Sitting perfectly still, focused on one spot she knew as the source, waiting in the dark for that one moment of glory she had faith was coming.

There are so many lessons I learned from this experience. Can I be determined enough to watch, focused intently on the mission, for prolonged periods of time without reward? Can I overcome my normal impatience and fleeting attention to be still and wait? When I don't understand someone, can I remember to try to see it through their eyes? At their level?

Most of all, I must never lose faith. Nellie knew the light would come eventually. She believed in what she could not yet see. She wasn't crazy. She had true faith. Focused faith. I must have faith, too, that there is still light to be found even if it seems far away. I must always be ready to jump at the chance when I find it.

— Shannon Leach —

74

Duct, Duct, Loose

*You call to a dog, and a dog will break its neck to get
to you. Dogs just want to please. Call to a cat,
and its attitude is, What's in it for me?*
~Lewis Grizzard

Frankie was once a skinny cat with a dull, burr-covered black coat. She lived in the forest next door to our family business. Occasionally, she'd come out of the woods to beg for food and companionship, and then she would vanish again. My husband often saw her disappear into a rock pile.

I was a bit wary of the stray cat. My kids were not. "Don't touch that cat; it might have rabies," I'd tell them.

"But we *have* to touch the cat."

Clearly, the cat needed a rabies shot. I took her to the vet. She strode from the carrier like she'd just accepted a job as a vet tech and was ready to impale her first dog on the end of a syringe. "That is a cool cat," the vet remarked.

"Yeah," I agreed. "That *is* a cool cat." By the end of the visit, we were cat owners.

Frankie's first days with us were spent in cat-sized hiding places. She hid in the gap between my desk and the wall, in the space just under the pipes behind the washing machine, and inside the sofa footrest. Those corners and crevices probably reminded her of the rock pile where she kept her mouse bones and spider friends. She felt safe in small spaces.

Just three days after we brought her home, my ten-year-old dropped a toy into the vent on his bedroom floor and pulled off the register to retrieve it. To Frankie, it was another cat-sized space.

"Mom! The cat is in the vent!"

I reached my son's bedroom just in time to watch our brand-new pet disappear into the darkened corridors of our home's HVAC ductwork. She did look back at me once, her yellow eyes bright. She meowed hoarsely as if to say, "This is where I live now." Then, she was gone.

What does one do when the cat is in the ductwork?

First, I called the HVAC people. I think they wanted to be helpful, but they told me our HVAC system was non-disassemblable, so there was nothing they could do. They did say they could suck her out with some kind of giant vacuum thing if she ended up dying in there, which was not comforting.

Next, I called the fire department. They sent someone out to have a look, but they couldn't do anything either. The HVAC system was still as non-disassemblable as it had been the day before.

I pulled every register out of the floor. I went to our local animal shelter and rented a cat trap, which I filled with stinky cans of tuna and salmon, just in case she decided to emerge late at night, and I wasn't there to catch her. Two days later, the trap was still empty, and I was starting to have nightmares about looming, giant vacuum things.

On the third night, after my kids went to bed, my daughter said she heard something in the vent. We shone a flashlight into the darkness, and yellow eyes stared back at us.

I tried to coax Frankie out. She looked at me and meowed hoarsely as if to say, "Yes, I'd like to place an order for a tuna sandwich and a Diet Coke, please."

My daughter opened a fresh can of tuna. I put some of it on my fingers and stuck my whole arm into the duct. Frankie ate the tuna, just enough of it to remind her that HVAC systems are not Best Westerns, and the continental breakfast is only served aboveground.

She crept forward for more tuna. I moved my arm a bit farther away until the scruff of her neck was in reach.

After I pulled Frankie out of the duct, my kids replaced the vents on every open register and bolted them back into place. Frankie, who was covered in several years' worth of dust and whatever else gets sucked into a duct, got a bath and the rest of the tuna.

Frankie never went back into the ductwork, mostly because we never took a register off unless she was locked in another room. Eventually, she also stopped crawling into the gap between my desk and the wall, the space just under the pipes behind the washing machine, and inside the sofa footrest. Now, she feels safe when she's perched on top of a kids' bunk bed or curled up in my lap.

Frankie lives indoors now. The forest and the rock pile where she used to live are distant memories, if she remembers them at all. Sometimes, though, she sits in front of the screen door to get some fresh air and a sunbeam.

We can open the door, but she won't go out. She just looks at us and meows hoarsely, as if to say, "This is where I live now."

— Becki Robins —

75

I'll Have to Meet Kitty

A cat is a puzzle for which there is no solution.
~Hazel Nicholson

The converted basement I'd been living in for the better part of a year flooded every time it rained. It was so frequent and so bad that I kept a pair of rainboots instead of slippers beside my bed. I probably should have broken my lease and moved after the first time it happened. Or, if not then, then definitely after the second or third. But I was a stickler for finishing what I started, even if it wasn't in my best interest.

With the end of my lease on the horizon, I spent the summer looking for a new apartment. But, with the budget of a grad student, everything within my price range came with roommates, was cramped, or lacked essential appliances. Or they didn't allow pets. And I had a cat.

I had resigned myself to another year with a flooding floor when, on my way back from a hike, I saw it: a red "For Rent" sign staked into the ground in front of The Bookhouse. At first glance, I thought it was for the bookstore, but in small print scribbled in black marker it read, "1 bedroom."

I dialed immediately.

The apartment was ideal. The living room had perfectly dated carpet. The tile in the kitchen was a blue-and-yellow checkerboard. Plus, there was parking in the lot across the street. And I could afford it.

Then I asked the question, "Are pets allowed? I have a cat."

"Well, I'll have to meet kitty to see."

I laughed. But Ginny wasn't kidding.

"Yeah, that's no problem," I stammered and arranged to bring Patches by the next day.

But it was a problem. It was a *big* problem.

This cat had all the worst characteristics that cats get branded with. She hated most people. She hissed. She bit. She clawed. She was, in general, a complete jerk, and she was not shy about letting anyone know it.

We'd gotten her as a kitten from a farmstand when I was eleven. Patches, as my sister named her for her calico fur, was small, extra fluffy, and cute. On the ride home, she curled up in my sister's lap and slept while purring softly, causing us all to say, "Awww."

But the aw factor was short-lived because, as soon as we got home, she started to bully our exceptionally sweet, geriatric tabby. And when that bored her, she yowled and clawed at the doors relentlessly. If that didn't quell her seemingly endless rage, she attacked us at random.

After years of this, my family started talking about trying to rehome her.

I balked when my parents mentioned their plan to me. Besides the fact that no one was going to want an eight-year-old cat with a bad attitude, I thought the plan was to give Patches a forever home, not to rehome her because she was difficult. They told me if I was so insistent on it, I could do it. So, later that year when I moved out, I carted her off with me to my studio apartment in the city.

Things didn't go well at first. Her behavior was much the same as it had been at my parents' house, only now I was the sole object of her aggression. A few days in, I was scratched up and full of regret but determined to make this work. And, after a year, we had come to an understanding: As long as I didn't enter her space without permission, she would tolerate my existence (and only mine) and keep her claws and teeth to herself.

So, when my prospective new landlord said she wanted to meet Patches, I braced for the worst, knowing that in one day I'd have to make her do two things she despised: ride in her crate and meet a new person. But I had to try.

"Patchy." She'd clearly heard the crate come out the night before and was now, thirty minutes before I was supposed to introduce her to Ginny, cowering under the bed. "Come get a treat." I shook the bag.

She didn't budge.

I got a cushion from the couch and pushed it toward her to try and force her out. She hunkered down and emitted a low growl. I persisted, pushing the pillow gently into her. Then, in a flash, she sprinted for the door, and I grabbed her, receiving several kicks and angry screams for my efforts, which continued once the lid of the crate was closed.

"I'm sorry. I know this sucks, but you're going to love this place, so please, please, please, just be as nice as possible. Just this once," I tried to convince her. "I know you can do it. You're such a good girl. Just do this one thing for us, okay? Please?"

By the time we pulled up to the apartment, I felt nauseous and couldn't help but think of how stupid it was that the landlord wanted to meet a cat she would literally never see again. But we were already there, and I said I'd bring Patches to her, so there was nothing left to do but finish what I started.

By the time we made our way up to the apartment, my heart was racing. I imagined Ginny putting her face close to the crate, and Patches launching at her and latching onto her neck. I could picture the blood, the screaming, and the horror

I placed the crate on the kitchen floor, and Ginny looked in.

"Hello, kitty," she cooed.

"Patches," I mumbled.

"Hi, Patches, aren't you cute?" She put her fingers closer to the cage, and I could hear the growl starting.

"She's a little cranky after the drive," I murmured, and Ginny backed away.

"Well, let's have her out then."

My nightmare was about to come true. I hesitated. I had not anticipated letting her out.

"Open it up. It won't hurt her."

Little did she know that was not my concern. I felt my face flush, and the sick feeling in my stomach got worse. I swallowed hard and opened the crate.

I could hear my heart beating.

And then Patches started to move. She slowly wandered toward the open crate door, soundless and cautious, almost like she was stalking her prey with one paw and then the other on the kitchen tile.

And then, she stopped and just stood there.

My mind was racing, anticipating her launching forward at any moment.

"Oh, she's so cute!" Ginny inched her hand closer.

This was it.

"She doesn't really like being touched," I whisper-yelled as Ginny's hand lingered within striking range.

But Patches, instead of doing as she always had — biting, hissing or clawing — simply backed into her crate. Disinterested.

"Oh, she's shy. Well, that's okay then." Ginny laughed.

Had we done this? I wasn't sure. But as I closed the crate, I was relieved that, at least for now, it was over, and we'd finished what we started. Lease or no lease, there was an accomplishment in that.

— Lindsey Esplin —

76

Fetching Catnip Mice

Our perfect companions never
have fewer than four feet.
~Colette

"Good job, buddy! Can you bring me a red one?"

I glanced over the top of my book at my husband. "What will you do if he actually brings back the red mouse?"

"He doesn't understand 'red mouse.'" All the same, my husband leaned over the edge of the bed to pat Firefly's head, rewarding the tabby for his superior mousing skills.

I shook my head, watching out of the corner of my eye as Firefly headed down the hall, intent on his mission.

At almost fourteen, our oldest cat no longer showed an interest in playing with the catnip mice he delivered to our feet. The distinct meow preceding his appearance merely heralded the arrival of the fuzzy cat toys to our workspaces, the bedroom, or the living room. Firefly patiently carried one mouse at a time for our inspection. Once satisfied with the quota — the number depending on his whim — he curled up beside us, content with a job well done.

It was an advanced version of the game he and I started in his kittenhood.

As with most foster kittens, I never planned to keep Firefly. He arrived with his brother in the early morning hours, delivered under my bed despite the careful preparations of a queening box. Their mother, Panda, decided a discarded sweatshirt ranked as a superior nest. So, I woke up to tiny squeaks, leaning over to find two healthy kittens eagerly nursing from their exhausted mother.

Through the following months, I gave myself stern lectures on the fate of my new striped roommates. Cute as they were, and as entertained as I was by their antics, mine was a temporary housing situation. As soon as the rescue found them permanent homes, they'd disappear from my life forever. I knew better than to grow attached.

Except Firefly — named for the white tip of his tail — insisted on burrowing into my life. When I found him scrambling out of the kitten box, determined to scale the side of the bed and reach my pillow, I knew I was in trouble. He'd elected me as his person, and no one would convince him differently.

I recognized our connection with that first impromptu game. Attempting to distract him from the tassel on my bookmark, I tossed a catnip mouse across the room. Firefly launched himself after the toy, quickly pummeling it between kitten paws. Then, to my surprise, he picked it up and delivered it back to my lap. Wide green eyes looked up at me, with that white-tipped tail twitching in anticipation. I sent the mouse in an arc down the hall without a second thought. He repeated his catch and return.

Now, he had my attention.

I knew cats could learn to fetch, of course. Provide the proper incentive, and it was possible to train a cat in any manner of tricks. But I wasn't employing any operant conditioning techniques so familiar from my years at the zoo. Instead, Firefly seemed to have the knack down on instinct.

He continued to fetch the mouse with kitten abandon, finally collapsing on my lap to purr himself to sleep.

The game of fetch became our favorite routine. Whenever I managed to scrape together more than five minutes, he presented a catnip mouse at my feet. And only the tiny, fuzzy mice would do. While other cat toys were acceptable for random kitten games, the plush mice with their internal rattles were reserved for fetch.

As we aged, I noticed the mice making strategic appearances.

Firefly only asked to play when I found myself distracted by relationship problems, concerns with work, or troubles with family. The repetitive motion of tossing that simple cat toy down a hallway or toward the stairs granted me the mindless oblivion to piece together whatever conflict occupied my thoughts. And once I stumbled my way toward a resolution, the mouse would lie forgotten. Firefly could settle into my lap, content with his work.

When arthritis started to prevent his mad dashes the plush mice lay forgotten in the bottom of the toy box. Only rarely did they appear when one of the younger cats decided to pluck a mouse and chase it around the room. I watched as Firefly waited for them to finish their game before he retrieved the mouse and brought it to me. The few times I tossed it, he watched me and then ignored the invitation. He no longer wanted to engage in the game.

Then pancreatitis struck, leaving him sicker than from any of his previous ailments. I sat up with him most of the night, asking questions neither I nor my husband had an answer to. I knew fourteen was a reasonable, even respectable age for a cat. But I wasn't willing to accept that fourteen years was enough. Firefly had already battled and overcome so many other medical challenges throughout his life. I refused to accept that things ended here.

Staring at the television without seeing the program, I heard a soft rattle near my foot close to 3:00 A.M. A glance down revealed a now-familiar gaze turned up to face me. He didn't always make perfect jumps anymore, but he landed beside me with unerring aim. The mouse was dropped beside me, and Firefly settled into my lap. Within moments, he was asleep.

The message was clear, "I'm okay, Mom."

After that, the catnip mice continued to find their way to one of us — sometimes in groups of three or more, other times just a lonesome mouse. Firefly left his colorful calling cards for us, hailed by a loud call we couldn't miss. Then, he curled up in our laps — message delivered.

One evening a few days later, when every catnip mouse made a trip into the bedroom, I reflected on the history of those games of fetch. As I laughed over his persistent antics, fumbling out of the dark spaces in my mind, I realized his words had always been the same with each mouse delivered: "It's okay."

Firefly meowed loudly, pacing down the shadows in the hall. I glanced over at my husband, but he remained lost in his book.

A rattle and thump announced the arrival of a new mouse. Firefly jumped into my lap, finished with his deliveries for the evening. A peek at the floor sent my lips curving.

A red catnip mouse rested at the edge of the blanket.

— Andria Kennedy —

77

The Purr-fect Host

Like all pure creatures, cats are practical.
~William S. Burroughs, The Cat Inside

So many years have passed that I don't remember if the Bible study at my house was my idea or if someone else suggested I host it. I only remember that I was more than a tad nervous when I was told that seventeen women had signed up and would be coming to my home every Wednesday afternoon for the next dozen weeks!

Because our dining room was larger than any we'd previously owned, and the kitchen was also good-sized, my husband had encouraged me with a hug and said, "You can do this, babe. We have the room, and you have a way of making people feel welcome."

I shook my head. Actually, he was mistaken. Just the thought of so many women coming to a house I had trouble cleaning? At my age, keeping up a fair-sized home was becoming a serious problem. What if every woman who walked through my door sensed how ill-at-ease I felt?

Still, I'd agreed to do this, so I really had no choice. I needed to make my list and start preparing. I was well aware, though, that at 1:00 in the afternoon — when the women would begin to arrive — the sun would have begun to cover the entire west-facing front of our home. It would also fill the entire dining room and highlight every nook and cranny. Because we hadn't yet purchased window treatments, there would be visible "dust fairies" dancing, and anything that hadn't been polished to a high shine would be showing up like a black mark on my housekeeping!

On the other hand, my husband had reminded me before he left for work that I'd already become acquainted with most of the women who would be attending the study, and I'd immediately liked all of them. In addition, I was grateful for the way each one had instantly made me feel a part of their close-knit town.

But now, the afternoon had arrived for our first study. I had baked the night before and earlier that morning. I'd also gotten out my best dessert dishes and the silver my husband's mother had given me. There would be cloth napkins and fresh flowers in the center of the table. I'd again polished the buffet, and I'd employed my long-handled feather duster to make certain there was no dust lurking under the serving cart in the corner.

"Still…" I breathed, spotting the first woman making her way up my front walk. What if Scotty was wrong? What if not one single woman felt welcome? What if they all thought I was a terrible housekeeper? What if I'd made the coffee too weak or too strong? What if my dessert wasn't up to their standards? What if our powder room wasn't exactly spotless because my husband had been the last one in there? "What if…?" I whispered for my ears alone when my plump, fluffed-up cat shot out from the top of the stairs and then behind my denim skirt. His previous owner had named him Simba, and he had become so comfortable in my home that he had all but taken over.

And that's exactly what he was now doing. I almost couldn't get to the door for having to watch that I didn't trip or step on the tail that was whipping back and forth like a baton in the hands of an orchestra conductor. I reached beyond him and barely grabbed the doorknob when he suddenly dashed to the porch and then back inside again. Then, he brushed his warm striped fur against the chilled legs of first one and then another guest who'd braved the North Dakota weather. He loudly purred and strutted exactly like the perfect escort, just as if he'd been trained for this very important position. Once greeted, each woman was led first to the kitchen where the fresh-ground coffee perked and then to my well-prepared dining room.

That first afternoon, I swear my confident feline was smiling as he made his mad dash every time the doorbell announced another arrival. He did so until each guest had gotten her coffee and dessert and tucked herself around my harvest table. And then, as we began to study, my amazing pet stretched himself out on the windowsill. The sun was streaming in, making his thick coat shine. He'd done his part; he'd made everyone feel welcome. Meanwhile, not one woman had mentioned my immaculate home, but, to a person, each had suggested that, if I didn't watch out, someone would be sneaking my Simba into a tote and taking him to her own home.

And me? I began to reflect on the Bible's Martha and Mary that we were studying — the Martha who'd done the fretting and the Mary who sat at the feet of Jesus and simply enjoyed the listening and sharing. I realized I'd become a distant cousin to Martha — fretting myself into a frenzy, fearing nothing would be exactly right or as polished as the others would be expecting. Maybe I should have added a dish of pink mints to the table. But Simba, like Mary, had found himself the perfect spot where he could recline in his own calming way. And, in doing so, he'd put everyone at ease.

That Bible study went on for three months, and every Wednesday, Simba — a name that means power, and surely he'd shown me his power to make others feel welcome — did what Simba was good at. He welcomed each woman at *his* front door. He even escorted each of *our* guests to *his* kitchen and then to *his* dining room table. Stretched nearly the full width of his perch in the warm winter sun, he made everyone — including me — feel at ease in *his* cozy setting. Not only that, he made it clear that he enjoyed their company, and he showed me that, more important than a house that was spotless from bottom to top, I needed to sit back and relax. I needed to become more like him and Mary — and less like Martha and me.

— Nancy Hoag —

78

The Birds and the Bees... and the Cat

*My relationship with cats has saved me
from a deadly, pervasive ignorance.*
~William S. Burroughs

One of the sounds of summer, growing up in my New Hampshire town of six thousand people, was the howling of horny cats. The house I grew up in, with its white aluminum siding and black shutters, didn't look like a haven for feline romance. Our cat Blackie, a black domestic shorthair, was the runt of a litter of kittens produced by Princess, a tiger cat, who had adopted us after the children of the family who owned her tried to push her around the neighborhood in a doll stroller.

After getting off to a slow start in life, Blackie matured quickly and soon attracted a chorus of noisy suitors to our back yard. I was only seven that first summer and knew nothing of feline mating habits when I was jolted awake in the middle of a humid night. I was sleeping at the foot of my bed, hoping to catch a breeze through the only window in the bedroom I shared with my twin sister. The high-pitched howls coming from directly below my window sounded too horrific to be coming from cats that, to my knowledge, only meowed and purred. Thinking some wild animals were chasing Blackie, I screamed. My mother, with her hair in pink curlers and bobby pins, smelling of Noxzema skin cream, appeared in the doorway asking what the ruckus was about.

"What's that noise?" I cried, suddenly regretting sleeping near the window.

"That's just cats. Go back to sleep," my mother said wearily, as she attempted to make a quick escape. I was not satisfied.

"What are they doing? Why do they sound like that?"

"That's how boy cats fight over a girl cat. They are here to, uh, play with Blackie."

"But how does a boy cat know he's the one that Blackie likes? How does she show him?"

"I don't know. It's just what they do," she said, clearly exasperated. Then she made the mistake of adding, "That's how we get kittens. Go back to sleep." My mother then rushed out of the room, and I later heard her yelling at the cats as she sprayed Blackie's potential suitors with the garden hose. Blackie was soon pregnant anyway, much to my delight.

Blackie could be quite aloof, but she had a special bond with my father. My mother insisted that Blackie go outside for the night, and we knew from the smell of hay and cow manure that she slept in a neighbor's barn down the street. Blackie would only let my father open the door for her when it was time to go out. She would prance past my mother, sister, and me watching television in the living room and quickly climb the stairs to the bathroom where my father would invariably be taking a shower. Normally a quiet cat, she would meow loudly and persistently outside the door. Every night, the ritual was the same, as my father, wrapped in two towels and wearing squishy-sounding flip-flops, would follow her down the stairs and to the front door. He said that Blackie thought he was the butler, and, given her personality, the image fit.

It was not surprising when, several months after the ruckus in the back yard, Blackie appeared at the front door one Saturday morning after clearly having delivered her kittens. She refused to come inside when I opened the door and stood there staring at me and meowing. I called for my father and, when he appeared at the door, Blackie took off at a run for the barn. She returned a few minutes later with a newborn kitten in her mouth. When my father opened the door, she headed straight into the den where there was a bookshelf with just enough room for her to squeeze underneath with her slimmer postpartum body. She placed the kitten under the bookshelf and then hurriedly set off to repeat the process three more times while my father waited dutifully at the door.

With the next litter and every litter thereafter, Blackie decided to do some nesting before the kittens' arrival. We knew the time was near when she pulled the towels off the drying rack between the shower and the wall, making a cozy bed right there where she always summoned my father. She would deliver her kittens at the barn and then bring them one by one and drop them at my father's feet when he came to the door. He then knew he was supposed to take each one to the towels in the bathroom while she returned to the barn to get the rest of the litter.

Blackie had chosen well when she decided that my father was the one she would entrust with her kittens. My father respected all living things. One of my favorite memories of my father was watching him climb a ladder perched against the garage while gently cradling a baby bird. He was trying to put it back into the birdhouse after it fell out, and he nearly fell off the ladder when the mother bird came tearing out of the birdhouse after him. My father was the one who checked the yard for garden snakes before mowing the grass, gently picking them up with a rake and moving them to safety. He even gingerly picked up worms from our driveway after a rain shower and put them on the edge of the grass so he wouldn't squish them when he backed the car out of the garage.

Blackie lived a long and fertile life. The only times I saw my father cry were when he got the phone call telling him his cousin was killed in Vietnam, and when he took Blackie to the vet at the end of her life. It was fitting that he should be the one to do this one last thing for her, when there were no more doors that needed to be opened.

As for my mother, she finally did attempt to talk to my sister and me about sex. No doubt, Blackie had been there as a constant reminder of the threat of hormonal males, and spraying male suitors with a hose was an ineffective method of birth control. Years after that fateful night with Blackie, my mother was still so flustered talking about reproduction that she got a lot of the anatomical terms incorrect. My sister and I were left so confused that we secretly checked out a book on sex from the school library. Thankfully, Blackie had already shown us that choosing the person you trusted with your offspring was the most important part.

— Shirley M. Phillips —

79

Chicken Cat

Attitude is a little thing that makes a big difference.
~Winston Churchill

He was one tough kitty, rescued when just months old from a drainpipe at a local dam. Though illegal, it wasn't unusual for people to dump their unwanted kittens or bunnies in the shrubbery near the dam. Even after we rescued him, he still had a tough-guy attitude and was one of pets that ruled the neighborhood, that was until the morning we found a chicken in our back yard.

Up until that morning, Augie had properly defended our home from the neighborhood's cat bullies. He'd harassed the local birds, and he'd caught his share of mice. He was definitely our guard cat.

Then came the morning he didn't blast out the back door to perform his normal duties. An unfamiliar noise stopped him. I heard and saw it, too: a rusty-red chicken going "cluck, cluck" as it strutted back and forth. Where in the world did it come from? The other side of our back fence was a vacant lot where a tree service dumped its cut wood to cure and later sell. On either side of us were regular homes.

We knew of two "urban farms" within two blocks, but they had a horse, goats and a geriatric donkey with a severe sway in its back. No chickens. But here it was, cluck-cluck-clucking the length of our yard, back and forth. Augie finally streaked out the back door and clawed up the five-foot fence to escape this alien creature.

I debated opening the gate so the rogue chicken could find its way out — and maybe home. But if he didn't tangle with Augie, he might end up under cars on the busy street just two houses away. I left it shut.

I put some wild bird seed in a cup, made sure the chicken had some water, and decided on the "found pet" ad route. An ad I placed through a popular online ad service brought immediate results — from scammers inviting me to participate in amazing business opportunities. I placed another ad in the local newspaper and then called The Humane Society with a "found animal" report. Once the animal-control officer quit laughing, I got the report filed.

In the meantime, Henny Penny (as I was now calling the chicken as it apparently fell from the sky) had settled in to a back-and-forth pacing in our yard. The sky wasn't falling, but Augie was traumatized, not daring to get close to this alien animal. It was my laundry day, so I came out with a basket of just-washed clothes to hang on the clothesline. As Henny Penny came near, I put my cat-owner experience to the test and reached over to pet it. To my surprise, it squatted as though wanting more. This had to be somebody's pet — but whose?

The answer came when the newspaper ad was published, and the chicken's owner called. I was surprised to learn that Henny Penny and a few siblings lived quietly in a little coop around the corner, with thick trees and wild blackberry vines separating us. Why I never heard them, I don't know. Ditto why I didn't hear the fracas one night when this hen's family was massacred by an unknown wild animal. Somehow, Henny Penny had managed to fly up and over two fences into the safety of our yard.

The caller arrived with some chicken food and lured the chicken into his arms. I learned Henny Penny's real name was Kibbles because she liked dog food. Tucked into her grateful owner's arm, Henny Penny — er, Kibbles — left our yard.

For several days, Augie still hesitated when he was let out the back door in the morning. Yes, our warrior cat had turned "chicken." The dreadful animal that paced and clucked had to be somewhere, but where? Eventually, he forgot about the intruder and went back to defending our yard from the neighborhood bullies and the occasional wicked raccoon.

And I decided that was the end of our Henny Penny story. I was wrong. The next year, I spotted some white oval objects while I was weeding. Henny Penny had laid them there while she was on the lam. Carefully, I lifted them in a plastic bag and buried them in the garbage bin.

I dumped them for Augie's protection, too. He'd been known to bat around balls. If he'd tried that with Henny Penny's year-old eggs, there's no telling how much more he would have been traumatized.

—Jeanne Zornes—

Chapter

9

Opening Hearts

80

Lockdown with Kittens

Kittens can happen to anyone.
~Paul Gallico

I n the second week of March 2020, on the same day my area went into Covid-19 lockdown, my family brought home kittens. This timing was not intentional. I had been the victim of a relentless, targeted campaign for a cat, spearheaded by my five-year-old son, who has a marshmallow heart for anything that mews.

While my family was not in a position to commit to a long-term pet, we finally determined that fostering from the local animal shelter might be a decent option. The process involved months of training sessions, background checks, orientation and, finally, approval.

I envisioned fostering one cat — probably an overweight, grouchy senior that would sprawl with me on the couch to watch Netflix or an ugly cat that deserved his own Instagram account. But the shelter sent a mother and her tiny kittens who needed an immediate home.

"You won't even have to do anything," the foster-pet coordinator assured us. "Mamas take care of their babies."

"Doesn't that seem like a lot of cats in an 800-square-foot condo?" I wondered aloud.

"You won't even notice they're there," the coordinator promised.

So, our family expanded by six kittens — Gobi, Mojave, Agave, Wildflower, Foxtail, and Joshua — three days old, eyes closed, ears flattened, fur slicked. Then there was the mama, Sydney, a fierce miniature panther.

In the corner of the living room, we made a home for the cats. We positioned the crate in a place that was warm but not too warm. We laid out food bowls, filled the water dish, and put out the litterbox. Then, we opened the door.

You know the cartoons where the Tasmanian devil is delivered in a wooden box that says "DANGER!"? And, as soon as the box is opened, it unleashes a tornado of chaos? That was Sydney.

She bolted for the bedroom, spiraled into a closet door, bounced off the wall, and squeezed herself under the bed, wedging herself between plastic tubs of photos and sweaters. We tried everything to lure her out, but she refused to budge. After a frantic text, the shelter coordinator said we could leave her be; she'd come out on her own.

Almost twelve hours later, the kittens howled with hunger. Sydney continued to hunker under the bed.

I understood this because I had postpartum depression, too. However, somebody needed to feed these babies, and it wasn't going to be me.

We blocked the perimeter of the bed with boxes and prodded Sydney out with a broom, ushering her back into the crate with her children. Because she continued to run and hide, the shelter gave us another crate, a larger one, where Sydney would stay caged for the remainder of her time with us.

It didn't go without notice that I put another creature in lockdown while I was in lockdown.

My work transitioned to home. My son's school didn't return e-mails. My group text with other moms grew long and panicked as we tried to patch together lessons for our kids using YouTube videos and craft glue. I started and did not finish many books, but I read dozens of articles about Covid-19, as if the act of reading was actually doing something, as if I'd reach the end of *The Atlantic* and discover the cure.

While the world burned, we weighed kittens every morning and night. They grew by measurable ounces. This was a reliable thing.

Outside, people got sick. My area became a hotspot. I drove past the hospital where tents for patient care had been erected in the parking lot. My nurse friends wore face masks until their cheeks were tender and raw. A friend had emergency surgery for a brain tumor, and she was alone in her recovery room.

Sydney needed to return to the shelter for surgery, and the shelter opted to keep her. She was unadoptable, they said, but she'd live the rest of her life on their catio — a patio enclosed by chicken wire. It was a shame, I thought. She never struck me as undesirable, only afraid.

The six babies were older by this point, eyes open, ears perked, fur puffed. They became spunky and boisterous. On my Zoom meetings, the background filled with kitten tumbleweeds.

I launched my debut book, and all my events were held online. They were attended by people who love and support me and have spent years cheering me on, but I couldn't touch them, embrace them or celebrate. It was surreal. After nine years of work, I could finally hold my words in my hands, but I couldn't see my book anywhere beyond. I couldn't share the same air with another reader. I had nothing to sign. I grew suspicious and wondered if the book only existed in my condo.

My screentime skyrocketed. I lived a screen life, Tetris-ing my schedule with Zoom work, Zoom school, Zoom readings, and Zoom happy hours. I ordered groceries on the computer and had real-life food delivered to my door.

I also held Wildflower until she fell asleep in my hand. Gobi swatted my hair while I wrote. Agave was the frisky guy, the one who attacked my toes.

The animals made me feel human.

Our neighbors on the right side drove to Canada and never returned. Our neighbor to the left, the seventy-nine-year-old man in recovery from cancer, stopped leaving his house. But, each week, he rolled our recycling bin from the street back up to the garage — a simple kindness but also a necessary update. As long as the bin was rolled up the drive, this man was alive.

In May, it was time for the kittens to return to the shelter. They were nine weeks old.

The emptiness was endless. I no longer complained about kittens destroying my decorative pillows. I complained about the silence.

A couple of weeks passed, and we received another litter of kittens, this time just three: Chipmunk, Rabbit, and Mouse.

Yes, a cat named Mouse. He was the color of smoke and moved like fog. He tucked himself along my legs whenever I sat and wound infinity symbols around my ankles when I stood.

My family expected the reliable thing, the experience of nurturing a living soul, of growing something from small to big, of loving something and being loved in return. It was unexpected then the morning my son giggled and said, "Silly Mouse is sleeping in his litterbox."

Mouse was limp, his fur wet and matted with urine. He did not open his eyes.

The veterinarian said that kittens can crash; it happens all the time. It's called Fading Kitten Syndrome, when a previously healthy kitten gasps for breath and begins to fade. Sometimes, they don't make it. Sometimes, they do. There's no way to predict this. You never know.

"Not all who are born will live," we were reminded.

It was embarrassing, this extravagant assumption that the hearts around me would continue to beat simply because I wanted them to; this misguided notion that if I gave something my care, it would thrive for that reason alone. I thought our condo was safe. In lockdown, nothing could come for us. We were untouchable. We relied on that, and it was true until it wasn't.

Mouse made it. After three days with the vet, he returned to our condo, where every one of his tiny, hot breaths felt like a magic trick, a mystery. We tended to him and his siblings for another couple of weeks. Then, it was time for them to go.

It was a Groundhog Day of farewells. Again, we put kittens in a crate and toted them out the door. Again, we cried. But I've learned that to foster an animal is to become acquainted with goodbye.

These days have so many goodbyes.

On a scale of grief, a house without kittens hardly ranks at all, let alone a neighborhood without neighbors and a book that isn't on shelves. This is trivial stuff.

There's no reason to carve out a slender space for nano-sadnesses when sorrow is plentiful. But these minor mournings accumulate, hour upon hour, until I wonder how the earth itself doesn't crumble from the weight.

Someday, perhaps, the sadness won't feel crushing and inevitable. Someday, perhaps, I'll tell my son that I'm allergic to cats.

—Maggie Downs—

81

Bob, the Free-Range Cat

*If we treated everyone we meet with the same affection
we bestow upon our favorite cat, they, too, would purr.*
~Martin Buxbaum

"Excuse me," I said to the gray cat with piercing green eyes who stared up at me. She was lying on the stairs, blocking the entrance to my new apartment on the second floor. She only blinked her response, refusing to budge. Though I was anxious to put down my oversized box and start unpacking, she didn't seem to care.

I couldn't help but notice her chopped tail — not the kind of chop a veterinarian might give but a rough, jagged slice that left her with a pitiful-looking stump. I wondered what had happened to her.

I had moved with my own two cats all the way from Alaska to Tennessee. Having retired from a career as a probation officer in my fifties, with a small pension and two self-sufficient daughters in their thirties, I knew this was my time. But what I hadn't thought about was how hard it would be to make new friends, especially during the pandemic.

People in the South are friendly, that's for sure. Within nanoseconds, my college-aged neighbors popped over to introduce themselves and give me the lay of the land. "The cat is called Bob because of her tail."

A quick summary of the other building residents revealed that, in total, we were a motley crew. A single father turned fitness guru with three daughters lived directly across from me. There was a young mom and her grade-school-aged daughter. Directly below me was a former model in the flower-child era who had turned retail maven in her sixties and fed all the wildlife and stray animals that came by. A boisterous, disabled vet in failing health who'd wallpapered his place with photos of his favorite presidential candidate lived directly across from her. And so on.

I was glad to meet the young couple, for whom I developed an instant affection, but it was clear that everyone around already had busy lives complete with friends, families and jobs. Everyone, except me.

It took a few days, but Bob the cat began to hang around my apartment door. Too skittish for petting, she trailed me to my car and sometimes accompanied me up the stairs to my front porch on the way back.

Two months in, Bob allowed me to pet her. By then, I was adding to her food supply after a water and food dish appeared within three feet of my door. When I saw any of my neighbors, the conversation was all about her. "Has it been you who's changed her water out lately? I haven't had time." Or, "Have you seen Bob this morning? She's not been around."

After gaining her trust, I even invited Bob into my home to meet my cats: seven-year-old litter mates named Oliver and Lou who normally didn't like other cats. But Bob was the exception. When she tentatively entered the living room, both boys gently greeted her and let her walk the length of the apartment. After she was satisfied that she'd seen all that interested her, Bob stood at the door to be let out.

"She doesn't want to be owned," my downstairs neighbor told me one morning. "We've tried to adopt her, but she likes roaming free." By now, I was having at least four conversations a week with neighbors about Bob.

I could see that Bob had become slightly paunchier after the holidays, and her food and water dishes were being replenished like the bottomless French fries at Red Robin. Why would she want to settle for just one home?

But I worried that she'd get hurt in the elements or by wildlife on the property.

One day, as I headed out in the morning for a walk, I saw that my fear had been realized. Bob had a deep wound in one eye, and she was barely moving.

My across-the-hall neighbor popped out of the door. He was on it. "Can I help pay the vet bill?" I asked as he told me the plan for Bob's medical care. "Nope," he said. "It's already covered by the downstairs neighbor."

Upon her return, Bob's eye had been treated, and she looked as if she'd been to the spa, groomed, vaccinated, given flea medication, and sent home with a treatment plan.

I bought her some toys with catnip. Another neighbor bought a luxury cat bed. Still another supplied a soft blanket. Faux houseplants completed the look of her outdoor palace.

No longer were we neighbors exchanging idle chitchat on the status of politics or the pandemic or the many other things we didn't always agree on. We were bonding over Bob. Co-parenting conversations on the right food, preferred toys, and Bob's bowel habits led to other issues on which to connect. Day by day, we were becoming a family.

Rushing upstairs one night, with my arms filled with groceries, I found Bob perched next to a raccoon by her food dish. They looked at me with the guilty expressions of teens at a house party. The raccoon stayed a little longer to finish the meal before reluctantly returning home. Soon after, my neighbor across the hall came onto the deck to visit. As we talked about Bob, he let his large dog and cat onto the deck to say hello. I opened my front door to let Oliver and Lou join the fun. Another neighbor appeared with two small dogs. A rabbit bounced out of an apartment and onto the scene. Each animal greeted Bob and then one another as we humans remained in a circle, talking and laughing like old, dear friends.

"She's not a stray," I told some new neighbors recently who were unpacking their U-Haul. They'd stopped me, concerned about Bob's tail.

I thought about how Bob had opened the doors to conversations and connections I'd likely have never had otherwise as a transplant to

Tennessee after more than fifty years in Alaska. She brought out the best in all of us by granting us the chance just to love her.

"This is Bob," I told them, "our community's free-range cat."

—Lizbeth Meredith—

The Power of Love and Patience

Cats choose us. We don't own them.
~Kristen Cast

The meow was so quiet at first that I wasn't certain what I had heard. The second meow was louder and unmistakable.

I was taking my daily walk on a perfect March morning about a month after Covid effectively shut down tourism on the island of Kauai. A plumeria-scented breeze gently blew as I strolled past a resort a few blocks from my home. The hotel would typically be bustling, but now it was a ghost town.

I stopped to look for the source of the meowing. A tortoiseshell-colored cat emerged from a bush and perched on a black lava rock. She gazed up at me with bright yellow eyes, and I could see that she was emaciated. Her ribs poked through her dull, mottled fur. Her plaintive cries seemed to be imploring me to help. They cut straight to my heart.

The stray and feral cats that live on the grounds of the resort were accustomed to getting plenty of tasty tidbits tossed to them by tourists. But the tourists stopped coming when the pandemic arrived — and the cats were starving.

I rushed home and returned with a sack filled with dry cat food and several cans of the food I feed my three adult cats — all foster failures. The hungry cat was waiting for me, as if she knew I would return. She devoured the first can of food that I set down for her and then chowed down on the dry food.

I assumed the cat was feral, as there are an estimated 10,000 to 15,000 homeless or feral cats on the island. So, I was surprised when, after wolfing down a second can of food, she sat beside me. I took a chance and reached out to pet her, wondering if she might bite or scratch me. Instead, she purred rapturously, pushing her face against my hand.

I returned shortly before sunset that evening, and there she was waiting for me on her rock. She seemed to want affection even more than food. I gave her plenty of both. I was getting ready to head home when another tortie pushed her way through a thicket of fuchsia-colored bougainvillea. This cat appeared to be in even worse shape than the first. She was skeletal, with cloudy eyes. She was wheezing and had a nasal discharge.

Unlike my new friend, cat number two was extremely skittish. She flinched when I approached her and then ducked back into the safety of the bushes. I backed off, but soon hunger won out. She devoured the food that I set out.

This was the beginning of what would become my daily routine. I named my new friend Mildred after the title character in my mother-in-law's favorite childhood book about an abandoned orphan. A friend's little girl dubbed the other cat Beanie.

I fed Mildred and Beanie twice a day for the next eighteen months. Mildred became more loving than ever, trotting beside me when I walked away. Cars stopped on the street, their passengers asking me, "How do you get your cat to walk with you?" I would retort, "She's not my cat—but she thinks she is—and I can't get her to stop walking with me."

I would have been happy to have Mildred tag along and maybe even adopt her, but when she followed me home, my indoor cats lunged at the windows, hissing and growling at the interloper. The only way I could stop her from camping out on my doorstep and causing a ruckus was to drive the few blocks to where I fed Mildred and Beanie and make my escape in my car when our time together was finished.

Mildred and Beanie both had the tips of their right ear snipped, signifying that they had been spayed. A friend's microchip reader revealed that, eight years earlier, Mildred had been spayed, microchipped, and released by an organization that works to keep down the feral and stray cat population. It had been fifteen years for Beanie.

A kind neighbor, who is a veterinarian, looked at Bean and diagnosed a chronic respiratory illness and a sarcoma on one of her paws. She said that being feral and at an advanced age, the best thing to do would be to simply allow her to live out her remaining years without the stress of having to hunt for food.

Kauai is a pretty good place to be a homeless cat. There are sheds where the cats can escape the rain, and the weatherman's idea of chilly weather is seventy degrees. The tourists and resort workers returned, and many of them shared food with the cats, but I continued feeding them. Morning and evening, Mildred and Beanie would come running to meet me, meowing their greeting. My time with them became a highlight in my day. Mildred grew even more loving, sitting pressed against me each evening as we watched the sunset paint the sky.

A year and a half of twice-daily feedings did nothing to allay Beanie's fear of me. Occasionally, I would rest my hand on her for a moment while she was eating, but she would pull away or swat me, clearly uncomfortable with it. I accepted that with her being at least sixteen years old, the old girl was set in her ways and would never trust a human.

Then, one evening, Bean sat beside me. From then on, she sat close to me every night. I respected her desire not to be touched. I assured her that I loved her and would always take care of her. Then, one morning, when she was through eating, she tapped me with her paw. I set down more food, but that was not what she wanted. She tapped me again and, impossible as it seemed, I sensed that she wanted to be touched. I gently stroked her side, noticing how much she had filled out in the time that I had been feeding her. She seemed to like being petted. I began petting her every day, moving up to her head and neck in time.

This morning, as I sat petting her, I heard a faint rumbling and then a gentle vibration. Beanie was purring. It brought tears to my eyes. It took almost two years, but Beanie has decided to trust me and enjoy being loved.

—Jason Blume—

83

Fostering Kindness

In this life we cannot always do great things.
But we can do small things with great love.
~Mother Teresa

As soon as I entered the animal-control building, I could hear the yowling. The clamor of many cats crying at once echoed down the long institutional hallway. As I stepped inside the cat room, I saw that every cage from the floor to the ceiling was full. Some cats were at the front of their small cages, crying for attention. Others were curled up, frozen in fear. My heart sank, seeing all the beings in need, scared and confused.

I was there to bring home my first foster cat, Snow. I hoped she would be a bright spot in a year of great loss for me. I had left my job, boyfriend, and home, and lost my darling cat Annie to cancer. Annie had been my companion for eighteen years. Her presence had been a constant comfort, and her absence was the greatest of all my losses that year.

I wanted to adopt another animal, but I wasn't financially ready. With the encouragement of a friend who had previously fostered and told me about the great need for fosters, I signed up with a rescue organization. Ellie from the organization told me to go to Animal Control to pick up Snow, who was young and friendly, a great choice for a first-time foster. When I walked into the cat room, I quickly realized that taking just one was only going to make a small difference. But, I told myself, it still would make a difference.

I was grateful that someone had already chosen Snow for me. I don't know how I would have picked. However, it would have been hard not to notice her as her cry may have been the loudest of all. She was desperate to get out of her cage. When I put my fingers through the metal grate to pet her as well as I could, she leaned into them, craving affection.

Snow was a tuxedo cat, nearly all black. She had a white chest, white paws, and a tiny white half-mustache that melted my heart the instant I saw her. She was still a kitten herself but had already given birth to a litter of three. She was found soon after, a stray nursing under a porch and likely getting little nutrition. Snow's kittens had already found forever homes. Now it was her turn.

When I got Snow home, I was amazed at her energy. She ran all over my apartment, pouncing on toy mice and jumping impressively high when I waved the wand toy. Her energy was way too big for that small cage! She quickly learned how to play fetch. I would throw Annie's toy mice, and she would bring them back to me over and over. I loved seeing Annie's things put to use again.

When it was time for rest, Snow was a great snuggler. We would take naps together, and she would always find a way to wrap her body into mine. She loved being held and she rolled over for belly rubs. No matter who came to the door, she was there to greet them and ask for affection. Everyone loved her.

During our first trip to the vet, I found out something else about Snow. She had a disease: feline immunodeficiency virus (FIV). I learned it is a disease that attacks the immune system. Many infected cats live full, normal lives, but everyday illnesses can become severe for them. When the vet delivered the news, I panicked. How was I going to find an adopter now?

Many times, I thought of adopting her myself. She was a wonderful companion. But every time I would consider it, the image of that crowded cat room came to mind. I thought of the ones frozen in fear and knew that if Annie had been in that shelter, that's how she would have been. And I would have wanted someone to save her. If I found Snow a home, I would make room for another cat in need.

I posted Snow's adoption profile through my organization, trying to attract a family that would love her as much as I did. And I waited. And waited. And waited. All the while, I watched cats without diseases get adopted quickly.

One day, I posted a link to her profile on my Facebook page, and I got a reply from an old friend saying, "We may be interested."

I was excited — and also uncertain. We had been together for seven months. Would I be able to part with my darling? My friend and his wife had three older kids, lots of people to give her the love I wanted for her. They had lost their cat and were ready to open their hearts to a new one. I explained the FIV diagnosis, and my friend said they did not mind. He said that they were not perfect either and had not always had easy lives. Others had always helped them. This was a chance for them to help another being. All five came to meet her and voted afterward. It was unanimous; they wanted Snow to join their family.

When I dropped Snow off at her new home, I cried. And I cried for several days afterward, too. But I was also comforted, knowing she went to a house full of love. The day after the adoption, I got an update. Snow had gone from room to room, giving and receiving love from everyone. She was home.

A few years later, I got a message from my friend. Did I think Snow would like a friend? Yes, I most certainly did! They adopted another one of my fosters, a gorgeous kitten named Vegas. She was mostly white with an unusual black streak down her nose and mouth, and brown spots on her ears and back. The pair quickly became best friends. Snow was gentle with Vegas and helped her grow up by setting boundaries and teaching her how to play. Four years later, I still get pictures of them playing or cuddled up together in a kitty ball. Happy. Safe. Loved. Every time, it warms my heart.

I've continued to foster. When I'm struggling with whether to keep or adopt out a foster, as I often do, I think of that crowded cat room. And I think of Snow's happy ending and how, if I had kept her, I wouldn't have been able to save the thirty-seven additional cats that I have since. I can make a difference, one at a time.

— Mary Christine Kane —

84

Toby, the Biting Feral Cat

Volunteers do not necessarily have the time;
they have the heart.
~Elizabeth Andrews

I was trapped in my pint-sized home office with a snarling cat during the Covid lockdown. This had become our nightly ritual ever since he'd arrived. I would take a sip of wine to brace myself to face this tiny terrorist whose neck wound needed treating. I'd gather my cotton wool, iodine spray and a large towel to throw over him once he was safely contained in a corner. Once I caught him, I would swaddle him like a baby so that he couldn't escape, which made him look comical with his angry head poking out.

He was barely two years old, but his ears resembled a boxer, and tufts of his fur were missing. This little fighter had been found on a rough street around the corner from my house and trapped by a local cat charity. I collected him from the vet, who was relieved to be saying goodbye to their most difficult resident. After a few weeks in my spare room, he came and sat next to me, so I thought he wanted to call a truce.

I put out my hand to greet him and gain his trust but was rewarded with the sharp pain of his teeth penetrating my skin. My finger sported four angry, red marks, and I had to go to the emergency room to get it treated.

Walking back into the room, my nemesis hissed at me as I poured food into his bowl. I wondered what the world had done to him and pondered whether he'd be in my office forever, haunting me with his bad attitude. Phone in hand, I texted the cat charity and asked if there was space at a feral colony if he couldn't be rehabilitated. They said they would ask around, but it didn't sound promising.

I decided that tomorrow would be another day and closed the door, leaving him to blend in with the darkness. After another month, his wound started to close up, which meant that I no longer had to harass him with the iodine spray. It also meant that he could wander around the house more and explore new territory beyond his office den. He started to tolerate my presence in his space and moved around freely without keeping an eye on my whereabouts.

Again, he came and sat next to me on the love seat. I wasn't taking any chances, so I kept my arms firmly by my sides. Each evening, he edged closer to me, even getting himself featured on my daily Zoom calls with colleagues who commented on his intense expression. One night, he put his mouth to my arm and opened his mouth. I felt something and jumped a foot in the air. He hissed and jumped away, but I realised he'd licked me. He'd forgiven me for the journeys to the vet and the iodine spraying, but now I'd been the one to give him a scare.

After a few days, he came back to me and sat on my knee. I didn't know if I dared upset the fragile equilibrium by touching him, so I picked up a spoon and gave him a light scratch on the head with the handle. He started to purr. After a few false starts, I experienced what every cat rescuer hopes for — the moment when the cat chooses to trust humans again.

But there was still work to be done. After all, he was a biter, and I had the scars to prove it. He continued to come and sit on my knee, so I started to stroke him on the head. Arching his head into my hand, I could see the scar on his neck, curved around like an upside-down smile. It was a badge of human cruelty that had taken nearly three months to heal. The question of whether his soul would do the same would soon be answered.

Toby started to climb up to my shoulder and lay his head on me. I put my arms around him, and he purred. He put his face against my face and rubbed his cheek against mine. A street cat with the worst possible start in life had become more affectionate than the pampered cats I'd grown up with. I looked into his yellow eyes to see that he had softened. His capacity to love had been unlocked by my hours of patience. He was no longer a "lost cause." In fact, he was now someone's ideal pet. I just needed to find that person.

There was still one more bump in the road, though. Potential adopters need to visit the cat after they've made their application. An excited woman came to visit. I told her that Toby was jumpy and to let him come to her, but she was determined to force his affection. He hissed at her when she approached, and she continued to try to touch him until he bit her in frustration. Needless to say, she passed on him, and it was back to the drawing board.

Thankfully, another would-be adopter got in touch after some further rehabilitation where Toby learnt to relax with myself and my partner. I told her the same thing, and she sat quietly with him and didn't force contact while he assessed her. She was very quiet, so I didn't know if she was interested, but I told her all about his loving ways. Once he trusted you, I said, he longed to be held like a baby. He didn't show any of his affection to her that day, and I didn't know if I would hear from her again.

When she got in touch with the charity to say she was interested in adopting him, I was over the moon. In four months, Toby's luck had changed. His new mom turned up at my doorstep to collect him. I told her to leave him alone, and he would warm up in his own time. After that, I didn't hear anything. I crossed my fingers that no news was good news, and they were a match. Weeks went by until she posted a picture of herself cuddling up to Toby with his cheek on her cheek. They both had the love they deserved, and he wasn't a biter anymore. My heart filled; it had all been worth it.

After the intensity of spending eight to twelve hours a day working in the room with Toby, I wondered what I would do with the free time. Little did I know that sleeping under my hedge was my next project: another black cat from the same litter who needed the same chance I'd given to his brother.

—Jennifer Sizeland—

85

Gracie

When I am feeling low, all I have to do is watch
my cat, and my courage returns.
~Charles Bukowski

She was never my cat. She was my husband's in every way. She played with him, watched TV with him, and curled up next to him when she slept.

I scooped her litterbox and fed her twice a day. I cleaned up when she launched a hairball. But she ignored me. That was our relationship. I was the handmaiden to the king's mistress.

Gracie was beautiful. She had the looks of a domestic shorthair mix. You often see her clone on cat-food commercials. She was gray and black and had the classic "M" shape on her forehead and large emerald-green eyes.

As time went on, Gracie put on weight. Our vet was concerned. I'm sure he suspected that we were sneaking her extra snacks. I examined my husband's face for signs of guilt. He didn't flinch under pressure. But then my husband died, and I was left alone with Gracie. Life went on in a crooked kind of way as we both missed our companion, and then, two weeks after I became a widow, the next bad thing happened. Gracie developed diabetes.

I was overwhelmed. The young vet began to explain to me how to correctly use the syringe to give Gracie her twice-daily shots. What? I was in no condition to do anything. I had already gotten a ticket going through a stop sign the week before, which made it clear I was out of my mind. But this? I have to say this was not my finest hour. When I got the ticket, I was calmly polite as if in a fugue state.

But when the vet delivered her bad news, I was Medea and Lady Macbeth. "Do you mean to tell me I have to give this cat a shot twice a day for the rest of its life?" I yelled. The vet just nodded. The young tech holding Gracie looked frightened, but, under fire, he kept a tight hold on her. I was immediately embarrassed. I apologized and listened to the information like a regretful child. Then I took Gracie out to the car in her carrier and didn't speak to her the entire trip home.

We continued to live our separate lives, with Gracie sleeping on my husband's slipper and me sullenly taking care of her needs. The twice-daily shots tethered me to home on a twelve-hour cycle. Her special food, insulin and needles were expensive, and if I wanted to go away, her boarding fee was high. My thoughts turned dark. Who would take a diabetic cat? Could I give her away if I paid her fees for a year? Should I return her to the shelter where we got her? I even considered allowing the disease to take its course. I wrestled on and off with this moral dilemma for weeks, but then I stopped. Gracie was a living thing, so that was that.

This odd coexistence could have gone on forever, but it didn't. One morning, I woke up as if I hadn't slept. I went to feed Gracie and set up her shot. I waited until she was occupied eating, and I inserted the needle in a handful of skin and delivered the three units of insulin. Or had I? I became unsure if I had twisted the dial to three or two, which was her evening dose. I panicked. The vet warned me that an incorrect or late dose could cause hypoglycemia, which could cause seizures and even death.

I called the vet and imitated a crazy person to the receptionist. She grasped the problem and told me to bring in the cat. Grabbing Gracie and putting her in her carrier was a nightmare. She resisted with all her feline strength. Finally getting her in, I risked another ticket as I sped to the vet. Gracie was whisked into the examining room, and I sat in the waiting room looking stonily at the enormous fish tank.

When the vet emerged, she told me that Gracie's sugar level was in perfect balance. The relief I felt was like finding your lost child at an amusement park.

From that day on, I began to cherish Gracie. Because I was lavishing her with affection, she began to warm up to me. It's amazing to me how much I like this cat. I have conversations with her as I go through my day. Before dinner is a time to cuddle. She's the only living thing I can sing to who doesn't leave the room. I guess you can say we saved each other. I protect her from the ravages of her disease, and Gracie gave me a meaningful purpose at a time when I was rudderless. My original complaints are still operational, but affection will always trump inconvenience. Ask any cat lover.

— Meg Fitzgerald —

86

Furry Angels

A meow massages the heart.
~Stuart McMillan

An American shorthair cat raking her claws across the old couch on the front porch was the last thing I would have expected that morning in March 2020. Standing there with a steaming cup of chamomile tea in one hand, I could only stare at this peculiar visitor. Alternating black, gray, and brown stripes covered her body, and she had delicate white mitten paws. She turned brilliant golden eyes, dark pupils as wide with curiosity as my own, to study me before scampering away toward the safety of the nearby bushes.

We glimpsed her over the next couple of weeks, but at first my parents, brother, and I thought she was visiting us to chase after the ground squirrels and rabbits in our yard.

The cat that we took to calling Dinah came at one of the roughest points in our lives. I had moved out of my apartment and come back home amid the pandemic. My father was undergoing chemotherapy treatments for colon cancer, and my grandmother was fading away at a distant hospital.

It felt like the world was crumbling around us.

Dinah was a wonderful distraction. She loved to roll around on her back at the base of the porch steps and snooze nearby. It was as if she had life completely figured out.

She took to trailing after us in the yard at a distance with her tail held up. She even took to meowing at the front door — as if she had faith that we would eventually give in and put out bowls of food and water (which we did).

Then, my mother reported hearing high-pitched meows from our partially enclosed patio area in the back. I peered out the laundry room window into the patio and noticed Dinah sitting beside an old washing machine. She blinked at me as if to say, "Good, you're watching," before making a trilling sound I had never heard before.

A black puffball with golden eyes waddled out to join her from behind an overturned flowerpot.

The entire situation snapped into perfect focus.

Heartless individuals were known to drive out and abandon unwanted pets in the countryside from time to time. Pregnant cats would be especially vulnerable to this mistreatment. Even so, we spent the next several hours scouring various boards online and around our community for reports of missing cats with her description, without success.

My parents expressed concern that my father might catch something from the cats if we took them into our home, given his weakened immune system while undergoing chemotherapy. So my brother and I called various shelters to ask if they might take the cats. But they were all full.

We decided the back patio area was at least a safe place for Dinah and the kitten — who we named Salem — to stay until we decided what to do next, and we sought to be much more attentive to their needs.

Dinah gently taught me various little lessons about interacting with cats, including just how affectionate and social they can be toward humans. I grew close to Salem as well, who overcame her skittishness.

Each session with the cats was like therapy as things continued to fall apart. I stepped outside on the afternoon my grandmother passed away with tears rolling down my cheeks, and Dinah immediately streaked over to offer comfort. She always seemed to know the right way to soothe or comfort me, and she became especially gentle over the next several days as preparations took place for my grandmother's funeral. We watched the burial via a livestream feed on Facebook.

Then, our lives took another twist.

Dinah's belly started to swell.

We looked up the veterinary clinic that had just opened in the nearest town and made an appointment with them. The vet was friendly and understanding, but she delivered some troublesome news. Dinah was pregnant, and she was due to "pop" at any time. She dispelled my parents' concerns that bringing the cats indoors would affect my father during his chemotherapy treatments, though, which was great news.

Then the vet told us we would need to somehow separate Dinah and Salem, or Salem would continue trying to nurse from Dinah and suck away all the nutrition needed for the litter. Our home was small and keeping them apart inside would be difficult. We couldn't leave Salem outside on her own in the back patio area, and we didn't trust the wilder critters in our yard to leave the newborn kittens alone if Dinah gave birth to them there.

It was another dire situation until one of the assistants gave us the number for a woman named Natasha who ran a private "cat sanctuary" about a mile away from the clinic. We would never have found her just by doing an Internet search or flipping through the phone book.

We called, and when she heard of the situation, Natasha rushed over for Dinah. Meeting and speaking with her, we knew she would be the best person to take care of Dinah and her new kittens. I knew we would all miss her dearly, but she would have the best care and plenty of space at the sanctuary. Natasha would ensure that Dinah safely delivered her babies, and she had well-established ways to help all of them find loving homes.

As for Salem, our home was all she had known most of her life so far, and I had formed a special bond with her through our play sessions. I asked to bring her back home with us, gave her a bath, and — alongside my parents and brother — tried to comfort her the way Dinah had comforted me. Before too long, Salem began to trail after me and beg for attention, so I suppose I became a kind of surrogate mother for her (a role that I assumed gladly).

Having Salem around the house gave all of us fresh purpose, I believe. She was constantly curious and even managed to make my father, usually so stern, laugh at her antics — something that she still does to this day.

Dinah delivered her litter of seven healthy kittens the day after Natasha brought her to the sanctuary. Through text messages, I saw photographs of all the sweet kittens from the litter, glimpsed the pride in Dinah's expression, and felt glad she had been a part of our lives for even a short period. When Natasha later told me, a few weeks later, that Dinah was helping the veterinarian care for two newborn kittens who had lost their mother, I wasn't surprised in the least.

Angels come in all shapes and sizes, after all.

Some are just fluffier than others.

—Joyce Jacobo—

87

A Role Model for Resilience

I have felt cats rubbing their faces against mine and
touching my cheek with claws carefully sheathed.
These things, to me, are expressions of love.
~James Herriot

My husband Sid and I were heartbroken when we learned that our cat Andy had diabetes. His veterinarian explained that older cats usually do not do well with the disease, so our eight-year-old feline might only live six more months.

We dutifully gave him insulin shots twice a day and painfully watched Andy struggle as the vet constantly adjusted his dosage. On two occasions, Andy had such violent seizures that he lost consciousness. Both times, he miraculously survived.

We began to talk about ending his suffering but then Andy dramatically improved. The seizures stopped and he resumed most of his normal activities. Thankfully, six months turned into many more years.

Cats are generally considered creatures of habit and don't usually adjust well to changes, but Andy did. On top of dealing with diabetes, he weathered several other storms, including some major events we went through together.

We were both devastated by Sid's sudden death. Andy curled up in his master's favorite chair for weeks, while I cried endlessly after such a tragic loss. We had always had a strong bond, but our shared sadness brought us even closer.

Almost a year after my husband's death, I decided to relocate to a different state. My furry friend adjusted beautifully to a move across the country where he encountered new surroundings and an entirely different lifestyle.

I think he knew that I was struggling to make it on my own and needed to lean on him. He took all the traumatic changes in stride, and his example helped me roll with the punches as I started over.

There were many times I did not think I could make it, but my tabby was always there for me. On top of his own challenges, he had to wear a lot of hats as we traveled down the road to recovery. He seemed to intuitively know when he needed to be my best friend, grief counselor, rescuer or protector, and sometimes had to wear all those hats simultaneously. My precious pet became an emotional caregiver and did whatever he had to do to help me deal with a deep hurt.

He sensed what I needed and responded accordingly. He would gently nuzzle me whenever I got completely lost in my grief. When I needed a laugh, my companion's mischievous nature emerged, and he became quite the clever comedian. He also proved that cats — despite what some people believe — are indeed capable of unconditional love.

As he aged, Andy's steps became slow and deliberate, and he no longer ran or jumped. He seemed content as we both inched closer to the new normal. We settled into a routine that included giving my ailing feline extra nurturing. Needless to say, he got used to being the center of my world.

A few years after my first husband died, I met Tom. He embraced Andy with all his problems. At first, my pet wasn't too receptive. He would often pull back and turn away if Tom tried to pet him. Andy would also sprawl out beside me to make sure there wasn't enough room on the couch for Tom. If we were already sitting next to each other, Andy would crawl up, wiggle his way between us, and push the new guy away from me with his back paws. My aging cat's overprotective nature often made us laugh out loud. When Tom and I were focused on each other, Andy would play the "feeble card," sometimes letting out a helpless, pathetic cry in an attempt to regain my full attention.

One day when Tom entered the house, he gave me a big hug. My sick, old cat miraculously sprang into action, leaping across the floor like a lion cub. He raced past us and sailed into the air, landing on top of my hutch. He had never jumped that high before, even as a kitten. I guess Andy was trying to demonstrate that he was still the king of the castle, despite his frailties. I screamed his name in total disbelief. Andy stared down at me from high atop the hutch and proudly bellowed a meow that sounded more like a roar. I felt like he was announcing, "Nothing is impossible when you are determined. Just look at me!"

His burst of energy didn't last that long, but Andy made his position clear. There was only room for one "Tom" in my life, and that was an able-bodied tomcat named Andy.

It took a long time, but after Tom and I married, Andy did eventually accept the new addition to the family. My stubborn feline probably realized that the outsider wasn't going anywhere, and he must be okay if I cared for him.

The two of them developed a morning routine. Andy would roll over for his daily tummy rub and affectionate words from Tom. He even allowed my new husband to give him his insulin shots.

At the age of sixteen, almost eight years after the prognosis of six months, Andy died. I sobbed over the loss of my beloved pet, but I was grateful that he had lived as long as he did.

Thanks to Andy, I learned to be resilient, determined and face the most difficult challenges head-on. My loving, loyal cat also taught me that, when life knocks you down and moving forward seems impossible, you can always reach deep inside you and muster the strength to pull yourself up, stand tall and overcome overwhelming odds. Together, we found the new normal at the end of the road back to happiness.

It's hard to imagine a cat as a role model, but Andy was. He miraculously overcame his challenges. His example, coupled with his devotion and tender loving care enabled me to triumphantly conquer grief and emerge as a stronger woman.

— Melinda Richarz Lyons —

88

Chicken Soup for the Soul

The Love They Deserved

*I love cats because I enjoy my home; and,
little by little, they become its visible soul.*
~Jean Cocteau

The little cat came into our lives via our porch. Someone must have dropped her off to fend for herself. We named her Grey because her fur was a beautiful light gray, which was velvety to the touch. Although she remained skittish, and we couldn't pet her, she did learn to trust us.

One afternoon, I heard Grey uncharacteristically hissing. I went out onto the porch to see a large male tabby stealing Grey's food. I chased him away.

We heard a rumor that a neighbor had moved and abandoned the cat. I was upset that Grey had to endure intimidation from this furry trespasser. She had enough bad things happen in her life. For the next two weeks, I continued to chase the insolent tomcat. I told him that there would be no fighting on my watch. I thought he would move on, but he didn't. He knew I meant business, so his demeanor changed. He became more loving toward Grey. He began sharing the food and using his manners. Soon, the two felines became inseparable.

I empathized because he had been abandoned, too. Just because he was large in size didn't mean he wasn't frightened and hungry. He was desperate for food, water, and a place to belong.

Laughingly, my sister called him a lard ball because he weighed seventeen pounds, and the name stuck. He eventually wormed his way into our hearts and became part of the family, too.

In the spring, our family enjoyed hunting for wild mushrooms. Morel mushrooms were delicious in recipes or dredged in flour and sautéed in butter. There was a place in the woods where we knew we could find them. One morning, after an overnight rain, we decided to set out with our teenage daughters to pick some morels.

Our family of four started hiking through the woods, and Lardball decided to tag along. Nature had awakened from its winter slumber. Our trek was filled with wonderful sights and sounds. The woodland had started to burst with greenery. The chilly spring air smelled fresh and new. We enjoyed the nature walk as much as the hunt for mushrooms.

We carefully scanned the countryside for the delicious harvest that was highly sought after. You had to focus your vision on the groundcover and look under dried leaves and twigs. Mushrooms were hard to find because they camouflaged amongst the lush foliage of the forest floor.

We noticed that Lardball stayed with us and meowed loudly if any of us got too far apart. Our girls were gathering lavender wildflowers and must have wandered too far away for Lardball's comfort because he cried and rounded them up like a Border Collie. After finding our bounty, we decided to head home. Our gentle giant led the way. He walked a few feet ahead of us and then sat down and turned his head toward us. He meowed loudly until we caught up with him. He continued this pattern the whole way home. He was making sure we all stayed together and returned home safely. I have never seen a cat do this, but I understood his motivation.

This poor kitty who had been thrown away and abandoned was keeping his new family together and safe. He was leading us back to our home. The home that he chose. The home that he loved. The forever home he never wanted to lose.

After a long life, Lardball and Grey have since passed on. They lived out their lives in a loving home and never again experienced hunger or uncertainty. In the end, they found the love they deserved.

— Robin Howard Will —

Connected

One must love a cat on its own terms.
~Paul Gray

He doesn't sleep on a silk cushion or curled up on my lap. He doesn't twine himself around my legs wanting to be fed or demanding my attention. He is not a house cat. He likes living alone — outdoors. He has a name, Sox, although he doesn't know it or answer to it. He is not a pampered pet.

Sox is just, well, a cat. Yet this story is about Sox because I identify with him. I love him — from afar. And I laugh at him. A lot. When he's happy, he performs as if no one is watching. We have an understanding, Sox and I: I don't try to impose my friendship on him. In return, he accepts my food and shelter.

Sox is feral. He lives by his wits and, for the past two years, by my kindness.

When I first met him, he ran and hid behind a mugo pine in a corner of my back yard. It was the beginning of fall, and the temperature was on the decline. I was concerned about his survival. Because I was cat-less, I didn't have anything to feed him. I didn't even know what cats ate. I had noticed products with cat pictures on them at the grocery store, so I bought the ones with the prettiest cats — a bag of dry chow and several cans of stuff that promised "real seafood," "beef chunks," "shreds of real meat," and "gravy"!

At dusk, I put out a kitty smorgasbord and a bowl of water. I left the drapes open on my patio door. Just as daylight faded, Sox appeared — black with four white feet, a white bib and almond-shaped eyes. He wasn't big on manners; he ate fast, drank from the birdbath and ran. It became routine — a plate of food, a sip or two of water every evening before dark and a quick exit. He saw me through the open drapes and regarded me with typical feline disdain — until I opened the door to make friends with him. Then he was over the fence and gone in a New York minute.

Yet, there was progress. Home late one evening from school — and late with Sox's routine feeding — I saw Mr. Independent staring at me, accusing me through the patio door. "Where's my supper?" But when I opened the door with his food, he retreated to a safe distance and stared at me. I put down the plate and waited, thinking he might approach. Maybe we could actually be friends. No, it was a standoff. I could have waited until dawn, and we would have been staring at each other in the daylight.

With winter coming, what would he do for shelter? I was sure he had made arrangements... under someone's porch, under a portable shed, inside a crawl space. But I felt responsible. I knew he would never come inside, so I bought him an expensive "cat house." (Yes, that's what they called it, so don't laugh.) It guaranteed the seal of approval for feral cats — a way in and an exit when it was necessary. I padded it with old towels and threw in some kitty treats. By morning, the towels had been rearranged, and the kitty treats were gone. I haven't seen Sox inside the house, but I know he spends nights there. I wash the towels periodically — separate from my laundry.

On weekends, I watch Sox play by himself in my back yard and on my patio — running, jumping and chasing shadows. Summer afternoons, he likes to sleep under a patio chair. It's obvious he feels comfortable and safe in my yard. Now he stays long enough after supper to clean his paws, whiskers, and mouth — Sox is super hygienic. Then he goes somewhere for an evening's entertainment, coming back late at night. Like a short-order cook in an all-night diner, I leave a "midnight snack" for him. And, like a parent, I worry about his safety.

Maybe we will just be distant friends, Sox and me, forever or however long feral cats live. Or humans. We have an arm's length relationship, but there is a connection. I feel it, and I believe Sox does, too. There are times when I think it goes beyond the supper and the cat house. But his distrust of humans is so strong that it's like a constant warning: Beware of that guy. Sometimes, I feel the same distrust with my fellow humans. Where does it come from... that distrust in a cat that wants to feel connectedness and a human who sometimes feels too much?

For now, we are both okay with our unique relationship. I take it one day at a time, and I suppose Sox does, too. He doesn't let me know his feelings unless the menu doesn't please him. (I discovered he doesn't like tuna.) Someday, from inside my patio door, I'll look him right in the eye and ask him point blank where we need to take this relationship. In the meantime, we're connected.

Sort of.

— David Tarpenning —

Letting Love In

Your heart knows the way. Run in that direction.
~Rumi

n the fall of 2010, my two-year-old cat Chulo was a typical only child. Rescuing him two years prior had transformed both of our lives. I wanted to give other cats the same chance at happiness, so I became a feline foster mother to prepare other cats for their forever homes. I'd heard about other foster parents getting attached to their foster pets, but my heart was already taken. There was no way I could love another animal the way I loved Chulo.

The shelter started contacting me with requests to foster, but the timing was always off. My husband (then boyfriend) Johan and I were always traveling or hosting guests. Then, in the spring of 2011, they contacted me with a proposal: A one-month-old kitten needed foster care until she was big enough to adopt.

"I'm here to pick up Lena," I told the woman behind the desk.

She disappeared into an adjacent room and emerged with a pet carrier. Lena announced her presence with a high-pitched squeak. I crouched down to get a good look at the stray. She was small enough to fit in the palm of my hand, much smaller than Chulo had been when I'd adopted him.

"Bring her back for a checkup in about a month," the woman said. "When she weighs two pounds, we can put her up for adoption."

We all took to Lena right away. Even Chulo found her irresistible, grooming her soft gray belly. Over the following weeks, Lena brought much light and laughter to our little family. Despite her tiny size, her rambunctious energy was larger than life, and it transformed the way all of us interacted. For her part, she also seemed to feel right at home with us.

Lena was always challenging her foster brother to a play fight. When I was in the bath, she swatted at the running water. After a long day, she sought out her foster father for cuddles and naps.

As I prepared to return her to the shelter, I noticed that one of her eyes was irritated. Her doctor gave me some ointment and asked if I could keep her for two more weeks "just until the eye heals." I agreed. By that time, she'd been with us for a month. What were another two weeks?

Or so I thought.

When the shelter told me to write a summary about Lena for their website, I gushed about her outstanding qualities: "bunny-soft," "playful," and "sweet as can be." But all anyone had to do was look at that adorable face. Lena would find an adopter right away, no matter what I wrote.

But who? That question began to haunt me. One night, it woke me from a dead sleep. I turned on the bedside lamp, and Johan groaned.

"What if Lena's owners abandon her?" I asked him in a panic. "What if they let her outside, and she gets hit by a car? Will they keep an eye on her while running a bath?"

Johan rolled over to face me.

"You know why you're worried, don't you?" he asked. I didn't respond. "Because you love her."

"Ridiculous!" I said, turning off the lamp.

But I couldn't fall back asleep. I'd been so sure that my heart couldn't accommodate another pet that I'd never worried about loving Lena. The truth was, I couldn't imagine giving her back to the shelter. Not now. She felt like part of our family. Johan was right. I had fallen in love with her, and I didn't even know it.

"It's okay," Johan whispered in the darkness. "I love her, too."

Bean, as we would come to call her, taught me about the heart's limitless capacity. She showed me that my heart could expand to let love in. I realized that I was never really her foster mother. I was always just her mother. I'm a foster failure. And it's one of the best things to ever happen to me.

— Laura Plummer —

Chapter
10

Natural Therapists

We Got a Cat

Not all angels have wings.
Sometimes, they have whiskers.
~Author Unknown

My phone pinged, and I picked it up to read the incoming message. "We got a cat," my sister wrote. Underneath, an image of a small black kitten appeared on the screen. Another ping. "Her name is Verity," followed by a smiley-face emoji.

"Cute," I replied nonchalantly. I was not much of a cat person. Although I didn't dislike them, I had never really warmed to them either. That, combined with the fact that I was currently living on the other side of the world in London — whereas my family's home was far away in Sydney, Australia — meant that I didn't give this news much thought.

Flash forward a year, and I was leaving London to return to my home country. I was broke and jobless but grateful that moving back in with my parents and sister for a while was an option. I was sad to leave London as I had made friends and a life for myself there. On my first night back, my flight got in late, and I was extremely tired. I gave my family some quick hugs before crashing in bed. I am sure I was asleep before the lights were even out, but at 3:00 A.M. I found myself wide awake. This is normal when experiencing jet lag from travelling over time zones, but I could still feel myself begin to panic.

Questions began flooding my brain. What was I going to do

with my life now? Where would I live? How long before I ran out of money? I could feel my heart racing and knew that a panic attack was starting to rear its ugly head. Suddenly, I heard a thud and the weight of something land on my bed. I shot up, peering down toward the end of my bed to see what had made that sensation. I realised it was my sister's cat, Verity, and it was strutting toward me.

"Hello," I said apprehensively, uncertain what to do or say to this unfamiliar cat. Verity's response was to nuzzle my face with her soft, velvety head before emitting a slow, warm purr. What I felt next was like something I had never experienced before. It was almost as if her purr was emanating from her body and sending waves through mine right to my chest and the centre of where all the panic had been coming from. It was like the sound was unknitting all the tightness in my chest, and I could feel myself slowly relaxing as I sank back down into my bed. The next thing I knew, she was on top of me, right in the spot where I felt my panic attacks the strongest, and she gently kneaded me before plopping down and falling asleep. Before I knew it, I was fast asleep too, and when I woke in the morning, I found her lying next to my pillow.

Every night after that, Verity would sleep in my bed. She began following me around the house, and if I sat down on the couch, she was on my lap in an instant. I loved being around her, and my family joked that she was no longer my sister's cat but mine. Because of her, I became a cat fan and would buy cute trinkets, clothing and jewellery adorned with adorable cat faces. When it was time for me to move out again, I was sad to leave Verity behind, but I was moving somewhere much closer than London, so I knew I would still see her often. I eventually got a cat of my own, and even though she is nowhere near as affectionate as Verity, I adore her.

I visit my family most weeks, and Verity is still there waiting for me. I spend most of my time at the house cuddling her on the couch, and my family insists that I probably come to see Verity more than them. I don't always disagree. I love that little black ball of fluff, and I am forever grateful that she helped me through that night. I don't know if she knew what she was doing, but I do know that she turned a person who was lukewarm about cats into a red-hot fan for life.

— Hannah Castelli —

92

Max's Lesson

If there were to be a universal sound depicting peace,
I would surely vote for the purr.
~Barbara L. Diamond

everal years ago, I lived with a curious orange cat named Max who taught me a very important life lesson. Max's curiosity took him to many places — the bottom of my sewing basket, my clothes hamper, my dresser drawers, and under the kitchen sink. But Max wasn't the only one who got into everything. I did, too. I was as unpredictable and flighty as Max.

I've had lots of jobs — telephone operator, tin-can inspector, radio copywriter, secretary, receptionist, HR director, marketing director and dog groomer. I also owned a few businesses. When I went to college, I couldn't stick with one major. I switched from Sociology to Business Management to Women's Studies to Creative Writing.

I moved a lot, too. My friends used to tease me that whenever I went anywhere on vacation, I considered moving to that area, and sometimes I actually did.

I was fickle with dating as well, which is fine when you're young and first start dating. But then, as the years go on, you realize you may have made the mistake of walking away from the perfect relationship.

Years later, in my forties, I worked at a job I didn't really like, bought a new car at least every two years, and was not in a committed relationship with anyone except Max. Max drove me crazy with his antics. I couldn't iron my clothes without him pulling on the iron's cord or jumping on the ironing board. And trying to eat without him jumping on my lap was almost impossible.

Then, one day, when I left a cabinet door ajar, he pulled it open and climbed inside. I was at my wits' end with him that day and yelled, "Max! Just because a door is open, you don't have to walk through it."

And then I stood still and replayed those words in my mind: *Just because a door is open, you don't have to walk through it.*

Oh, my gosh, that's what I had been doing my entire life — walking through every door, taking every opportunity, and never giving a thought as to whether or not I was making the right decision.

Thanks to Max, I learned a very important lesson that day. Since then, whenever an opportunity comes along — a new job, a new relationship, a new place to live — I recall those fateful words I said to Max. Just because a door is open, you don't have to walk through it.

I have now lived in Florida for thirty years, in the same apartment for seven, and have been driving the same VW Beetle for eleven years. And I've been in a committed eight-year relationship with a very conventional cat named Raven. I've never been happier.

—Joanna Michaels—

93

Chicken Soup for the Soul

Catlike

*Who among us hasn't envied a cat's ability to ignore
the cares of daily life and to relax completely?*
~Karen Brademeyer

heard her yowling before I saw her. "Boots?" I said, looking around. She trotted to the end of the driveway and twisted her body around my ankles. Boots knew me from the many times I cat-sat for Ruth.

"Did Ruth go off and leave you?" I wasn't surprised. During my last conversation with Ruth's daughter, I had asked about Boots.

"Well," Debbie said, "I told the new owners that the house comes with a free cat." She laughed.

"Meow." Boots told me all about it.

"Well, I bet you're starving."

I fed her on Miss Ruth's porch, left her a fresh bowl of water, and did this for several days. The new owner, who was flipping the house, kept tossing out the trays and then posted a note telling me to stop using his stoop to attract cats. I explained about Boots's abandonment, and that I was coaxing her down to my place.

Each morning, I moved the food tray. I shook the bowl of kibble and called her to the end of Ruth's driveway, then to the next house, then to Ms. Betty's old house where her grandson Timothy now lived, then to the edge of my yard and, finally to the sidewalk at my place.

Although I offered, Boots would never come inside — her trust didn't reach that far. Instead, for two years, Boots took up residency under Ms. Betty's abandoned Cadillac. I asked Timothy's permission to use his driveway as a landing pad. I constructed kitty houses for her out of boxes. The following winter, I coaxed her into using a warming box under my magnolia tree. Beside it, I put an igloo designed for cats with a wider opening for extra surveillance and quick escapes. Inside, I placed a large, puffy cat bed lined with a warming pad. To see her climb into the nest, cozy and safe, was thanks enough.

She had a way of reinforcing my behavior to take care of her just by eating the food with gratitude or using the items I made for her. Unlike people, she seemed grateful for every effort I made. Caring for her was a simple pleasure and sacred act. I wouldn't be that person who let her down.

What began as a simple, moral imperative grew into a rewarding stewardship. We developed an understanding. I would provide food and a place to camp out, and she would accept the effort. Boots was my cat, yet not anybody's pet. I liked this about her.

In February, the biggest snowstorm we'd had in decades hit hard. Sleet and freezing rain were followed by seven inches of snow. Boots was content in her snow-encased igloo. And even though I was undergoing chemotherapy treatment, I shoveled a path from her house to my front stoop so she could eat without getting too cold.

One afternoon that spring, as I sat outside too weak from chemo to do much else, she came to the porch and allowed me to pet her. This was three years into our arrangement. In a way, I felt we were kindred creatures. Boots had become my charge during the lowest point of my divorce, and I admired her independent nature and resilience after being abandoned. I wanted to be more catlike myself.

When I opened the door one Sunday morning last October, no cats were around. A heavy quiet hung in the darkness. "Boots?" I called, instinctively looking toward her house. I called to my house cat, "Whitman?"

Then, I saw her lying in the grass.

"Oh no, Boots!"

I knelt over her small body. My tears fell on her already dew-soaked coat.

The new neighbor, Lisa, came to the edge of the yard. "Is everything okay?"

"No, my cat is dead," I said. She joined me in the center of the grass and reported that she had heard barking. Armed with a can of pepper spray, she had come out to investigate and saw two German Shepherds running from my yard.

I went inside to gather a towel. Returning, I knelt again and lifted Boots's body, already stiff with death, onto the green terrycloth. "This is the first time she'll allow me to pick her up," I said. The irony made me cry harder. I understood her mistrust. Her wariness had kept her alive — until now.

My shirt grew damp as I snuggled her. I carried her to the back yard and held her for a time. I let her rest on the picnic table while my boyfriend dug her grave. As the dirt covered her body, my partner sobbed, making guttural noises from some wild place. "With all the times I worried that she wouldn't make it through a bitterly cold night, I never imagined… Boots shouldn't have died like this," I said.

Days later, I planted yellow chrysanthemums on her grave. Watering the mums was a poor replacement for tending to her. Alone, I felt safe to let out my grief. It took the form of gratitude. Caring for her gave me purpose when I was so lost without my former life and not yet into my new one, and then again from health to battling cancer. "I am so grateful you trusted me enough to take care of you, Bootsie."

As I put away her feeding bowls and extra cushions, I considered donating her igloo to a rescue center but thought better of it. I decided to keep the igloo in place — just in case another kitty adopts me.

— Catherine Berresheim —

CAThartic Therapy

The cat does not offer services. The cat offers itself.
~William S. Burroughs

When my parents bought a rundown house, we had no idea it came with a bonus — a small litter of kittens that we discovered while mowing the back yard. Thankfully, they were unharmed, but only one dared to stick around and see what humans were all about. I named her Nykyta and was instantly hooked on this little black cat with white accents. She was borderline feral, but we became fast friends.

One summer day, I came home from work and discovered a wonderful gift. Nykyta had three kittens. One didn't survive, one disappeared, and one remained, a little gray fluffball whom I named Xena.

She started sleeping in the crook of my arm as soon as she could make the leap. She worked hard at it, making pathways over furniture and obstacles until she could make it in one leap. She slept there every night.

She was attentive and independent, and I swear she was mute. She never made a sound. It's unusual for a cat, but I guess she didn't have anything to say. She would greet me at the door when I came home, lie on my lap while I watched TV or read, and sit on my desk as though watching me work. She watched the words fly across the screen as I wrote a story or essay and would lie near my papers if I was doing homework. She even loved to help me check my e-mail, and I swear she loved working on dialogue scenes with me.

Then, ten years later, everything changed. I received a devastating diagnosis, and my life changed forever. It's amazing how a few simple words can do that. I had an arteriovenous malformation (AVM) and needed brain surgery. It was a terrifying and stressful time, but my ever-faithful companion took on a new role. She became my confidante and Kleenex as I cried myself to sleep most nights. It was the most emotional and physically challenging time in my whole life. She was my constant, my rock, and my self-imposed therapist; she never batted a whisker.

After the procedure, she changed her behaviors to accommodate the new normal for Mommy. After a decade of silence, she began to meow — only one meow at a time and so softly that it was barely audible. It served as a gentle reminder that I had forgotten to check her food or water bowls or clean the litterbox. Her behavior changed again when my seizures started, maintaining a position around my head, monitoring but out of harm's way. She would immediately curl up as close as possible when they subsided, with her head on my shoulder, purring softly until I recovered.

When strokes left me with chronic migraines and weakness, she again adjusted her behavior. The only time she didn't sleep in my arms was during those migraines. For these, she assumed a new position. She curled up on my pillow beside me and pressed her forehead against mine. It was a silent attempt to comfort Mommy, or maybe she was trying to take away the pain.

Three years later, she suffered her own stroke. My constant companion and portable purring tissue box now cried in pain. She could no longer reach the litterbox or aim properly. She vomited almost everything she ate, and her head permanently tilted to one side. I now faced the hardest decision I have ever made — even more challenging than brain surgery. Should I let her go?

"I don't know if I can do this," I cried to my dad. He wrapped his arms tightly around me, offering the only comfort he could. "I don't want to lose her."

My dad shared the pain. He was usually the one who saw our animals to their final rest. It is a job I don't envy and will never make him do alone again. "You have to do what you think is right," he offered. I think he was fighting tears himself, as his voice choked just the slightest.

As her mom and best friend, I had to put her needs first and now I miss her every day. I still see Xena when I close my eyes at night. She is there in my happy place, waiting for me to scoop her up, cuddle and get smothered with kisses as I used to do. She is her youthful self again, full of energy and playfulness, and I can't help but smile at the memories of our many years together.

If I knew then what I know now, would I change anything? I am asked this a lot when I share this story.

My answer is always a resounding, "Yes, absolutely. If I had known how well she would treat my migraines, I would've named her Excedrin."

— Angela Celeste Atkinson —

95

Who Rescued Whom?

There is no such thing as "just a cat."
~Robert A. Heinlein

The day my life changed started like any other during the decade I'd been fighting anorexia. I'd stayed up most of the night before, very slowly eating something, prolonging the time I got to eat. At that time, to me, food was love. It took me six hours to eat a sandwich. When I finished eating, I was always filled with sadness and loneliness.

But that day I came home from grocery shopping to find a four-pound, silver tabby kitten hiding under the deck by my front door. He seemed so tiny and so overwhelmed by his surroundings.

We sized each other up. There was a connection that I couldn't define right away. But the cat and I saw something in each other. He seemed just as starved for love as I was. He demanded I stop and pet him.

I named him Bear because he wrapped his paws around my wrist and moved my hand to his belly to be rubbed — just like a bear hug. Here was this tiny, homeless, hungry, and scared kitten, and all he wanted from me was ear and belly rubs?

I trusted my heart for the first time. From that day on, I began to recover from anorexia. Recovery wasn't a straight line — it required treatment three more times. But with Bear's steady love, and the peace that came from living with him, I eventually got better.

Day in and day out, Bear made me smile — usually when I needed it most. His ridiculous antics made me laugh and admire the little guy with the ginormous attitude. Bear was confident and lived with his whole heart. I thought that one day I might be that bold, too.

Bear changed everything for me. He taught me to accept love and to realize that I could be happy. I could feel safe. I could finally determine who I was and what I wanted in my life without interference or judgment. Other than expecting my love, Bear had no expectations, didn't judge, and didn't hurt or betray me. When I cried, he never complained about my tears wetting his fur. When I had nightmares, he sat on my back until I became grounded in reality. When I felt unsettled in my body, he acted no differently toward me. He loved me whether I weighed seventy pounds or a hundred and seventy pounds.

Bear increased my self-esteem enough that I overcame my eating disorder. And while it took several years, he was the seed that launched my recovery, and I never looked back.

My life didn't change in a moment — or even a year. It was an everyday decision to do the hard thing — motivated by Bear to do better for us both and step outside my comfort zone. I healed by persevering when things got difficult, giving it my all, and remembering who I was on the day Bear and I met and what he meant to me over the years. Loving Bear made me a better person — a more loving and understanding person, someone I am proud to be.

Bear taught me that love has the power to truly change everything. And our love did change everything — not only for a tiny, homeless kitten but also for the human who opened her heart to him. Life is funny in that we often get exactly what we need when we need it.

— Katherine E. Kern —

96

A Cat Named Cake

There is something about the presence of a cat... that
seems to take the bite out of being alone.
~Louis J. Camuti

I often joke with people that I have all five Love Languages. But the reality is that I have a three-way tie for first place: receiving gifts, quality time, and physical touch. As you can imagine, Covid and the lockdown have drastically affected me in that area because there is no touch or quality time when you live alone. And the lack of having my needs met in that way affected me so much that, on a Friday night in March, I logged onto Google and typed, "How much prescription medication do I have to take to end my life?" and "Will it hurt if I overdose on medication?" Thankfully, when you have queries like this on Google, this automatically pops up: "You're not alone. Text this number. Call the National Suicide Hotline." And, well, clearly I'm here and I just ended up crying myself to sleep that night.

A few weeks prior to my unfortunate Google search, I had applied and been approved to be a foster pet parent. So, the morning after my disastrous night, I woke up and went to the shelter, and they gave me a foster cat!

The only thing I really knew about cats was that they are very solitary beings, they don't like affection, and they think they're better than any other human on the planet. At least that was what I thought.

The cat they gave me was named Patty Cake, which I believed

was a terrible name — way too many syllables for a pet! So, I shortened her name to Cake. Cake the cat. I brought her home, and showed her the litterbox, scratching pad, and food area. I sat down on the couch, expecting her to go hide somewhere, but she jumped in my lap. Imagine my surprise! This tiny creature that I wasn't even sure I wanted to foster, that I fully expected to ignore me and tear up my furniture, just wanted to cuddle. She'd lie on my lap and shoulder, purr and sleep.

I don't know how to adequately explain what it feels like when you are not having your needs met. The desperation. The grief. The emptiness of not being touched. Bereft. Desolate.

I also don't know how to describe what it feels like when you get that first warm body that touches you after weeks of nothingness. Joy, perhaps. Hope.

Suffice to say, it was exactly what I needed, and Cake and I went on to have many adventures! I trained her like a dog because that was all I knew. I taught her to come when her name was called, sit, get up and other simple commands. I now have scratches on my furniture in places that weren't there before, but we're just going to say it gives my couch character.

About a month into fostering Cake, I got a call from the pet shelter, and they told me they had a forever home for Cake. My initial thought was dread. I wasn't ready. What if my emotions and thoughts began to tumble into dark spaces again?

I gave it a second thought and realized that, in that specific moment in time, I needed warmth, care and touch. And Cake provided that for me. Cake needed a warm and loving home away from a scary and loud shelter while her forever home was being finalized, and I provided that for Cake. And so, while I'm sad she's gone, I'm happy she's with an amazing forever family. I can now say that the best roommate and grief counselor I've ever had in my life was a cat named Cake.

— Courtney Tierra —

97

How My Cat Changed My Life

If purring could be encapsulated, it'd be the most
powerful anti-depressant on the
pharmaceutical market.
~Alexis F. Hope

You know how when you're a kid, you just beg and beg your parents for a pet? That's what I did. From the time I was seven years old, I begged my parents for a dog. Any kind of dog — it didn't matter. I was an only child and wanted a companion. My parents grew up with pets but didn't feel they had the time or attention to devote to a puppy. Occasionally, they'd consider it a little bit, and we'd go to The Humane Society to donate some old blankets and look at pups. But they never found one they thought would fit into our little family, and we always left without a new friend. Eventually, I gave up asking and grew up with a few goldfish and a lot of stuffed animals.

Fast forward to my college years. Living in a dorm was not something I enjoyed. I've always been an introvert, never really enjoyed parties, and I found myself in therapy to work through my anxiety. I tried yoga, meditation, medication, and more, but nothing seemed to help much. I went home from school on weekends to see my friends and work my job, but I wasn't happy.

During a therapy session one day in early summer after my

sophomore year, my therapist looked at me and said, "Have you ever considered getting a pet?"

"I always wanted a dog as a kid, but my parents always said no," I responded.

"What would your parents think about a cat? I really think having a pet would benefit you," she said.

I'd never really thought about having a cat before. I had some friends with cats, but I'd never considered having one of my own. I'd always found them to be a little aloof. But I went home that day and asked my parents what they thought about getting a cat. Since nothing else seemed to be helping me through my anxiety, they agreed to look, but only if we found the right fit for our family.

That weekend, we went to a shelter and I looked at their cats. I didn't know what I was looking for, but you know what they say: You don't choose a cat; a cat chooses you. And that's exactly what happened. I looked at a few kennels in the shelter, trying to see if one had a cat I liked. One had two small kittens who were very intrigued by my dad's jingly keys. They seemed very entertaining and energetic, but didn't really seem interested in me. The next kennel had a larger white cat with one eye. She refused to come forward to us and watched from afar.

In the final kennel was a little gray tabby, eight months old. The shelter staff said she was shy, but she stared right into my eyes and stood on her hind legs to watch my mom and me whenever we walked away from her kennel. I opened her door and picked up a toy to play with her, but she didn't care about the toy at all. She just kept jumping up against my leg and staring at me with huge, loving eyes.

I pointed her out to my parents, and she seemed to have the same effect on them that she had on me. Her golden eyes stared right into our souls, begging us to take her home. Finally, at the age of twenty, I found myself holding a cat carrier while my dad paid the adoption fee and signed some papers. Her name was Lucy, and she was now ours.

Because we hadn't expected to take home a cat that day, we stopped at a pet store on our way home. My mom stayed in the car with Lucy while my dad and I ran into the store. We quickly picked out a litterbox, litter, food, a bed, bowls, a scratching post, a collar, and toys.

I even picked out a little purple tag shaped like a heart and had her name engraved on the front and our information on the back. Seeing her name engraved on that little heart made it feel even more real.

When we got Lucy home, her adjustment took a little time. We quickly figured out which toys she liked and didn't like, and she explored the house very carefully. But the first night that she crawled into my lap on the couch and started purring was the night I knew we had made the right decision. This cat was going to become my best friend. Taking care of her helped me to take care of myself, whether I knew it at the time or not.

Lucy is now six years old and has done her job as an emotional-support cat very well. She's queen of the castle at my parents' house, and they love and spoil her like another child. She spends most of her days curled up by the side of one of her humans, purring and soaking in the love and affection. Since adopting her, I've graduated college, found a job, and moved to an apartment. Lucy, although technically *my* cat, was so comfortable in my parents' home, and my parents had grown so fond of her, that we decided to let her stay where she is most comfortable. I have now adopted a young, affectionate and energetic kitten named Colby Jack, while Lucy enjoys her days reigning over my parents' home.

Lucy changed my life for the better, whether she knows it or not. I don't know what my life would have been like without her.

— Katie Wagner —

98

The Cat Nobody Wanted

Beauty is not in the face; beauty is a light in the heart.
~Kahlil Gibran

Could a cat save me? It seemed unlikely. I thought of the vet bills and the cost of pet sitters and all the cat necessities. Still, loneliness was threatening to devour me. I was closing in on seventy, and my two best friends had passed away. I figured my only hope for companionship might be a cat, so I made the trip to The Humane Society.

Once there, I slowly scanned the cages. One cage held two cats. That cage was the same size as the others that held only a single cat. I was told the cats were a bonded pair and must be adopted together. The bigger cat's appearance was riveting. The markings on her face looked like permanent eyeliner was traced around her already beautiful eyes.

I guessed they must have come in that morning, but I was told they had been there for three months. Three months in one cage together? Really! I thought they would have been snapped up by the first adopter.

Then, I noticed that the smaller cat moved a bit awkwardly. "Is she sick?" I asked. No, I was assured. She was born that way. Her mother probably had distemper. Her sister was protected by the placental barrier, but she wasn't. She was expected to live a full life, though.

I looked more carefully at the smaller cat. Her fur stuck out in all directions, and her little face had an almost cranky expression. She made jerky, almost convulsive movements, while her sister seemed to float gracefully even in the confines of the small cage. The smaller cat looked broken beside her sister's perfection, and my heart went out to her.

I have always been a sucker for anyone with a lot to overcome. My tutoring business was full of courageous, special-ed kids whom I adored. When it came to deciding whether to adopt these cats, the answer seemed obvious.

"I want these ones!" I announced.

"Are you sure?" asked the worker.

"Yes, I'm absolutely sure!" I exclaimed.

We loaded them into the carrier for the trip home. On the way, I decided to name the disabled cat Jazz and her more perfect sister Jessie.

The next day, a neighbor came over to check out my new companions. She looked dubiously at Jazz and inquired, "Did you know she was like that when you adopted her?"

"Yes," I replied. "I was told she would improve a bit with time."

"Yeah, sure," my neighbor huffed and left shortly thereafter.

The first weeks marked a period of adjustment. If I tried to pick up Jessie and cuddle with her, she fought to get away. I could pick up Jazz, but she would often leave at the first opportunity.

At playtime, though, Jessie, the healthier cat, responded enthusiastically, jumping and flipping agilely after the toys dangling on strings. Jazz, while enthusiastic, sometimes seemed to play with the shadow of the toy. If Jazz was chasing something, she often couldn't stop in time and collided with the furniture. When I mentioned this on a vet visit, I was told she would learn. Not a fan of painful learning, I purchased enough pillows to completely encircle the room we played in. Jazz still couldn't stop herself at will, but now her little face would plop into a pillow, and her tiny bottom would go up. At least it was a soft landing.

Time went on, and Jazz's mobility improved markedly. Soon, she could hop up on the bed instead of just slamming into the side of it. She also figured out that running flat-out chasing toys was better replaced by attacking them fiercely when they came flying over to the place where she was sitting. She began to crave cuddles, and the sour expression on her face gave way to a look of fascination with everything in her environment. Grooming by me and her slightly bigger sister made Jazz's fur silky to the touch. Jazz became relaxed and transformed into a gorgeous kitty.

The fur babies definitely lifted my mood, but sometimes I still got stuck in deep depression. During these times, it felt like I had been swallowed into a dark place where hope was nonexistent. Then, one day, when I was feeling especially down, I noticed an unusual movement out of the corner of my eye. I turned and saw Jazz, with all her mobility problems, trying to climb up the post into the window seat I had made for them. I knew that the chances of Jazz making it to the top were slim. In some ways, Jazz and I seemed permanently stuck and unable to surmount the last barriers holding us down.

I watched unhappily as little Jazz kicked and struggled up the post. I kept telling myself to get up and rescue her, but with the weight of my depression, I felt as if I was welded to my chair. When Jazz got near the top, to my absolute amazement, she became fiercer than ever and kicked and fought her way onto the platform. Then, she settled down comfortably to enjoy the view of the city spread out beneath her.

Suddenly, I realized that a lot of my beliefs about the things I had always designated as "just reality" might not be true at all. Of course, I had read about "limiting beliefs," but how they could really play out had eluded me until that moment.

Now, I was inspired to make a number of changes in my life. I exchanged my big, clunky computer for a laptop and moved my workspace from the inside of my cupboard office to a self-built desk/table that I placed by the window so I had a view of the city and the lake. I sought out therapy and began working hard on myself.

Today, Jazz still has a bit of an awkward walk, and I still have moments of sadness. Jessie will cuddle on her terms only. For the most part, though, we are content.

Every morning when I awaken, it is not long before I feel a small plop at the end of my bed and little feet moving up toward my face. Jazz then snuggles close, purring a cheery good morning. Each time she greets me this way, I feel my whole body relax, and I sink into a deeply peaceful state. Against all my gloomy predictions about how things could only get worse, a small and once-ugly Jazz, the cat nobody wanted, gave me the love and example I needed to help me reinvent my life for the better.

—Jodi Anne Joyce—

99

Comfort from a Kitten

When a cat chooses to be friendly,
it's a big deal because a cat is picky.
~Mike Deupree

The days following the unexpected death of our six-year-old Great Dane, Thor, were quiet and sad. We all felt his absence, including his mom, Simi. Thor had been one of a litter of fifteen (yes, fifteen!) Great Dane puppies delivered in our garage on a Sunday afternoon. He was a goofy, clumsy, loveable dog who grew up with our children and brought us joy and laughter. We wanted to be sure that we showed Simi extra attention and love as we grieved, with hopes that we could help her through the pain of the loss of her son, playmate and friend. We noted that she was sleeping more and eating less, although she was still engaging with her humans and enjoying the increased cuddles and treats offered to her.

About two weeks later, my husband noticed cat prints on his car before leaving for work. Few animals are brave enough to enter a fenced yard with a Great Dane, but Simi had been spending more time indoors, so that offered a possible explanation. We didn't think anymore about the evidence of a cat until the next evening.

While tinkering in the garage, my husband heard a "meow" from nearby and soon felt a rubbing against his leg. Imagine his surprise to spot a brown tabby kitten at his feet, meowing and purring as she leaned against him. This was the first sign that this little kitten was special since my husband is not a "cat person." He called for me to come to the garage, and I was surprised to see the little one. The kitten purred as I lifted her and determined that it was a little girl. She was a brown tabby and looked like the cat version of Simi, who is a brindle Great Dane.

I went inside and returned with milk and cold cuts for her as I wondered what we would do for this little kitten. I snapped a picture of her to check with the neighbors to see if she was simply lost, but no one claimed her or offered to adopt her. Where had she come from? Kittens don't just appear from thin air. With her little belly full, she began exploring the garage and the people in it. She was comfortable around people, leading us to believe she'd once had a human family. Had they put her out on our little dirt road? Did she wander away from a neighboring area? Was she underneath a car that was passing through and dropped when it became heated? What would we do about Simi? We agreed that we'd see if the kitten stayed overnight and determine our next steps in the morning.

The next morning, our little kitten was meowing for breakfast on the front porch. Simi perked her ears and turned her head as if to say, "What is that?" We devised a plan for my husband to walk the kitten down the driveway near the gate so she'd have an escape route if needed. Meanwhile, I led Simi outside and down the driveway for the two to meet. Admittedly, we didn't have high expectations for this encounter. As Simi caught sight of the kitten, she crept toward it, tail wagging and head tilted to the right with her ears up. The kitten bristled and held her ground but showed no fear. To our amazement, the two continued to examine one another inquisitively and began moving back toward the house. It was another sign to us that this was a special kitten.

The two continued to slowly become acquainted throughout the day, growing increasingly more comfortable with one another and sharing spaces. This was, by far, the most active Simi had been since Thor's death. Whether it was the similarity of their appearance or simply having another fur baby, Simi was once again wagging her tail and happy to be outdoors. She had a new buddy, and while she couldn't wrestle and play with this one as she'd done with Thor, she quickly became smitten with her new friend.

The following day, we agreed that this little visitor was having a positive effect on Simi and us. We scheduled a veterinary appointment to have her examined and spayed. Now, what to name this brave kitten who had appeared unexpectedly and brought us all comfort and laughter after some dark days? As we tossed around names, we kept thinking back to Thor and how much this kitten reminded us of his bravery and affection for Simi. Could this kitten have been sent to us to help with our grief? Do those things really happen?

We may never know how that adorable kitten came to us, but now we can't remember life without her. However it happened, and wherever she came from, we are thankful for our Sunshine and how she brought our family comfort and light.

— Laura Vertin —

100

Robot Cats

Dementia care — it's not rocket science;
it's heart science.
~Gail Weatherill, RN

L et me begin by saying that I have never been a cat person. To be quite honest, cats always intimidated me. They seemed so sultry, sleek, and mysterious. They reminded me of fast girls in high school. Secretly, I longed to be in that elite club, but with my awkward gait and innate gawkiness, I was certainly not in their elite league! I felt more at home with an overgrown puppy — somewhat awkward, a bit slobbery, and always tripping over its own feet.

That is why I was so astounded when I began working with patients afflicted with dementia and discovered that cats — yes, cats, with their mysterious, sophisticated mannerisms and pretenses — often provided the best solace and comfort available.

For nearly a decade, I worked in a continuing-care retirement community that had a unit dedicated to those suffering from Alzheimer's, memory loss, and other types of dementia. In addition to private bedrooms with full baths, this twenty-bed memory-care unit also housed an elegant dining area, shared activity rooms, living rooms, and fenced outdoor gardens. At the end of each corridor was a Snoezelen room. This quiet area was dimmed with soft lighting, equipped with continuous sounds of nature like babbling brooks or chirping birds, and contained tables of soft, scented items to hold, like felt-covered, weighted bean bags or small pillows filled with lavender.

If a resident became agitated, combative, or overwhelmed, it sometimes helped if they were brought to the Snoezelen room to calm down. In most cases, handling these memory challenges in a holistic manner by providing a calming environment was preferable to resorting to medications. And I can attest that, at least half the time, the Snoezelen room had a positive outcome, particularly during that difficult time around 4:30 P.M. when the sun began to set.

To those not familiar with the term "sundowning" in regard to those suffering from dementia, it refers to a state of confusion occurring in the late afternoon and can last into the nighttime hours. Sundowning can result in behaviors such as increased confusion, anxiety, aggression, pacing and wandering. Sometimes, a calming atmosphere, like that provided in the Snoezelen room, can alleviate some of these symptoms.

Of course, not every resident responded well to "snoezeling." I distinctly remember one late afternoon when a granddaughter came to visit. She brought her newborn baby to the memory-care unit to introduce the infant to its great-grandmother. That first encounter did not go well as both the baby and the great-grandma became agitated. When both members of the family began crying, the stroller and wheelchair were rolled into the Snoezelen room. After twenty minutes, only the baby calmed down. The great-grandmother continued to cry, much to the disappointment of the granddaughter.

That occurrence fired up the clinical team. What other interventions could be put in place to mitigate some of the emotional distresses of those suffering from dementia?

And that quest marked the beginning of when I began to change my perception of cats.

For quite some time, I witnessed firsthand the therapeutic benefits of pet therapy. Every Wednesday, several certified dogs, along with their handlers, would visit our residents with the goals of providing entertainment, offering comfort, and relieving boredom. Those visits were certainly the high point of Wednesday afternoons, and if no one was agitated or sundowning, everyone enjoyed those visits.

Then, one day, a certified dementia practitioner overseeing our community presented a challenge. Could the benefits of pet therapy be expanded to address the needs of an agitated patient, perhaps even more than a typical Snoezelen room? And, if so, how could we make that happen?

Fortunately for us, as well as for so many other communities working with patients with dementia, some of the groundwork had already been laid. Yes, pet therapy was beneficial, but due to the fact that many of these patients became extremely agitated, this technique needed one vital tweak. Rather than using live animals, patients were given robotic companions, which were just as furry, cuddly, and responsive as the live ones. And these robotic animals were amazing. They looked, felt, sounded, acted, and even moved like their real-life counterparts.

When our first "litter" of robotic animals arrived, our staff went wild over the adorable puppies. However, not surprising to feline lovers everywhere, it was the robotic cats — not the dogs, rabbits, kittens, or even puppies — that were the most successful when it came to working with our patients.

That said, I don't mean to criticize the other robotic pets as they were all beautiful, sweet, and lifelike. But there was something very special about the cats. That first "litter" was comprised of three cats: an orange tabby, a black-and-white tuxedo, and a silver with white mitts. All of them were equipped with a "vibrapurr," that sounded and felt like a real cat when held. Each cat opened and closed its eyes, raised its paw, opened its mouth, and moved its head and body in that same sophisticated manner as a real cat. And all of them responded to motion when petted and touched.

I distinctly remember the day when the cats arrived. Our administrator had taken the tabby, inserted the batteries, and placed it on a countertop during our morning staff meeting. As we were reviewing the upcoming daily activities, the cat seemed to listen, nod its head, wave its paw, and then let out appropriate purrs during the thirty-minute session. My colleagues and I were astounded. It was as if the cat were actually participating in our meeting. But the real test was about to unfold. How would our patients react to "Tabby"?

As fate would have it, we didn't have to wait long to find out. By lunchtime, one of the gentlemen was having a difficult time — agitated, angry, and upset — and the Snoezelen room was not working. I was elected to give Tabby a try.

I remember entering the room, gently holding the cat, and petting it while I carefully set it down on a cushioned chair next to the wheelchair. Speaking softly, I said, "Looks like you have a visitor." And, right on cue, the cat moved its head, blinked its eyes, and raised a paw. I don't think the patient registered my voice at all, but he became fixated on the cat. Immediately, he quieted down, rolled his wheelchair toward the cat, and stroked its fur. The cat responded with a vibrapurr, and the patient actually smiled.

Over the next few months, I witnessed that same scenario as it was repeated many times. As I mentioned previously, the robotic dogs, puppies, and rabbits sometimes soothed the agitation, but the cats really worked wonders. Why? I really don't know.

Maybe it was their allure, their mystery, their self-sufficiency? Maybe it was that they seem to be so self-contained in their own world that they could somehow recognize another world of confusion and anxiety, break through that wall, and bring solace, calm, and even smiles?

Then again, maybe the reasons don't matter at all.

— Barbara Davey —

Wildest Cat?

> *As anyone who has ever been around a cat for any*
> *length of time well knows cats have enormous*
> *patience with the limitations of the human kind.*
> ~Cleveland Amory

Yikes! My cat had turned into a wild thing. In just a week or so, my calm, sweet, affectionate, longhaired Rusty had morphed into the attack cat of the century!

It was not what I needed at all! Wasn't the rest of my life in enough chaos? Changes at work. Changes in relationships. Changes in every nook and cranny of my days. I already felt as if my entire world was on its way to hell in a handbasket.

Nothing calmed my cat down either. He ran and leaped and dove in every direction. He howled and whined and hissed. He broke every single rule we had ever had to keep peace in the home we shared. He'd turned into a cat I'd never met before!

I could not get through to him. Not by coaxing or whispering. Not by threats or scoldings. Not even by promises of dire consequences like, "If you don't behave, I will go into a rehab facility where they don't allow cats, so goodbye to canned tuna and catnip mice (a special favorite)."

Finally, I took Rusty to the vet. After lots of poking and prodding, unhelpful, sympathetic, squeaky noises (from the vet) and endless kitty treats, the vet shook his head. "Nothing," he told me with a cheerful grin. "Not a thing wrong with him. He's doing great."

"No," I argued with my fiercest glower, "he's not great. He's absolutely awful." I almost burst into tears.

Vet did his very best "poor kitty" sympathetic nod and "sweet kitty" noises.

Then the vet asked the most insightful question that anyone had ever asked me — at least, anytime recently. He asked the wisest question that anyone had thought to ask me in decades. He asked the question that turned our lives around — Rusty's and mine.

"So," said my cat's kindhearted vet, "how has your life been going lately?"

Shock shot through me from the tip of my toes to the way-too-wild and frizzy ends of my hair.

"Me?" I gasped. I stared at him, essentially speechless, tempted to burst into tears and throw myself into his cat-cradling arms.

I managed a relatively coherent response.

"Not so good," I admitted, while a rebellious, inner voice supplied a list of options. *I'm terrible, wretched, miserable, in chaos, desperate, dreadful...* The list went on and on in my head.

The kindly cat doctor nodded and replied, "Just what I suspected. Often, the human-to-cat bond is so powerful that a perfectly healthy cat will act out in response to his human's emotional stresses."

I nodded along, thinking, "Yes, yes, yes, yes, yes!"

Our doctor had nailed it exactly. I was going through a truly and deeply terrible time in my life, and Rusty was right there with me. We shared such a close bond that my emotional chaos had overflowed onto my cat's otherwise normal and contented life. We were sharing my misery.

I resisted the impulse to throw my arms around this wonderful cat doctor and instead listened carefully to his instructions.

He wrote out a sort of prescription for us. For me, it was a list of good people therapists. For my cat, he made a list of kitty encouragements and affirmations.

"Do your best," our doctor told us both, "to be calm, patient and kind. Once you're doing better" (this to me), "then Rusty will do better, too. His behavior issues reflect your own anxieties."

He gave us smiles and pats on the back. Rusty got another cat treat, too, but I did not.

We both left feeling much better, my Rusty and me.

That day turned us around. I got some good, professional therapy for my super stressors. Rusty got a kinder, gentler me with more ear scratches and throat rubs.

As therapy eased my stresses and anxieties, Rusty and I both got back to our better selves, thanks to a vet who understood much about that amazing and wondrous bond between humans and the animals they love. He was an expert at understanding deep, personal cat relationships and how the cats we love can reflect our fears and struggles.

— Karen M. Leet —

Meet Our Contributors

Kristi Adams loves sharing the humorous side of military life, including traveling the world with her Air Force husband of sixteen years and a very willful cat named Tiki. This is Tiki's third appearance in the *Chicken Soup for the Soul* series, and Kristi's fifteenth story in the series. Learn more at www.kristiadamsmedia.com.

Angela Celeste Atkinson lives in the state of Washington. She has multiple furbabies and loves mochas, peanut butter, and chocolate. She is currently working on a romance trilogy and a mystery novel.

Anita Aurit is an award-winning blogger and writer. She has written three books in the *Feline Opine* series and is finishing her first cozy mystery featuring her cats. Anita has diplomas in cat behavior and pet bereavement counseling. She continues to learn life lessons from her three feline muses, Alberto, Oliver, and Lily.

Dave Bachmann is a retired teacher who taught English to special needs students in Arizona for thirty-nine years. He now lives and writes in California with his wife Jay, a retired elementary teacher, along with their fifteen-year-old Lab, Scout.

Zoa Ann Beasley lives on Maryland's Eastern Shore. After a career in banking, and later as a child-support enforcement officer, she enjoys traveling with her husband. When her dear Snickers died of old age, Zoa Ann eventually rescued Misty, a beautiful Angora kitty, named for all the tears Zoa Ann cried when Snickers was missing.

Krista Behr lives in the rural foothills of upstate New York's Adirondack Mountains with her family, four-legged friends, and about a bazillion plants. A full-time writer, Krista runs a gardening website of articles and advice on gardening for northern zones at yankeedirt.com.

Catherine Berresheim earned her MFA in creative nonfiction from Spalding University's Naslund-Mann Graduate School of Writing in November 2013. She has three adult children and teaches English for a community college in the Nashville, TN area. Her true passion is leading workshops on writing as a way of healing.

Sandy Kelly Bexon has worked as a journalist and communications strategist in Alberta for over twenty-five years. She is a widely published freelance writer and author of two books. She lives with her daughter and a motley crew of rescue animals, including a tiny cat with a huge personality!

Wife of a USMC "Knight in Shining Armor," and DiL to his super-centurion mom (the other Mrs. Bingham in their PA country house), **Diane S. Bingham** loves being grandma to nine enchanting children, and two great-grands. She dabbles in genealogy, and animal rescue with all thirty-six inches and thirty pounds of Gentleman Jake being her last "rescupade."

Jason Blume, a songwriter with fifty million album sales, has photographed 2,500 cats for the Kauai Humane Society and fostered forty neonatal kittens. Billboard Books published his three songwriting books and he is working on a book about lessons learned from rescued cats. Visit jasonblume.com for weekly cat photos and stories.

Deborah J. Bollinger loves cats and gardening and, as an accomplished watercolorist, uses paint in place of print. This, her first story in the *Chicken Soup for the Soul* series, was shared with and ghostwritten by Capi Cloud Cohen.

Carolyn Bolz was born and raised in Southern California. She earned her bachelor's degree (with a major in Spanish) and a bilingual teaching credential from the University of California, Riverside. For many years, she taught in the public schools. During her spare time, Carolyn enjoys spoiling her nieces and nephews.

Skyler Burns-Cranfield is a young wife and mother to three boys. She graduated in 2009 from McMinn County High School in the small town of Athens, TN. She and her husband have a small family-owned flooring business there and she enjoys writing on the side. This is her first published story, but she hopes many more will follow.

Kait Carson is the nationally published author of cozy and traditional mysteries. Learn more at www.kaitcarson.com.

Hannah Castelli is a freelance writer from Wollongong, Australia. She enjoys getting out and exploring the world around her. For Hannah, the best part about experiencing life is documenting it afterwards and sharing it with readers both locally and all over the globe.

Tilly Clark works as a veterinary nurse and officially designated cat advocate at a sizable pet clinic just outside Oslo, Norway. She spends her free time writing, watching movies from the 1930s, and playing the ukulele for her elderly cat Linni and a ball python named Nero.

Annette M. Clayton is a writer of children's literature and an environmental activist. When she's not clicking away on her keyboard you can find her drinking lattes, hiking, or at her twins' soccer game. Learn more at www.annettemclayton.com or on Twitter @AnnetteMClayton.

Leslie Colburn is a mom, an educator, and the author of three children's books. She writes parenting articles and material that encourages those in the waves of grief. Leslie visits Christian schools, churches, and conferences, teaching kids that they are created on purpose for a purpose. Learn more at www.lesliecolburn.com.

Cory Conner graduated from McNeese State University with a degree in business administration. He has had a lifelong interest in history that led him to the hobby of creative writing. He is currently working on a historical fiction novel, but his favorite hobby is spending time with his wife and two children.

Gillian A. Corsiatto is a cat lover and Canadian author. She has one published book and various excerpts from her work published in magazines. She has future plans for a sequel to her book, *Duck Light*.

Sherri Daley has established herself as someone who will write about anything, from new cancer treatments to the lives of Broadway stagehands, tuning up your oil burner, that new car smell, or Joshua Bell's violin. She's author of *High Cotton*, an account of the life and death of Philip Hehmeyer, who committed suicide in 1982.

Barbara Davey is a frequent contributor to the *Chicken Soup for the Soul* series, having had her first story "A Legacy in a Soup Pot" published in 1998. She is a graduate of Seton Hall University. Recently retired, she and her husband, Ron Becker, live in Verona, NJ.

Denise Del Bianco is a retired widow living with her son and daughter-in-law in Aviano, Italy, after travelling the world with the love of her life, Pietro. After meeting in France, he and Denise raised two children in Italy and Canada. She enjoys cooking, reading, and cuddling her furry grandkids. Follow her on Twitter @DeniseBecht1.

Mary DeVries has lived on three continents, in four countries, fifteen cities, and seven U.S. states. Along the way she has raised three children and remained married to the handsome guy she met at college freshman registration. She loves to write about anything and everything. E-mail her at marydj03@gmail.com.

Eileen Joyce Donovan's debut historical novel, *Promises*, won the Marie M. Irvine award for Literary Excellence and her historical novel, *A Lady Newspaperman's Dilemma*, won the When Words Count national competition. *The Campbell Sisters* has a 2023 release date. Eileen is currently living in New York City.

TaraMarie Dorsett is an animal behaviorist. Her life is full of happy, crazy, funny, and sometimes heartbreaking stories of the animals she works with. E-mail her at taramarie611@gmail.com.

Erin Downey started her career in radio, writing commercial copy and as an on-air personality. She later worked in tourism marketing, writing; she edited travel magazines promoting Northern Ontario throughout North America. She and her husband Glenn are lifelong cat lovers.

Maggie Downs is the author of the memoir, *Braver Than You Think: Around the World on the Trip of My (Mother's) Lifetime*. As a travel writer focused on meaningful adventure, her work has appeared in *The New York Times*, *The Washington Post*, *Travel + Leisure*, *Afar*, and others. She lives in Palm Springs, CA.

Gina du Bois, formerly of Santa Cruz, CA, lives with her husband in the Sierra foothills. Having a background in Egyptology, she works as an Egyptological editor. The memory of four special cats has inspired her first book, *Tiki, the Kitty Queen*, dedicated to the tabby-calico who showed up in the driveway and turned her life upside down.

Judith Eassa's writing endeavors began with "Writing Your Life

Story," an adult ed. session by author Cynthia F. Reynolds. Now retired, when not on her pontoon boat, gardening, birdwatching, or making memories with family, Eassa writes at her rural home on a lake in southeast Michigan. Her memoirs and a novel are current projects.

Stephanie Escobar is the author of *A Song Beyond Walls*. She resides in the Pacific Northwest with her husband and daughter where she enjoys rainy-dark days tucked away with a book, a hot cup of coffee, and a cat purring on her lap. Learn more at sescobarauthor.com.

Lindsey Esplin is a big fan of long walks through half sleepy cities and mossy forests. She has lived a little bit all over, most recently keeping company with the local cats in Scotland.

Karen Fayeth was born with the eye of a writer and the heart of a storyteller. Her work is heavily influenced by her New Mexico roots and continues to evolve in an urban setting. Karen has won awards for her writing, photography, and art. Now living in the San Francisco Bay Area, she can be found online at karenfayeth.com.

Meg Fitzgerald received her Master of Education from Rutgers University in 1984 and her Master in Liberal Studies, with honors, in 1994. She taught middle school for thirty-three years in North Jersey and then opened a tutoring service. She has two daughters and three grandchildren. She enjoys reading, aerobics and family time.

H L Ford received her Bachelor of Arts, with honors, from Southwestern State College, Weatherford, OK. She is a veteran newspaper reporter, columnist, member of Faith Writers, and an award-winning author of a three-book YA adventure/thriller series now available on Amazon.

Carol Gaido-Schmidt is a graduate of Penn State University with a Bachelor of Science in Nursing and a Master's in Business Administration. She works as a nurse and is currently a full-time student. She is actively involved in TNR and caring for feral cats.

Robert Grayson, an award-winning former daily newspaper reporter, writes books for young adults. Among his books are one on animal actors and one on animals in the military. He also writes magazine articles on professional sports stars. He and his wife have a fervent passion for rescuing and helping kittens and cats.

Amanda Ann Gregory, LCPC, is a trauma psychotherapist, national speaker, and author. She's been published in *Psychology Today*, *Psychotherapy Networker*, and *Highlights* magazine. She lives in Chicago with her partner and her sassy black cat, Mr. Bojangles.

Judith Gussmann taught English as a Second Language. She started writing in her retirement years. Since then, she has also been active in promoting and facilitating dialog between people with differing world views. She has two grown children and one wonderful (of course), grandson.

Vickie Hano-Hawkins lives in Louisiana bayou country. Her poetry and short story appear in the anthology, *Southern Treasures*, published by the Creative Minds Writers Group of Ponchatoula, LA. She is a graduate of Southeastern Louisiana University. Vickie enjoys writing, creating art journals, gardening and loves cats.

Nancy Hoag was a young mother of three when she graduated *cum laude* from the University of Washington in Seattle. Today she's a grandmother, the wife of a Montana cowboy, and author of nearly 1,200 stories and columns plus four nonfiction inspirational books.

Jennie Ivey lives and writes in Tennessee and has contributed stories to dozens of books in the *Chicken Soup for the Soul* series. Visit her website at jennieivey.com or e-mail her at jennieivey@gmail.com.

Joyce Jacobo received her Master of Art degree in Literature & Writing Studies from Cal State San Marcos. She loves to make people smile, resides deep in the Southern California countryside, and maintains "The Literary Serenity Archives," a WordPress blog of feel-good tales.

Jeanie Jacobson writes to share hope, humor, and Godly encouragement. In addition to her book, *Fast Fixes for the Christian Pack-Rat*, she's been published in the *Chicken Soup for the Soul* series, *Guideposts*, *The Upper Room*, *Focus on the Family*, Inspiration.org, and various other compilations. Learn more at JeanieJacobson.com.

Jodi Anne Joyce lives in Toronto, Ontario with her precious feline. She received her Bachelor of Arts with distinction from York University in Toronto. Her teaching experiences dealt mainly with special education children, who are still close to her heart. When not writing she enjoys yoga, cycling, and kayaking.

Mary Christine Kane lives in Minneapolis where she fosters cats through Pet Haven of Minnesota. Mary's poetry has appeared in numerous journals and her chapbook, *Between the Stars Where You Are Lost*, was published by Finishing Line Press. Learn more at marychristinekane.com.

Andria Kennedy never ceases to find inspiration for her writing from her four cats and Greyhound. They ensure her life is anything but boring. Her essays have been published in *Electric Lit*, *The Doe*, and *HuffPost Personal*. She lives in Virginia with her husband (the biggest fan of her writing).

Catherine Kenwell lives in Barrie, Ontario and is a regular contributor to the *Chicken Soup for the Soul* series. She is a writer and qualified mediator and advocate for mental health and brain injury awareness. In 2020, she co-authored *Not Cancelled: Canadian Kindness in the Face of COVID-19*.

Katherine E. Kern is a Professional Member of the Cat Writers' Association and an award-winning writer/blogger. Kat's writing celebrates the power of the feline-human bond and the unique essences of life with cats. Read more about Bear and living abundantly with cats at MommaKatandHerBearCat.com.

Helen Krasner has traveled, been a helicopter instructor, and lived in a Buddhist community. She has written about her experiences in the many articles and books she has had published. She lives in England with her partner David and five cats. This is her sixth story published in the *Chicken Soup for the Soul* series.

Mandy Lawrence is a Christian speaker and award-winning author of two books, *Wisdom from Wilbur* and *Replay*, in addition to being a nurse for more than twenty years. She and her dog Wilbur live in Lexington, NC.

Shannon Leach lives in Tennessee and is the owner of A Repurposed Heart. Her inspirational stories and books about leadership, life, and loving people focus on encouraging others and reminding them they are not alone. She holds a bachelor's degree in social work and is the co-founder of the nonprofit The Fostered Gift.

Karen M. Leet loves to write and has been at it since she was ten years old. Her writing has appeared in numerous publications. She has two books published by The History Press: *Sarah's Courage* and a civil war nonfiction.

Lisa A. Listwa traded life as a high school educator for life as a writer and hasn't looked back. She loves martial arts, all things bookish, and is a passionate home chef. Lisa is mother to one glorious handful of a daughter, wife to the nicest guy on the planet, and a reluctant but devoted cat owner.

Alice Lowe started writing after retirement. Since then, her personal essays have been published in more than a hundred literary journals and twice cited in *Best American Essays*. She lives in San Diego, CA with her husband Don and fifteen-year-old cat, Dody. Learn more at aliceloweblogs.wordpress.com.

Melinda Richarz Lyons received her Bachelor of Arts in Journalism from the University of North Texas. Her articles have appeared in numerous publications. She has also authored five books and lives in Tyler, TX.

Australian born author **Grant Madden** immigrated to the United States in 2005 and resides in El Cajon, CA. Grant has had cover stories appear in *Sailing, Cat Sailor* and the *San Diego Reader*. This is Grant's seventh story published in the *Chicken Soup for the Soul* series. Learn more at www.grantmadden.com.

Morna Murphy Martell has written articles, essays, plays, musicals, and TV/film reviews. She was New York Bureau Chief and Broadway Critic for *The Hollywood Reporter*. She is now theater columnist for senior magazine *Not Born Yesterday*. Her books *Classics 4 Kids* and *Shakespeare in an Hour* are available on Amazon.

Kim Johnson McGuire graduated from the University of California, Santa Barbara with a bachelor's degree in literature. She lives on California's Central Coast with her two mischievous felines. E-mail her at kimmycat2@msn.com.

Lizbeth Meredith is an author, speaker, and coach located in Chattanooga, TN. Her first indie memoir became a Lifetime television movie titled *Stolen by Their Father*. Lizbeth spent nearly three decades serving crime survivors and offenders, and now enjoys a life more ordinary with her cats and grown daughters.

Joanna Michaels writes fiction and memoir. She has been published in *CafeLit*, *Bright Flash*, and *Fine Lines*. She is a graduate of the MFA program at Queens University of Charlotte and is a member of the Florida Writers Association. Joanna lives with her cat, Raven, in Bradenton, FL.

Nicole L.V. Mullis is a storyteller of all trades, holding a degree in journalism and an M.F.A. in creative writing. She is a published novelist, journalist, and essayist, as well as a produced playwright. Other creative roles include mother, teacher, and chocoholic.

Carol Murphy has an M.A. in Speech Pathology and is retired from her pediatric practice. She writes about the ways language colors life's experiences. Her first book, *Slits*, was published in 2017. She realizes that lives can go awry, or be set straight, simply by a precise word at a pivotal moment. Learn more at www.carolmurphy.org.

Jesse Neve is a wife and mother of four who are all FAR taller than she is. She lives in Minnetrista, MN with her husband, whoever is home, and their turtle. Jesse's life goal is to bring a little smile to everyone she passes. E-mail her at jessedavidneve@frontiernet.net.

Steve Patschke is a retired elementary school librarian. Steve has published three picture books entitled *Don't Look at It, Don't Touch It*, *The Spooky Book*, and *The Nutcracker and the Mouse King*. Learn more at Stevepatschke.com.

A native Georgian, **Andrea Peebles** is retired after a thirty-five-year career in the commercial insurance industry. She enjoys travel, reading, writing, and spending time with family. She has been published in various magazines and has been blessed to be a part of the Chicken Soup for the Soul family for the past fifteen years.

As a long-time contributor to the *Chicken Soup for the Soul* series, author and novelist **Perry P. Perkins** has had stories in more than twenty books. He currently lives in the Midwest with his wife, daughter, and too many dogs.

Shirley M. Phillips received her M.A. in science writing from Johns Hopkins University in 2017. She is a former airline pilot, simulator instructor on the Airbus A320, and a college professor. Shirley enjoys spending time with her two daughters, attempting to knit socks, and reading nonfiction.

Laura Plummer is an American writer from Massachusetts. Her work has appeared in numerous print and online publications. This is her second story to appear in the *Chicken Soup for the Soul* series. Learn more at lauraplummer.me.

Kevin Porter is an energy consultant based in Maryland. He enjoys listening to music and going to plays and concerts, traveling, spending time with his two adult daughters and being outdoors. He lives with his wife and yes, four cats, in Elkridge, MD.

Connie Kaseweter Pullen lives in rural Sandy, OR near her five children and several grandchildren. She earned a B.A. degree, with honors, at the University of Portland in 2006, with a double major in psychology and sociology. Connie enjoys writing, photography and exploring nature. E-mail her at MyGrandmaPullen@aol.com.

Judith Quan is a retired nurse and lifelong animal lover who is cofounder of an animal rescue group, Petite Paws Pet Advocates.

Donna L. Roberts is a native upstate New Yorker who lives and works in Europe. She is a university professor who holds a Ph.D. in Psychology. Donna is an animal and human rights advocate and when she is researching or writing she can be found at her computer buried in rescue pets.

Becki Robins is a science writer, teller of stupid jokes, and embarrasser of her four children. Occasionally, she can be serious. She lives in rural Northern California and prefers the company of chickens.

Margaret Rowan's stories have been published in *Adelaide Literary Magazine* and *Potato Soup Journal*. She was a production artist/proofreader for several newspapers. With her husband, she owns an antiques business. In her hunt for the antiquated, the characters encountered and places visited spark her creativity.

Linda Sabourin lives in western Arkansas. She is an Ebay seller, specializing in vintage items found at local estate auctions. She enjoys writing and enjoys it even more when one of her stories makes it into a *Chicken Soup for the Soul* book!

Judy Bailey Sennett earned her M.S. in counseling and human relations from Villanova University at age forty-seven. She was a school counselor for twenty-four years. Now retired, her writing is inspired by her reflections on an interesting and rewarding life. Judy lives in Pennsylvania among many friends, near her two sons and her grandchildren.

Jennifer Sizeland is a freelance writer and assistant producer with twelve years of experience in the media industry. She has written for many publications including the *BBC*, *Independent*, *Metro*, *Manchester Mill*, *Get Me Giddy*, *Funny Women*, the Media Diversity Institute, and her own sustainability blog called "Land of Size."

CK Steefel is a former actor, most notably on two episodes of *Seinfeld*. She has been a screenwriter for twenty years and is currently writing her first novel. CK has been a fan of the *Chicken Soup for the Soul* series since its inception and is honored to be a contributor. Her pride and joy are her grown twins and her hubby of thirty-one years.

David Tarpenning retired from teaching at the University of Oklahoma after twenty-one years in the classroom. He is currently preparing three volumes of short fiction — including historical fiction — for publication. When he isn't running on the local trails, he is in front of the computer, writing.

Courtney Tierra is an author, expert giggler, and a firm believer in a healing hug. She is passionate about embracing self-worth, has written a children's book, has been featured in a previous *Chicken Soup for the Soul* book, and is an award-winning storyteller. E-mail her at worthy@courtneytierra.com.

For nearly a decade, **Poppy Tillbury** has enjoyed her fair share of glamor and excitement as an entertainment lawyer in California. Following her marriage, she moved to Mauritius. If she's not devouring a book, she can be found drooling in front of recipes or teaching her cat, Duchess, to be less haughty.

Jayne Thurber-Smith is an international award-winning freelance writer for various outlets including *Faith & Friends* magazine, *Sports Spectrum* and writersweekly.com. She loves tennis, volleyball and swimming, and leading her grandchildren on pony rides.

Brian Trent is the award-winning author of the sci-fi thriller

Redspace Rising, and more than a hundred stories appearing in the world's top fiction markets, including in *The New York Times* bestseller *Black Tide Rising* series. Trent lives in Connecticut. Learn more at www.briantrent.com.

Sheila Valesano writes screenplays, poetry, and short stories. Her work has been recognized in Table Read My Screenplay, Inroads Screenwriting Fellowship, NYC Midnight and *Unlimited Literature*. She is active with Barrington Writers Workshop and Chicago Screenwriters. Sheila enjoys time with family, historic homes, and art.

Laura Vertin graduated *magna cum laude* from Georgia Southern University in 1998 and obtained her Master's in social work from East Carolina University in 2001. She is a licensed social worker and lives in Georgia with her husband, two children, two dogs and a cat.

Katie Wagner has been a cat lover since she adopted her first cat, Lucy. She has a Bachelor of Arts in graphic design and works as a graphic designer. She makes cat toys and other pet themed products in her spare time. They are available on her website colbycraftsshop.com — affectionately named after her kitten, Colby Jack.

Juliann Wetz lives near Cincinnati with her four favorite felines. When she's not providing them a lap, she is writing for magazines such as *Highlights for Children*, *Boys' Life*, *German Life*, *Cappers*, *Reading Today*, and others or, she's vacuuming the avalanche of fur in her house.

SE White lives and writes from Nevada where she wrangles a bearded guy who only comes in from the garage when it's time for meals, three tiny house destroyers who randomly and erratically request snacks instead of meals, and one cat who denies her very existence until it's time for the food.

Marcia J. Wick is a blind, gray-haired grandmother retired from a professional writing career. She now writes freelance. Her essays reflect on parenting, caregiving, living with a disability, and adventures with her guide dog. E-mail her at marciajwick@gmail.com.

Robin Howard Will lives in rural Pennsylvania with her husband of over forty years. She is the mother of two beautiful daughters, and Gigi to two sweet grandbabies. She loves writing, reading, crafting, and baking. She is currently writing an inspirational memoir and will soon unveil a personal positivity blog.

Barbara Woods enjoys the company of her children and grand-children, as well as her work with Special Ed students within her local school district. With a B.A. in communication, she teaches communication skills to others and continues to write. Learn more at www.redbirdcommunication.

Patti Woods is a freelance writer based in Connecticut. Her work has been featured in *The Boston Globe*, *Business Insider*, *Parade* and many more publications. She is the author of *Lost Restaurants of Fairfield* and is the owner of Sandy Hollow Tarot found at sandyhollowtarot.com.

Christy Wopat is the author of three books: the award-winning memoir, *Almost a Mother*, a picture book, *Always Ours*, and *After All: Pregnancy After Loss*. Her personal essays have been featured in several different publications. Christy is a fourth-grade teacher and lives with her husband and children in Holmen, WI.

Linda J. Wright has been involved in animal advocacy and activism for over thirty years. She is the founder of The Cat People, a cat rescue and rehabilitation nonprofit. An award-winning writer, she is also the author of the *Kieran Yeats* series of animal rescue novels. Learn more at lindajwright.com.

Jeanne Zornes, from the state of Washington, is an eight-time contributor to the *Chicken Soup for the Soul* series. She has an M.A. from Wheaton College and has written seven inspirational books and hundreds of articles and short stories. Mom of two, grandma of four, she posts at jeannezornes.blogspot.com.

Meet Amy Newmark

Amy Newmark is the bestselling author, editor-in-chief, and publisher of the *Chicken Soup for the Soul* book series. Since 2008, she has published 188 new books, most of them national bestsellers in the U.S. and Canada, more than doubling the number of Chicken Soup for the Soul titles in print today. She is also the author of *Simply Happy*, a crash course in Chicken Soup for the Soul advice and wisdom that is filled with easy-to-implement, practical tips for enjoying a better life.

Amy is credited with revitalizing the Chicken Soup for the Soul brand, which has been a publishing industry phenomenon since the first book came out in 1993. By compiling inspirational and aspirational true stories curated from ordinary people who have had extraordinary experiences, Amy has kept the thirty-year-old Chicken Soup for the Soul brand fresh and relevant.

Amy graduated *magna cum laude* from Harvard University where she majored in Portuguese and minored in French. She then embarked on a three-decade career as a Wall Street analyst, a hedge fund manager, and a corporate executive in the technology field. She is a Chartered Financial Analyst.

Her return to literary pursuits was inevitable, as her honors thesis in college involved traveling throughout Brazil's impoverished northeast region, collecting stories from regular people. She is delighted to have come full circle in her writing career — from collecting stories "from the people" in Brazil as a twenty-year-old to, three decades later, collecting stories "from the people" for Chicken Soup for the Soul.

When Amy and her husband Bill, the CEO of Chicken Soup for the Soul, are not working, they are visiting their four grown children and their spouses, and their five grandchildren.

Follow Amy on Twitter @amynewmark. Listen to her free podcast — Chicken Soup for the Soul with Amy Newmark — on Apple, Google, or by using your favorite podcast app on your phone.

Thank You

We owe huge thanks to all our contributors and fans. We received thousands of submissions for this popular topic, and we spent months reading all of them. Susan Heim, Laura Dean, Crescent LoMonaco, Maureen Peltier, and Mary Fisher read all of them and narrowed down the selection for Associate Publisher D'ette Corona and Publisher and Editor-in-Chief Amy Newmark. Susan Heim did the first round of editing, and then D'ette chose the perfect quotations to put at the beginning of each story, and Amy edited the stories and shaped the final manuscript.

As we finished our work, D'ette continued to be Amy's right-hand woman in working with all our wonderful writers. Barbara LoMonaco, Kristiana Pastir and Elaine Kimbler jumped in to proof, proof, proof. And yes, there will always be typos anyway, so please feel free to let us know about them at webmaster@chickensoupforthesoul.com, and we will correct them in future printings.

The whole publishing team deserves a hand, including our Vice President of Marketing Maureen Peltier, our Vice President of Production Victor Cataldo, and our graphic designer Daniel Zaccari, who turned our manuscript into this beautiful, entertaining book.

About American Humane

American Humane is the country's first national humane organization, founded in 1877 and committed to ensuring the safety, welfare, and wellbeing of all animals. For more than 140 years, American Humane has been first to serve in promoting the welfare and safety of animals and strengthening the bond between animals and people. American Humane's initiatives are designed to help whenever and wherever animals are in need of rescue, shelter, protection or care.

American Humane is the only national humane organization with top ratings and endorsements from the key charity watchdog groups. The organization has earned Charity Navigator's highest "Four-Star Rating," the Platinum Seal of Transparency from GuideStar USA, and is one of the few charities that meets all of the Better Business Bureau's Wise Giving Alliance's 20 Standards for Charity Accountability.

American Humane's certification programs that verify humane treatment of animals are wide ranging, covering animals in film, on farms, in zoos and aquariums and even those in pet retailers. The iconic "No Animals Were Harmed®" certification, which appears during the end credits of films and TV shows, today monitors some 1,000 productions yearly.

Through rigorous, science-based criteria that are independently verified, American Humane's farm animal welfare program, Conservation program and Pet Provider programs help to ensure the humane treatment of more than one billion animals living on certified farms and ranches, in zoos and aquariums, and at pet provider locations. Simply put, American Humane is the largest verifier of animal welfare in the world.

Continuing its longstanding efforts to strengthen the healing power of the human-animal bond, American Humane also pairs veterans struggling to cope with the invisible wounds of war with highly trained service dogs, and also helps reunite discharged military working dogs with their former handlers.

To learn more about American Humane, visit AmericanHumane.org and follow them on Facebook, Instagram, Twitter and YouTube.

AMERICAN★HUMANE
FIRST TO SERVE°

Editor's Note: Chicken Soup for the Soul and American Humane have created *Humane Heroes*, a FREE new series of e-books and companion curricula for elementary, middle and high schoolers. Through thirty-six inspirational stories of animal rescue, rehabilitation, and humane conservation being performed at the world's leading zoological institutions, and eighteen easy-to-follow lesson plans, *Humane Heroes* provides highly engaging free reading materials that also encourage young people to appreciate and protect Earth's disappearing species. To download the free e-books and learn about the program, please visit www.chickensoup.com/ah.

Sharing Happiness, Inspiration, and Hope

Real people sharing real stories, every day, all over the world. In 2007, *USA Today* named *Chicken Soup for the Soul* one of the five most memorable books in the last quarter-century. With over 110 million books sold to date in the U.S. and Canada alone, more than 300 titles in print, and translations into nearly fifty languages, "chicken soup for the soul®" is one of the world's best-known phrases.

Today, thirty years after we first began sharing happiness, inspiration and hope through our books, we continue to delight our readers with new titles, but have also evolved beyond the bookshelves with super premium pet food, television shows, a podcast, video journalism from aplus.com, licensed products, and free movies and TV shows on our Crackle, Redbox, Popcornflix and Chicken Soup for the Soul streaming apps. We are busy "changing your life one story at a time®." Thanks for reading!

Share with Us

We all have had Chicken Soup for the Soul moments in our lives. If you would like to share your story or poem with millions of people around the world, go to chickensoup.com and click on Submit Your Story. You may be able to help another reader and become a published author at the same time. Some of our past contributors have launched writing and speaking careers from the publication of their stories in our books!

We only accept story submissions via our website. They are no longer accepted via mail or fax. Visit our website, www.chickensoup.com, and click on Submit Your Story for our writing guidelines and a list of topics we are working on.

To contact us regarding other matters, please send us an email through webmaster@chickensoupforthesoul.com, or fax or write us at:

Chicken Soup for the Soul
P.O. Box 700
Cos Cob, CT 06807-0700

One more note from your friends at Chicken Soup for the Soul: Occasionally, we receive an unsolicited book manuscript from one of our readers, and we would like to respectfully inform you that we do not accept unsolicited manuscripts, and we must discard the ones that appear.

Chicken Soup for the Soul

The Magic of Cats

101 Tales of Family, Friendship & Fun

Amy Newmark

Royalties from this book go to
AMERICAN★HUMANE
FIRST TO SERVE™

Paperback: 978-1-61159-066-1
eBook: 978-1-61159-301-3

More feline family fun

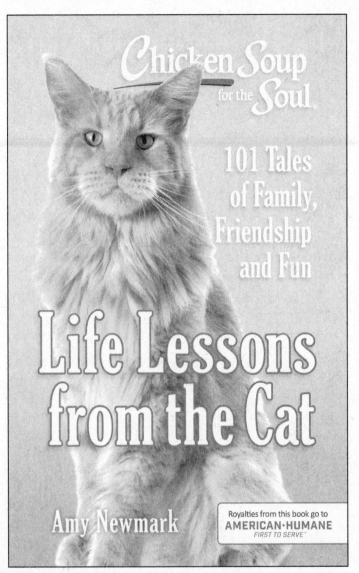

Chicken Soup for the Soul.

101 Tales of Family, Friendship and Fun

Life Lessons from the Cat

Amy Newmark

Royalties from this book go to
AMERICAN·HUMANE
FIRST TO SERVE

Paperback: 978-1-61159-989-3
eBook: 978-1-61159-289-4

and lessons learned from the cat

Changing the world one story at a time®
www.chickensoup.com